# Making Political Science Matter

# Making Political Science Matter

*Debating Knowledge, Research, and Method*

EDITED BY

*Sanford F. Schram and Brian Caterino*

*New York University Press*

NEW YORK AND LONDON

NEW YORK UNIVERSITY PRESS
New York and London
www.nyupress.org

Library of Congress Cataloging-in-Publication Data
Making political science matter : debating knowledge, research, and
method / edited by Sanford F. Schram and Brian Caterino.
p. cm.
Includes bibliographical references and index.
ISBN-13: 978-0-8147-4032-3 (cloth : alk. paper)
ISBN-10: 0-8147-4032-4 (cloth : alk. paper)
ISBN-13: 978-0-8147-4033-0 (pbk. : alk. paper)
ISBN-10: 0-8147-4033-2 (pbk. : alk. paper)
1. Political science—Philosophy. 2. Political science—Research—
Methodology. I. Schram, Sanford. II. Caterino, Brian. III. Title.

JC265.M274     2006
320.01—dc22     2006018397

New York University Press books are printed on acid-free paper, and their
binding materials are chosen for strength and durability.

Manufactured in the United States of America
c 10 9 8 7 6 5 4 3 2 1
p 10 9 8 7 6 5 4 3 2 1

# Contents

# Acknowledgments

The editors want to thank all the contributors for working with us to produce this book. Everyone was so cooperative. It has been a pleasure working with all those involved. Further, we want to thank Dvora Yanow for providing both sound advice and the title for the book, which she developed originally for a conference panel on the significance of Bent Flyvbjerg's *Making Social Science Matter.*

This book was started as a project that was hatched in discussions with Dvora and Patrick Thaddeus Jackson. Discussions with many others helped shaped the outline of the manuscript. In particular, we want to thank Fred Block, Barbara Cruikshank, Anne Dalke, Richard Fording, Chuck Green, Jack Gunnell, Bonnie Honig, Ken Hoover, Anne Norton, Ido Oren, Stephen Pimpare, Frances Fox Piven, Michael Shapiro, Rogers Smith, Joe Soss, and Keith Topper. In addition, we thank students in Sanford Schram's social theory seminar for offering ideas that help informed his thinking on the project: Page Buck, Wesley Bryant, Angie Campbell, Tom Duffin, Christine Hitchens, Linda Houser, Anchana Jetti, Gail Manza, Michael Pfeiffer, Sarah Podolin, Jennifer Stotter, and Tracey Uhl. We especially want to thank the anonymous reviewers recruited by New York University Press who engaged us effectively to improve the manuscript. Thanks are also due our great editor, Ilene Kalish, editorial assistant Salwa Jabado, and Despina Papazoglou Gimbel, managing editor, from the Press, who all worked methodically and judiciously to bring the book to publication. Last, we appreciate the permission from the following journals to reprint articles as chapters: *Politics & Society,* for the chapters by David Laitin and Bent Flyvbjerg; *Inquiry,* for the chapter by Theodore Schatzki; and *Political Theory,* for the chapter by Sanford Schram.

# Introduction
## Reframing the Debate

## Brian Caterino and Sanford F. Schram

In 2001, Bent Flyvbjerg published *Making Social Science Matter: Why Social Inquiry Fails and How It Can Succeed Again* (Flyvbjerg 2001). This book posed a unique challenge to the social sciences: to rethink the type of research they are best equipped to produce. Flyvbjerg, like others before him, called for the social sciences to reject pretensions that they could emulate the natural sciences. Given their unique subject matter, the social sciences would inevitably fail to follow the natural sciences in providing general causal explanations for why people do what they do. Instead, the social sciences were better equipped to help inform practical reason or phronesis, that is, the ability to make intelligent decisions in particular circumstances.

What is outstanding about Flyvbjerg's challenge is not the call to do social science that matters to real people in particular circumstances but the way he approached this familiar challenge by simultaneously doing two very disparate things that are rarely brought together. Flyvbjerg's book bridged theory and practice in a way that united philosophical and empirical subdivisions in the discipline. He thereby simultaneously provided a strong theoretical foundation for his vision of a politically relevant social science and illuminated his position with concrete examples from his own empirical research. He did all this in a way that demonstrated how research could engage political decision making so as to enhance democracy. Therefore, what was unique about Flyvbjerg's call for a renewed social science was the way that Flyvbjerg transgressed disciplinary boundaries to make a more compelling call for a social science that people could use to make a difference in their lives. The book was undoubtedly provocative, especially in political science, where it has helped fuel the Perestroika movement to make the discipline more relevant in understanding not just the problems political scientists address in their studies but also the problems political actors confront in the field of political struggle (Shapiro 2005; Monroe 2005).

That not everyone agrees with all that Flyvbjerg says is made evident by the rich set of responses we have brought together in this volume. At a minimum, Flyvbjerg's book has sparked a debate worth taking seriously. We have tried to do justice to that debate in this book. To begin, we provide some background on how political science has evolved in recent years, specify what is distinctive in Flyvbjerg's challenge, and conclude with an overview of the chapters that follow.

## The Persistence of the Naturalistic Model

For more than a century, the debates in Europe over social science were influenced by *methodenstreit,* that is, the methodological disputes between those who viewed the social sciences as following the model of the natural sciences and those who adopted a human-sciences approach that drew on historicism and hermeneutics as a basis for their conception of social inquiry. The development of social science in America took its own distinctive direction apart from what was being debated in Europe. In the United States, debate favored the selection of a naturalistic model of social inquiry that encouraged emulation of the natural sciences. Closely allied with liberal individualism, the naturalistic model became dominant at the end of the nineteenth century in America (Ross 1992, xiii). Debates over historicism and the historical nature of social science did enter into American social science in the years after the Civil War. The beginnings of this period still featured an interdisciplinary or, more accurately, nondisciplinary conception of social science (Haskell 2000; Lindenfeld 1997).While organizations like the American Social Science Association attempted to bring a professional status to social science, they still focused on solving practical problems via a reformist approach. This influence, however, waned by the turn of the century. Dorothy Ross notes: "Although they began that period [i.e., 1870–1929] influenced by German historical models, American social scientists determined by the end of it to orient their disciplines toward natural science" (Ross 1992, xiv).

In the United States, the professionalization of social science dovetailed with the rise of the large research university and its model of educating and training graduate students in specialized fields. The naturalistic model was adapted to these new conditions and to the aims of providing useful knowledge for social progress. While there were notable exceptions, the natural-science model dominated American social science through the first half of the twentieth century. This trend was accentuated in the post–World War II period with the emergence of behavioralism as its dominant manifestation, particularly in political science. With its emphasis on striving to be scientific by developing predictive causal models to explain human behavior, behavioralism was explicitly tied by its proponents to positivism in the philosophy science. Behavioralism also helped usher in the now well-accepted misconception that distinguishes between quantitative and qualitative research, drawing a line between positivistic approaches that focused on testing causal explanations and more interpretive approaches that sought to arrive at an understanding of the meaning of social events. This distinction largely worked to the detriment of the latter, with the emphasis on the former as the best way for political science to be scientific and to produce objective, empirically tested, generalizable knowledge of the political world. By the end of the twentieth century, interest had clearly increased in a political science that produced scientific knowledge regardless of its relevance for doing something about the problems political actors confronted. Universal, transcontextual, scientifically proven, objective knowledge was favored over more local, situated, contextual knowledge that embraced the contingencies of political life.

In recent years, there has persisted a push for a unitary discipline organized around the positivistic paradigm with the goal of growing knowledge of the causal relationships among political phenomena (King, Keohane, and Verba 1994). Some have envisioned a unitary discipline associated with the increasing influence of what is commonly referred to as rational-choice theory, which borrows the logic of self-interested behavior from economics to develop models that predict what a rational decision maker will decide to do in particular instances (Laitin 1995).

## The Constrained Pluralism of Post-Positivism

According to John Dryzek, James Farr, and Stephen Leonard, with the decline of behavioralism, political science entered a period of radical plurality with no central research focus but several hegemonic contenders (Dryzek, Farr, and Leonard 1995, 3). The current state of political science, however, can be better characterized as a constrained pluralism or a partial hegemony that limits methodological diversity. The current situation finds methodological pluralism itself as a highly contestible issue.

Keith Topper (2005) argues for appreciating the value of what he calls the "disorder of political inquiry," whereby researchers with different approaches can learn from one another in what Peter Galison (1987) refers to as "trading zones" that coexist in a disciplined field of inquiry. Such understanding of disciplines pushes past the idea popularized by Thomas Kuhn (1970) that "normal science" within any of the fields of natural science is done under a unifying paradigm. Yet, Topper is at pains to note that his post-paradigmatic understanding of disciplines is still not seen, let alone valued, by most political scientists, who remain wedded to the positivistic paradigm of emulating the natural sciences. Topper himself would like to see a critical pluralism that goes beyond both the current constrained pluralism or the "empty pluralism" of simply allowing a diversity of methods, good, bad, or indifferent. Drawing on the work of Pierre Bourdieu, Topper advocates a critical pluralism that offers a differentiated approach. It mixes methods as appropriate in ways that appreciate that all social phenomena, including politics, are human practices mediated through language that require both interpretation and explanation.

Ian Shapiro (2005) has added to this critique to highlight how the various subfields of political science do not help in this regard, since they have become disconnected not just from one another but also from the problems that confront political actors. Shapiro has called on political scientists to respond by being less wedded to their insular approaches and instead to practice problem-driven research that uses a diversity of methods in addressing problems in the political world as experienced by political actors. A rich debate has been kicked off by his call for reorganizing the discipline around problem areas. Researchers in this scheme transgress disciplinary boundaries, combine theoretical and empirical work, and mix methods to study political problems as effectively as possible. Others extend this approach to understand problems to change conditions for the better (see Wolfe 2005; Shapiro, Smith, and Masoud 2004).

In spite of such arguments, there remains resistance to appreciating the value of diversity within the discipline. While the dissolution of behavioralism no doubt opened the space for a variety of approaches, this opening has been challenged by those who have argued for a unitary model of political science (Laitin 1995) or have sought to assimilate alternative approaches to the positivistic paradigm (King, Keohane, and Verba 1994).

The attempt to assimilate alternative approaches has been necessary because they exist and have always existed. Even at the height of the behavioral revolution, there were voices in the wilderness that advocated an engaged social science. The work of Robert and Helen Lynd and of C. Wright Mills, along with the work of the early Frankfurt School in its residence at Columbia University, influenced scholars associated with the New Left and later the Caucus for a New Political Science. With time, the decline of behavioralism in political science by the end of the twentieth century opened the way for a variety of what today are often called "interpretive" approaches, such as critical theory, hermeneutics, post-structuralism, and feminism, that arose in the wake of these earlier influences.

These newer challenges have been explicitly self-reflective about what should be the object of inquiry in the social sciences and what therefore constitutes social knowledge. As a result, in political science, they do not simply advocate that the discipline engage politics as people experience it in particular settings but also link questions of engagement explicitly to methodological concerns about the source and character of engaged knowledge. Since our knowledge of the social world is inextricably connected to our meaningful involvements with others, social science is not primarily, as the naturalistic approach suggests, knowledge distinct from that available to participants in social life. Practical reason means more than a sphere of application or nonscientific understanding. Practical reason is the medium of both ordinary understanding and social scientific understanding. Therefore, to forgo the quest for general causal explanations and instead seek to understand what political relationships mean to people in particular settings inevitably improves both ordinary and scientific understanding.

While the alternative approaches have varied widely, they all challenge the primacy of positivistic models of causality. While causality generally refers to an account that "explains" an occurrence through the force of a variable that exists logically independent of any participant's understanding, causality as used by an interpretive theorist refers to the reason why an actor carries out an action. This does not exclude the influence of structural or unconscious elements or other constraints that limit understanding; it claims only that such constraints are not the last word or the terminus of inquiry.

Given this radically different view of what is meant by explanation, efforts to assimilate the alternative interpretive approaches to the dominant positivistic paradigm have faltered and end up highlighting the constrained nature of the supposed pluralism of the current era. A primary case in point is one of the major textbooks for the orthodox approach in political science, *Designing Social Inquiry* (hereafter DSI), by Gary King, Robert Keohane, and Sidney Verba (1994). While King, Keohane, and Verba claim to incorporate and legitimize qualitative work, they do so only by subordinating it to "causal" analysis. Interpretive work, rather anachronistically, is seen as "pure description" (King, Keohane, and Verba 1994, 34). Interpretation works by depicting the situation, as it is understood, without making any explanatory claims at all. King, Keohane, and Verba articulate an understanding of meaning in an objectivist way (41). In their treatment of the anthropologist Clifford Geertz's renowned account of understanding a gesture (Geertz 1973), they conclude that understanding the meaning of a gesture is a matter of observations and hypotheses that can in principle be understood by a solitary observer, independent of the cultural context, an idea that Geertz would undoubtedly reject. The mode of debate today at times involves trying to assimilate interpretive insights into the positivist paradigm, rather than seriously considering how these insights about the importance of contextualized reasoning pose a direct challenge to the idea of objective observation.

More recently, Henry Brady, David Collier, and their associates (2004) have published a critical assessment of *Designing Social Inquiry* that gained some currency as an effective counter to the DSI approach. The contributors to *Rethinking Social Inquiry* (RSI) raise a number of prescient objections against DSI, including its reliance on Karl Popper's model of social science that assumes that all social inquiry is dedicated to helping test hypotheses with large sets of data so to falsify those that the data do not support and to provisionally accept those the data do. Further, RSI criticizes DSI for employing, along with its narrow Popperian view of social science, a limited view of causality. Thus DSI assumes that large-n studies (i.e., those with many cases, as in sample surveys) are better for the purposes of testing hypotheses. As a result, DSI tries to make interpretive studies using qualitative data fit their model. In opposition, RSI advocates a more variegated philosophy of social science that recognizes a greater role for interpretive approaches to causal explanation. As a result, RSI gives greater attention to the case-study methods, which do not rely exclusively or even primarily on quantitative methods.

The opposition of large-n and case-study approaches certainly defines one of the major lines of cleavage in political science today. RSI's approach illustrates some of the shortcomings of the dominant DSI approach. The chapters in RSI most often offer an interpretation of this cleavage that, however, is far too narrow. Just as in DSI, some contributors to RSI tend to relegate interpretive work to the realm of description but not explanation (see, for instance, Tarrow 2004, 178). This approach leaves out much that is important to interpretive theory. While RSI does not present a monolithic view, some contributors help construct an opposition between a statistical view of causality and an inferential one. As a result, the analysis bypasses the crucial role of interpretation in helping understand the meaning of social realities as experienced by people such as those we study and even those who are doing the studying.

It is at this point that the question of assimilation becomes most challenging. The interpretive perspective defines the object of social inquiry in a distinct fashion (i.e., as dialogically meaningful action between and among people) and therefore requires a distinctively different view of causality and of explanation based on, but not restricted to, the actors' reasons for actions (e.g, see Taylor 1977; Bernstein 1978; Apel 1984; and Giddens 1986). Therefore, it is wrong to limit interpretive approaches that collect qualitative data to offering only descriptions but not explanations. They provide the basis for a different type of explanation—one that helps connect research to practical reasoning and, in this way, to social action itself. The case-study method, in fact, has to be based, in the first instance, on an interpretive account (not a description) of actors' worlds and can never be fully independent of that perspective. In the end, even the RSI response does not reframe the debate to the point where political science would be in the business of providing interpretations that could inform practical reason.

Interpretive approaches that emphasize understanding the meaning of social action in contexts continue to have growing impact on social inquiry. The search for explanation is increasingly seasoned with an appreciation of the need to understand meaning. For a growing number of social scientists, it is difficult to conceive of a pure social fact that is independent of the context of meaning. Could a political leader, for example, have legitimacy independent of the belief among the members of that political order that she is legitimate? More and more researchers accept that knowledge of the social world is impossible without understanding the meaningful involvement of the participants in the social world.

## Why Now Phronesis?

Flyvbjerg's *Making Social Science Matter* provides an opening for going beyond the constrained pluralism of the current era. Flyvbjerg did not seek to assimilate the quest to inform situated practical reason to the naturalist model and its quest for validating general causal theories. Instead, he put situated practical reasoning at the center of social science research. To justify this emphasis, Flyvbjerg drew on several strains of political and social inquiry to argue that social science is best suited to promoting the type of practical knowledge that Aristotle called *phronesis*. He relied heavily on Friedrich Nietzsche, Michel Foucault, and Pierre Bourdieu to center social inquiry on understanding and informing situated social practice. Flyvbjerg outlined how what he called "phronetic social science" could connect knowledge to power and inform efforts to improve social life. His vision for a renewed social science has resonated with various scholars in the social sciences who wish to move beyond the current dominant paradigm that emphasizes scientific causal modeling. It is this part of Flyvbjerg's analysis that has had a special appeal in political science, where the fledgling Perestroika movement has brought together a diverse set of scholars interested in promoting methodologically pluralistic discipline that will encourage "problem-driven" research in the name of a more relevant, civic-minded scholarship that can challenge power and change society for the better (Shapiro 2005; Monroe 2005).

For Flyvbjerg, the social sciences employ a version of *phronesis* that the natural-science model of social inquiry cannot accommodate with its emphasis on *episteme* and *techné*. This Aristotelian tripartite distinction is critical for Flyvbjerg in highlighting the comparative advantage of social science. *Phronesis* is, as Aristotle termed it, akin to practical wisdom that comes from an intimate familiarity with the contingencies and uncertainties of various forms of social practice embedded in complex social settings. *Episteme* is knowledge that is abstract and universal; *techné* is the know-how associated with practicing a craft. Flyvbjerg urges what he calls "phronetic social science" that can contribute to practical reason. Flyvbjerg emphasizes phronetic social science for five interrelated reasons:

1. Given the contingent nature of human interaction in the social world, social inquiry is best practiced when it seeks not general laws of action that can be used to predict courses of action but the critical

assessment of values, norms, and structures of power and dominance. Social inquiry is better when it is linked to questions of the
good life, that is, to questions of what we ought to do.

2. Social inquiry is a species not of theoretical reason but of practical
reason. Practical reason stays within a horizon of involvements in
social life. For Flyvbjerg, this entails a context-dependent view of
social inquiry that rests on the capacity for judgment.

3. Understanding can never be grasped analytically; it has a holistic
character, given that the social world is both historical and connected by narrative structures.

4. Understanding also has ineliminable subjective elements that require
researchers to forgo a disinterested position of detachment and to
enter into dialogue with those they study. Dialogical social inquiry
challenges traditional notions of impersonal objectivity and truth.

5. A dialogical social inquiry into a dynamic and changing social world
draws philosophical sustenance, in Flyvbjerg's view, from fusing
Aristotle and Nietzsche with Foucault and Bourdieu, while using
ideas from other significant philosophers and social theorists. This
combination emphasizes that interpretation is itself a practice of
power, implying an a priori involvement in the world that
researchers have take into account.

These five assumptions lead Flyvbjerg to propose what he terms "phronetic social science," which calls for mixing methods in the naming of
understanding and informing situated practice.

No man is an island unto himself; no woman, either. Flyvbjerg's challenge arises in part because the current terrain in political and social
inquiry therefore provides a more hospitable environment than previous
years for thinking whether and how we can build on Flyvbjerg's work to
build a more politically robust political science. Several antecedents have
helped till that soil to make it more fertile. There is first what we can call,
along with Mary Dietz (2002), the "turning operations" at work in the field
of political theory. Here, Dietz means for feminist theorists, in particular, to
turn to a more politically engaged, contextually sensitive, politically contingent kind of theorizing that has greater affinities with Niccolo Machiavelli
and Hannah Arendt than with Jurgen Habermas and John Rawls in its
attempt to theorize how politics in any particular situated community is
possible. In writing on citizenship, Dietze urges: "feminists should turn to
relations and practices that are expressly contextual, institutional, and

political, informed by and situated within particular cultures and histories, and oriented toward action" (Dietz 2002, 34, as quoted in Balfour 2004). Dietz is by no means alone, for many other theorists now join with her in explicitly eschewing Habermasian and Rawlsian attempts to envision the ideal political order in favor of working to create critical resources for making political action possible in contextualized settings. Flyvbjerg's work is informed by this growing theoretical sensibility, and he uses it in his own distinctive way to combine Aristotle with Friedrich Nietzsche and Michel Foucault to talk about how situated knowledge can challenge power, can be its own source of power, and can empower social change.

Another turning operation of its own kind informs the empirical side of Flyvbjerg's work. The "interpretive turn," first heralded by Paul Rabinow and William Sullivan (1979), has now been joined by the "linguistic turn," the "spatial turn," the turn to visual culture, and other turning operations, as well. All these turns are turns away from the positivistic paradigm that holds that political science must emulate the natural sciences and produce decontextualized, objective, scientific truth about the causal laws of politics. Instead, the growing turns away from the naturalistic model have helped bring to the fore contextual interpretations of what political actions mean to people. As a result, we can better not just describe subjective experiences but also explain them in terms of significance, understanding not only what these political actions mean but why people engage in them. The successive turns have provided in recent years, with increasing acceleration, multiple ways to contextualize political actions, making them not only interpretable but open to reinterpretation and thereby to revision and transformation. Once we see that we can reinterpret actions in a variety of ways, those actions themselves become subject to being practiced differently in the future. The alternative interpretive approaches are beginning to breach the boundaries set by the constrained pluralism of the field (see Norton 2004).

That said, interpretive understanding is itself a contested terrain for post-positivist social theory. While a variety of different theorists, including those who fall under such diverse rubrics as post-structuralists and neo-Aristotelians, argue that context sets limits to the scope of evaluation and critical reflection, other lines of inquiry, such as that found in contemporary critical theory and some forms of interpretive social theory, give a much broader scope to critique. Still others stress political, subjective, or cultural factors as limiting the terms of critique, by whom it can be offered, and from what standpoint. Some indication of the scope of this continuing dispute can be found in the contributions to this volume; our book is designed to help us take the Flyvbjerg debate farther.

## The Flyvbjerg Effect

The critiques and commentaries in this book respond to Flyvbjerg's challenge for political science and related disciplines, though rarely agreeing with all that he suggests. We are not all prepared to take all the turns he proposes, and some of us want to take other turns. Our goal is not so much to celebrate Flyvbjerg's book as the latest salvo in the *methodenstreit* of our times. Instead, it is to use the debate about his book to move the conversation further down the road in hopes that we might begin to see the emerging possibilities for a rejuvenated political science.

The first section of the book lays out the debate about Flyvbjerg's visions for a renewed social science. It starts with a chapter by Sanford Schram that provides a defense of phronetic social science that Schram says is "post-paradigmatic." Schram notes that Flyvbjerg himself prefers to call phronetic social science "nonparadigmatic." In either case, the idea is that phronetic social science is consistent with a methodological pluralism. It promotes problem-driven research that uses multiple methods as necessary to address a problem in ways that can inform and empower the people being studied. Next, David Laitin provides a critique of Flyvbjerg's book and his idea of phronetic social science. Laitin offers an alternative model that shows how phronesis can be and needs to be incorporated into the scientific approach to the study of politics, if it is to contribute to the knowledge accumulation process. Bent Flyvbjerg then replies to Laitin with a spirited defense of phronetic social science. Patrick Thaddeus Jackson then employs a very witty baseball analogy to further critique Laitin's model while highlighting the limits of mainstream comparative analysis. Corey Shdaimah and Roland Stahl end the first section by applying Flyvbjerg's concept of a value-oriented phronetic social science to a Philadelphia-area participatory-action research project on low-income home repair, demonstrating that some people are not waiting for the *methodenstreit* to end and are about the business of doing phronetic social science as we speak.

The next section of the book examines some of the larger theoretical questions posed by Flyvbjerg's work. First, Theodore Schatzki offers a judicious review of the theoretical dimensions of *Making Social Science*

*Matter,* while suggesting that we need to rethink its overly narrow use of the idea of phronesis for social science. Next, Brian Caterino's essay challenges the viability of Flyvbjerg's synthesis of Aristotelian and Nietzschean notions of virtue and phronesis. Mary Hawkesworth's post-positivist approach rejects the natural/social-science division in favor of a pragmatic analysis of the production of knowledge that centers on the notions of the audience and aim of knowledge. Stewart Clegg elaborates Flyvbjerg's conception of contextual or bounded rationalities by using Foucault's notion of power/knowledge and in the process demonstrates the relevance of Flyvbjerg's work to organizational studies. Leslie Paul Thiele provides an elaboration of Flyvbjerg's notion of intuitive knowledge, drawing on research in contemporary neurophysiology. With these chapters, we can begin to see how Flyvbjerg's work can be usefully engaged to consider enrichments across a number of fields in protean ways.

The third section addresses the disciplinary implications of Flyvbjerg's analysis for political science. Peri Schwartz-Shea offers an alternative to harmonistic versions of pluralism and advocates instead an agonistic version of political science in which researchers critically assess the political value of their research and its uses. Greg Kasza extends phronetic analysis further to the education of graduate students and in the process provides a program for graduate students to critically evaluate competing methodological claims. David Kettler harkens back to the Caucus for a New Political Science in the 1960s and to the critical theory of Franz Neumann to develop an alternative version of the relationship between political theory and research that can inform political science today. Tim Luke concludes the collection by suggesting while phronetic social science is a good start; we must go beyond it if we are to appreciate sufficiently how freedom and unfreedom are intertwined with a priori assumptions that inform the analysis of political power. Political analysis today, operating as it does in the shadow of what Luke calls the emerging "biopower regime," must reach down to examine the quasi-, proto-, and even pre-political practices of power that work through processes of subjectification, or what Michel Foucault called "governmentality." Political science must follow power into the biopolitical realm of subjectification if it is to serve efforts to resist it and even to turn toward fighting for freedom. It is at this point our volume ends, poised on the edge of the brave new world of the "proto-politics" of surveillance and discipline. The question that hangs in the air is what forms of political inquiry will help us not just interrogate but also maneuver in the emerging terrains of political contestation.

Our hope is that by examining the debate over Flyvbjerg's phronetic social science, we will be contributing to the ongoing ferment in the discipline. These are dark times politically, but the discipline is being revitalized. The conversation is robust, and Flyvbjerg's *Making Social Science Matter* is an important part of this conversation. We hope not just to replay Flyvbjerg's argument but to improvise from it. We therefore see the essays in this volume as part of a wider effort to create more opportunities for more diverse forms of political science. The larger hope is that politics, as well as political science, will be the better for it.

# Part I

# The Flyvbjerg Debate

# Return to Politics

## *Perestroika, Phronesis, and Post-Paradigmatic Political Science*

### *Sanford F. Schram*

Years ago, my good colleague Chuck Green enlisted me to teach a second section of an undergraduate research methods course in political science that we offered to majors. Chuck had organized his course around a simulation in which all the students in the class were to submit research grant proposals to a hypothetical foundation for funding. In his class, the hypothetical foundation was always called the Gnosis Foundation. As an alternative, I called mine the Phronesis Federation, which, given differences in the Greek names, was to be dedicated to financing research that informed practical reasoning about the real problems that confront society. I eventually dropped the simulation when teaching methods elsewhere, but the commitment to what Bent Flyvbjerg (2001) calls "phronetic social science" stuck. Years later, I got my hands on *Making Social Science Matter,* and, with the first reading, I was enchanted. Here was a book that was saying so much that I always wanted to say, and saying it so eloquently. By then, I was an active participant in a renegade movement to promote methodological plu- ralism in political science called Perestroika, and my research methods sem- inar was now called "Paradigms and Perestroika." The book affirmed my efforts. The circle had been squared. Yet, when David Laitin (2003) pub- lished his critique of *Making Social Science Matter* as a way of criticizing Perestroika, I knew that not everyone agreed and that there was an impor- tant debate brewing about the future of political inquiry (see chapter 2).

None of this is an accident. Political science is receiving increased criti- cal scrutiny as a discipline these days, and much of that scrutiny is coming from within its own ranks. A growing number of political scientists have signed on to efforts aimed at specifically challenging the dominance of positivistic research, particularly research that assumes that political behavior can be predicted according to theories of rationality and that such predictions underwrite cumulative explanations that constitute the growth of political knowledge. This movement to question such thinking is most dramatically represented in the network of scholars that has developed in response to the eponymous Mr. Perestroika letter that raised this challenge in poignant terms when it first circulated over the Internet back in October 2000.

Perestroika, it turns out, is a loose collection of political scientists, from graduate students to senior scholars, who do not always themselves agree on which features of the dominant approach they want to critique—some focus on the overly abstract nature of much of the research done today, some on the lack of nuance in decontextualized, large-sample empirical studies, others on the inhumaneness of thinking about social relations in causal terms, and still others on the ways in which contemporary social science all too often fails to produce the kind of knowledge that can meaningfully inform social life. As a group, the Perestroika movement, however, has championed methodological pluralism, charging that exclusionary practices have made graduate education less hospitable to historical and field research, qualitative case studies, interpretive and critical analysis, and a variety of context-sensitive approaches to the study of politics. The major journals of the field, perestroikans argue, have become preoccupied with publishing research that conforms to overly restrictive scientistic assumptions about what constitutes contributions to political knowledge. Perestroika is a healthy development for political science and all other social sciences as well, opening for reconsideration these very questionable assumptions about what constitutes political knowledge in particular and social knowledge in general.

From the vantage point of many perestroikans, the dominant paradigm in the field operates according to the following hierarchy of assumptions: (1) political science exists to help promote understanding of the truth about politics; (2) political science research contributes to this quest by adding to the accumulation of an expanding base of objective knowledge about politics; (3) the growth of this knowledge base is contingent upon the building of theory that offers explanations of politics; (4) the building of theory is dependent on the development of universal generalizations regarding the behavior of political actors; (5) the development of a growing body of generalizations occurs by testing falsifiable causal hypotheses that demonstrate their success in making predictions; (6) the accumulation of a growing body of predictions about political behavior comes from the study of variables in samples involving large numbers of cases; and (7) this growing body of objective causal knowledge can be put in service of society, particularly by influencing public policymakers and the stewards of the state.

This paradigm excludes much valuable research. For instance, it assumes that the study of a single case is "unscientific," provides no basis for generalizing, does not build theory, cannot contribute to the growth of political knowledge, and, as a result, is not even to be considered for publication in the leading journals and is to be discouraged as a legitimate doctoral dissertation project.[1] While there have always been dissenters to the drift toward "large-n," quantitative research in service of objective, decontextualized, and universally generalizable truths about politics, there is a good case to be made that the dissenters have increasingly been marginalized as the center of gravity of the discipline has drifted more and more toward reflecting these core assumptions about political knowledge.

Perestroika in political science has at a minimum provided an opportunity to halt this drift by questioning these assumptions and posing alternatives. At its best, the perestroikan impulse creates the possibility to question the idea that political science research exists as a unitary enterprise dedicated to the accumulation of an expanding knowledge base of universal, decontextualized generalizations about politics. In its place, Perestroika would put a more pluralistic emphasis on allowing for the blossoming of more contextual, contingent, and multiple political truths that involve a greater tie between theory and practice and a greater connection between thought and action in specific settings. Perestroika lays open the possibility that political science could actually be a very different sort of discipline, one less obsessed with proving it is a "science" and one more connected to providing delimited, contextualized, even local knowledges that might serve people within specific contexts.

Such a political science would therefore have very different standards as to what counts as meaningful political knowledge. It would, for instance, be less interested in studying such things as "development" or "modernization" in the abstract as objects of inquiry on their own, as when economics becomes the study of "the market" as opposed to the examination of the variety of markets. Instead of focusing solely on "development" or "modernization" per se, political science would be more about studying change in particular countries or using concepts like "development" or "modernization" in contextually sensitive ways to compare change in different countries.

This alternative political science would also be less preoccupied with perfecting method or pursuing research strictly for knowledge's own sake. As Rogers Smith (2002) has underscored, "knowledge does not have a sake"; all knowledge is tied to serving particular values. Therefore, this new political science would not be one that is dedicated to replacing one method with another. Instead, such a discipline, if that word is still appropriate, would encourage scholars to draw on a wide variety of methods from a diversity of theoretical perspectives, combining theory and empirical work in different and creative ways, all in dialogue with political actors in specific contexts. Problem-driven research would replace method-driven research (Shapiro 2002).

My own version of Perestroika would build on this problem-driven, contextually sensitive approach to enable people on the bottom, working in dialogue with social researchers, to challenge power. My perestroikan-inspired political science would be open to allowing ongoing political struggle to serve as the context for deciding what methods will be used in what ways to address which problems. This new dialogic political science would not find its standards for credible scholarship in arcane vocabularies and insular methods that are removed from local contexts and seem objective but are not without their own agendas. Instead, my political science would find its standards of knowledge in asking whether scholarship can demonstrate its contributions to enriching political discourse in contextualized settings.

Such a new political science, however, would at the same time recognize the risks associated with connecting to ongoing politics. It would guard against losing its critical capacity for the sake of achieving relevance. It would retain its critical capacity while in dialogue with ongoing political struggle, providing therefore a powerful "critical connectedness"—what Charles Lemert (2001) has called "global methods." It would, however, be less interested than the old political science in serving the state with objective knowledge. It would forgo the dream of scientific grandeur that aims to produce socially useful, decontextualized, objective knowledge, independent of politics.

A political science that forgoes the dream of a science of politics in order to dedicate itself to enhancing the critical capacity of people to practice a politics is, for me, an exciting prospect. A political science that does this to enhance the capacity to challenge power from below is all the more exciting. I would argue that the new political science would not just be more politically efficacious but also more intelligent, offering more robust forms of political knowledge.

Nothing, of course, springs full grown from the head of Zeus, and it is critically important to note that the potential of Perestroika has always been manifest in selected efforts in social science, if in recent decades more at the margins and most frequently outside the disciplines in interdisciplinary work and "applied" fields. I use the word "applied" hesitantly, however, since it reinforces the hegemonic perspective of a particular sort of epistemic privilege that assumes theory precedes action, that research is top-down in that first we study things as they exist objectively in truth and then we "apply" those understandings, grounded in theory from above, down to the real world of practice. This is to privilege decontextualized, universal knowledge over situated knowledges and only ends up reinforcing the idea that the social sciences need to ape the natural sciences in the pursuit of scientifically tested and validated generalizations about reality. Instead, throughout the relatively short hundred or so years of modern social science, there have always been practitioners of this craft who have been animated by alternative understandings of the kind of knowledge that social science can meaningfully produce. These practitioners have sought not just to criticize the Olympian perspective of the top-down hegemonic approach, and not just to propose alternatives, but to convincingly demonstrate them in their own work. These researchers can be found across the social sciences, employing a diversity of methodologies and studying a variety of topics. They situate their studies in the world of action, they insist on framing their work in terms of its relevance to ongoing human struggles and concerns, and they let their work emerge from the bottom up with the hope of producing not universal truths but poignantly relevant forms of knowledge that can help inform the human condition as it is experienced, fought over, and changed by the very same people being studied. A few examples are in order.

James Scott's writings, for instance, from *The Moral Economy of the Peasant* (1990) to *Seeing like a State* (1998), have looked at the world of power from the perspective of those on the bottom. He has, in *Seeing like a State,* demonstrated quite convincingly that the bottom-up perspective affords not only a different view but a better one, more attuned the needs of people in contextualized settings. A similar perspective is offered in the politically poignant analyses of Cynthia Enloe in such books as *Bananas,*

*Beaches and Bases* (1990) and *The Morning After: Sexual Politics at the End of the Cold War* (1993). Enloe highlights the gendered character of international relations in a world of superpowerdom and demonstrates in telling ways its particularly devastating consequences for women. Like Scott, she illustrates in her work that a bottom-up perspective produces a situated knowledge that can inform ongoing efforts to engage political power and produce political and social change.

The work of Frances Fox Piven and Richard A. Cloward represents an especially noteworthy example for my particular version of what Perestroika can bring to a revived political science. From *Regulating the Poor* (1971) to *Why Americans Still Don't Vote* (2000), their research grows from the bottom up, informed by ongoing political struggle, seeking to theorize and strategize about what is needed to feed back into those specific struggles. Like Enloe and Scott, Piven and Cloward employ a number of case studies, as in *Poor People's Movements* (1977), to tease out helpful lessons for those working to challenge power. Sometimes their theorizing is employed to inform a specific struggle, but it also offers more general understandings that could be applied beyond that struggle (see Schram 2002). Enloe, Scott, and Piven and Cloward are not alone; there are many other instances of such work scattered around the margins of political science and in other fields.

In fact, there is a rich tradition of several decades that is now leading to a growing number of studies in what is popularly called Participatory Action Research (PAR). The PAR approach emphasizes the alliance between researchers and those being studied so as to overcome the unquestioned assumptions and privileges associated with some people studying other people. Compelling examples here include Chester Hartman's 1974 *Yerba Buena,* which grew out of his activism working with tenants to resist their displacement in the face of land-grabbing developers. and William Foote Whyte and Kathleen King Whyte's 1988 *Making Mondragon: The Growth and Dynamics of the Worker Cooperative Complex.* The Whytes' analysis richly details how their research grew out of and effectively fed back into the struggles the Mondragon community was caught up in as its members sought to find a way to make socialism in a capitalist world sustainable. Within political science more than, say, sociology, this sort of work is still marginal, making the Perestroika challenge all the more necessary.

In addition, there is a strong philosophical base for the perestroikan perspective I am articulating that provides it with a intellectual grounding and ties it to broader movements for change that are roiling the human sciences across the board. One important source is Stephen Toulmin's *Return to Reason* (2001). Toulmin builds on his life's work in the philosophy of science, ordinary language philosophy, rhetoric, and the analysis of practical arts to offer a historically informed analysis of the problem of scientism in the social sciences. His primary argument is that since Descartes, and especially since Kant, western philosophical thought has been increasingly enchanted with the dream of realizing universal rationality as the highest form of knowledge and the basis for truth. Yet, Toulmin stresses that it was only relatively recently, in the twentieth century, that this dream came to be ascendant as the hegemonic ideal for organizing knowledge practices in the academy in general and the social sciences in particular. The dream of universal rationality as the gold standard for objective knowledge of truth became ascendant with rise of modern science and the growing influence of the argument that science, as best represented by particular natural sciences, was the best route toward achieving universal rationality, objective knowledge, and truth with a capital T. In its wake, the modern university was built and then increasingly compartmentalized into the multiversity, with growing numbers of specialized disciplines, each increasingly preoccupied with perfecting its own methodological prowess as to how to best arrive at truth.

Toulmin's main argument is that this derangement was a long time coming, involving arduous efforts as part of a campaign that achieved hegemonic status relatively recently. For Toulmin, before then, much of the history of modern Western philosophy can be understood in terms of striking a balance between universal rationality and contextual reason. The campaigners had to confront time and again the problem that what is universally rational may not be reasonable in particular situations. For centuries, the dream of universal rationality was counterbalanced by the practice of everyday reason. Humans experienced their lives and made sense of them between these poles. Yet, the rise of modern science increased the emphasis on the production of objective knowledge in the most abstract and generalizable terms possible. Theory was everything, and practice was subordinated to it. Theory-driven modern science's preferred discourse was mathematics, which, since Descartes, was the ideal idiom for expressing in abstract and generalizable terms the objective knowledge of universal rationality. Sciences began to be ranked by the degree to which they could produce universal rationality as expressed in mathematical terms. "Physics envy" spread. Then again, in the twentieth century, science in general became ascendant as the best way to produce such knowledge. The fact that "science as use" was conflated with "science as truth" helped greatly in vaulting science to the forefront as the supposedly superior road to truth as dramatic developments in technology were increasingly showcased as proof positive that science not only could do things but also knew the truth of what it was doing (Stevens 2002).

The idea that there is a distinctive scientific method that all sciences share began to gain greater currency, and all other forms of knowledge production came to be seen as inferior to the degree that they failed to conform to the dictates of the scientific method. Physics envy morphed into science envy, with the social sciences increasingly miming what was seen as the methods of the natural sciences in order to lay their own claim to scientific legitimacy. At this point, the precarious balance between abstract rationality and everyday reason was now seriously upset, and universal rationality in service of abstract generalizable knowledge, stated in the mathematical terms, was seen as the only real form of truth worth taking seriously. The wisdom of everyday reason was increasingly relegated to folklore or to applied fields, and it itself started to become a popular area of study, not so much for the truths it afforded but as an object of inquiry that could be used as data to test various hypotheses about which types of people in what cultures tended to think in what ways and why. The science of wisdom, as it were, whether studied in anthropology or philosophy, was a sure sign that rationality had triumphed over reason.

Toulmin effectively illuminates the rise of universal rationality, first in philosophy from Descartes on, then in the sciences, but also in the social sciences and applied fields. He highlights how a consistent bias in favor of abstract knowledge of universal rationality continued to work its way across disparate realms of knowledge production. Toulmin is not a social scientist, and in the past he has written about almost everything but. Yet, *Return to Reason* demonstrates a real feel for how the social sciences rose in the shadow of the preoccupation with the abstract knowledge of universal rationality and how that played out in selected fields. This is a wide-ranging book, written in a very inviting conversational style, from an Olympian vantage point; however, this is no mere dilettante rumination on the misguided project John Dewey called the "quest for certainty."

My favorite example in the entire book is Lancelot Brown, the famous nineteenth-century landscaper, who was also popularly known as "Capability" Brown because the designs for his quintessentially British gardens developed out of the available landscape, rather than, as with the French style, imposing an idealized image of a garden on the landscape and forc-ing it to conform to that ideal. Toulmin uses Capability Brown to demon-strate how British empiricism, in contrast to French idealism, pragmatically offers a way to "play it as it lays" and work with what is available within any particular context, rather than trying to impose abstract, universal ideals on situations. In Toulmin's hands, Capability Brown effectively illustrates the value in a return to reason as a counter-balance to the excessive emphasis on abstract knowledge of universal rationality.

Toulmin is most convincing when he notes that for the social sciences, the scientistic preoccupation with universal rationality was a particularly troubling turn. His primary case in point is the popular one—economics. He calls it the "physics that never was." Toulmin effectively shows that the history of the development of economics as a discipline involved the pro-gressive elimination of historical and social considerations, increasingly decontextualizing its subject matter in ever more abstract and mathemati-cal terms to produce its own universal rationality of market-related behav-ior. The application of abstract economic models to problems of public policy increasingly became the vogue. Theory dictated to practice in often ruthless terms, particularly when first-world lending institutions pre-scribed "structural adjustment" or "shock therapy" policies that required nation-states to retrofit their economies to conform to the models' requirements. The central problem here for Toulmin, as for so many oth-ers, is that these sorts of applications all too often assumed that contextu-ally specific understandings of predictable market behavior were universally applicable, abstracted them from their contexts, and imposed them in social settings, cultures, and political systems where they made very little sense at all, and did so all too often at great cost to the well-being of the people who were supposed to be helped by such "develop-ment" schemes. Toulmin counters these disasters of "top-down," theory-driven economic practice with the example of Muhammad Yunus, who works from the "bottom up" through his Grameen Bank, which pro-vides small loans in more than fifty thousand Bangladeshi villages so that local people can develop "appropriate" enterprises fitted to their commu-nities, values, and local practices. Yunus, a professional economist, is quoted by Toulmin (2001, 65) as saying: "If Economics [as it stands] were a social science, economists would have discovered what a powerful socio-economic weapon credit is. . . . If we can re-design economics as a genuine social science, we will be firmly on our way to creating a poverty-free world." Toulmin ends his tale of the disenchantment of economics by saying (Toulmin 2001, 66): "This message does not, of course, affect Economics alone: similar traditions in the other human sciences have led to similar misunderstandings and errors of practical judgment."

For Toulmin, the antidote to the twentieth-century hegemony of universal rationalism is respect for everyday reason, as practiced in contextualized settings, in ways that cannot be legislated by theory from the top down and are open to living with the uncertainty that such situated knowledges must accept as the ineliminable contingency of what Toulmin calls the "clinical arts." The social sciences are, for Toulmin, more akin to "applied sciences," but "applied" mischaracterizes the situation, suggesting that theory is applied in practice—an idea most significantly popularized by the reports Abraham Flexner wrote on professional medical education in 1913 and on social work in 1915. Instead, drawing on the work of Donald Schon (1983) and others, Toulmin wants us to learn that social theory is better seen growing out of practice, as an intensification of those meditative moments in social practice. Toulmin sees the need for social sciences, operating ever more beyond disciplinary boundaries, to be more about teaching practical wisdom, *phronesis,* as Aristotle termed it, as something that grows out of an intimate familiarity with the contingencies and uncertainties of various forms of social practice embedded in complex social settings. We need, therefore, to revise the standards for acceptable research methodologies, reincorporating context-sensitive research, such as case studies, not to dictate what is to be done but more to inventory infinitely unique cases from which social actors can learn to appreciate the complexities of social relations and practice various social crafts all the more effectively. Social science would be more like bioethics than like moral philosophy, basing itself on the insight that Toulmin provides when he notes that bioethics owes very little to moral philosophy, which, as theory, is incapable of specifying from the top down most bioethical decisions, which instead grow from the bottom up, in unlegislated form, varying with contexts, negotiating ambiguity, living with uncertainty, and still doing the necessary work of determining life and death every day. Case-study research for bioethicists and many others, often conducted in dialogical and collaborative relations with the people being studied, can help enable social actors to use knowledge to address their problems. Such participatory action research would, for Toulmin, be more fitting for a real social science that better understands its relationship to its contingent, contextual, and ever so thoroughly social subjects. For Toulmin, the return to reason will best be evidenced in the social sciences when wisdom of this sort is taught not as an object for scientific scrutiny, as evidence of cultural variation, but as the very goal of knowledge production itself.

It is at this point that the circle is squared for me in a most compelling way. In his Introduction, Toulmin cites another recent book as a sign that some social scientists are tapping into the themes he emphasizes. The book is none other than *Making Social Science Matter: Why Social Inquiry Fails and How It Can Succeed Again*. This is why Flyvjberg's book is so important. More than any other book I know, it provides solid intellectual justification for much of what Perestroika is about. Flyvbjerg's book takes us one step further down the road that Toulmin has laid out for us, and it does it eloquently, with its own impassioned argument that not only demonstrates what is wrong with the social sciences today but provides a detailed list of examples of how a phronetic social science is already possible and already happening here and there among the detritus of contemporary social science.

Flyvbjerg's book is such a breath of fresh air; he creatively uses Aristotle, Nietzsche, Foucault, Bourdieu, and others to make many of the same points as Toulmin, but in his own distinctive way. He fuses an Aristotelian concern for phronesis with a Marxist concern for praxis, adding a Foucauldian critique of Habermas's preoccupation with consensus to demonstrate that a phronetic social science that can offer a praxis worth pursuing is one that would work within any contextualized setting to challenge power, especially as it is articulated in discourse. Flyvbjerg's phronetic social science would be open to using a plurality of research methods to help people challenge power more effectively.

Flyvbjerg begins where Toulmin left us, in the present, with social science hopelessly lost, seeking to emulate the natural sciences with a quest for theory-driven abstract knowledge of universal rationality. Flyvbjerg adds a compelling critique that demonstrates convincingly that there is no symmetry between natural and social science in that natural science's interpretive problems are compounded by what Anthony Giddens called the "double hermeneutic" of the social sciences. By virtue of its distinctively human subject matter, social scientists inevitably are people who offer interpretations of other people's interpretations. And the people being studied always have the potential to include the social scientists' interpretations in theirs, creating an ever-changing subject matter and requiring a dialogic relationship between the people doing the studying and the people being studied. For Flyvbjerg, this situation unavoidably means that there can be no theory for social science in the sense that social science needs to forgo the dream that it can create time-tested theories of a static social reality.

As a result, argues Flyvbjerg, the social sciences should not seek to emulate the natural sciences. In such a comparison, the social sciences will always fare very poorly, being seen as inferiors incapable of producing knowledge based on tested theories that can evince prediction of the worlds they study. Instead, Flyvbjerg feels that the social sciences are better equipped to produce a different kind of knowledge—phronesis, practical wisdom—that grows out of intimate familiarity with practice in contextualized settings. Local knowledges, even tacit knowledges, that cannot be taught a priori, grown from the bottom up, emerging out of practice, forgoing the hubris of seeking claims to a decontextualized universal rationality stated in abstract terms of false precision. Add a sense of praxis, seeking the ability to push for change, leaven it with an appreciation of the ineliminable presence of power, and this phronetic social science can help people in ongoing political struggle question the relationships of knowledge and power and thereby work to change things in ways they might find more agreeable and even satisfying. Such a phronetic social science can contribute to what I have called "radical incrementalism," or the idea that praxis involves promoting change for the least advantaged by exploiting the possibilities in current political arrangements (Schram 2002).

Yet, what is most exciting is that Flyvbjerg not only goes beyond critique to offer a positive program; he demonstrates it in detail, pointing to a rich variety of contemporary work from that of Bourdieu, to Robert Bellah, to his own work. Flyvbjerg's research spanned fifteen years and focused on a major redevelopment project initiated by the Danish city of Aalborg, where Flyvbjerg continues to teach urban planning. His research on the project evolved over time, quickly becoming more phronetic as he came to appreciate how social science could make real contributions to the ongoing dialogue over the city's redevelopment efforts once his research was retrofitted to the specific context in which the issues of development were being debated. At first, Flyvbjerg was put off that decision makers rejected the relevance of studies about education elsewhere, and he came to be concerned with power. Without saying so, he evidently took to heart the idea that he had to work harder to produce research that, even while it challenged power, demonstrated its sensitivity to the Aalborg context. In the process, power relations got challenged in a very public way, the framing of the development agenda got successfully revised to include more grass-roots concerns, an ongoing dialogue with participants in the redevelopment process got richly elaborated, and social science research that gave up an interest in proving grand theories became critical to a very robust discourse on urban planning. As a result, the Aalborg planning project gained increased visibility as a successful project that went out of its way to democratize its decision making, in part by allowing social science research to help keep it honest, open, and collaborative.

Phronetic social science such as this would be very different from the social science that predominates today. Yet, I wonder whether it would be constructive to say that this would represent a new paradigm. This is because I am increasingly convinced that social science is ideally better seen as post-paradigmatic rather than as organized by one paradigm or another. For me, the idea of paradigm has no relevance to social science except as its own form of mimicry. Paradigmatic research is what natural scientists do. Social science, for the reasons provided in this essay, ideally should not be seen as amenable to being organized paradigmatically in any strict sense of the term.

The strict sense of the term is, of course, subject to intense debate, starting with its author, Thomas Kuhn. Paradigm started to become a critical idea for thinking about scientific knowledge in Kuhn's *The Structure of Scientific Revolutions* (1970) and served as the lynchpin for his theory that in any given field, "normal" science was periodically punctuated by "revolutionary" science that induced a conceptual transformation of the subject matter and initiated new ways of studying it. From the beginning, Kuhn struggled to respond to critics by relying in particular on two additional concepts—exemplar and disciplinary matrix (von Dietz 2001). An exemplar is an exemplary example, usually in the form of an innovative experiment or analytical treatment that, by its very success, implied a particular way to understand and study the subject in question. To the extent that they are contingent upon exemplars, Kuhn's paradigms are to a great degree therefore implicit in the very act of "learning by doing" in a contextually sensitive fashion, making them in their own way forms of phronetic reasoning, learned and elaborated through situated practice.[2] The disciplinary matrix is the social, institutional, and organizational side of the process, where cohorts of scientists were introduced to the paradigm and encouraged to practice normal science according to how they were socialized by the disciplinary matrix. It therefore is as if paradigms had both material and symbolic dimensions. Through learning to practice exemplars, graduate students became normal scientists. Natural science was its own form of phronesis, if only so as to practice natural scientific reasoning in the context of actually doing it.

Once a new exemplar arises that is seen as providing a preferred understanding of the subject matter in ways that the prevailing paradigm cannot, scientists have to learn the new rules for study implied by the new exemplar. Translation into the old system of study would not work because the paradigms were, in Kuhn's mind, to an ineliminable degree, by definition, incommensurable. Each paradigm's evidence is of a nature that it always has to be evaluated by its own standards, in its own context, making it impossible to use evidence to decide whether one paradigm was better than another. For Kuhn, knowledge does not grow cumulatively, with one paradigm building on another. We should never say that we now know more or better, only that with a paradigm change we know differently.

What was most radical, then, about Kuhn's notion of paradigm is that it unmasks the necessary fiction that the twentieth-century meta-story of science teaches us about the growth of objective knowledge. This Kuhnian claim led critics to charge him with relativism on the grounds that Kuhn seemed to be implying that one paradigm might be as true or right as another. Kuhn spent much of the rest of his life responding to critics with clarifications that more often than not moved him away from the relativistic implications of his work. Yet, I agree with Richard Rorty (1997) that when someone calls you a relativist, the best responses include saying thank you for highlighting your well-founded commitment to challenging the illegitimacy of the master narrative of science (also see Gunnell 1993).

Kuhn, however, left to the side whether paradigm has relevance to understanding social sciences. Given the subject matter, there ideally should be no normal science in any one of the social sciences. Regardless of the fact that both natural and social science are forms of learning in context that produce value-laden facts, social life, as opposed to the objects of natural scientific inquiry, involves multiple interpretive lenses that offer a cacophony of competing perspectives emanating from its origins in conscious, thinking human beings. Under these conditions, no one form of disciplined study of social life should be organized paradigmatically to exclude the consideration of multiple perspectives.

Ironically, the objectivists in social science themselves most often resist the application of Kuhn's idea of paradigm to their fields since it implies that their scientific work is value-laden. I agree with them about resisting its application to social science, but for the different reason that multiple perspectives are inherent in the subject matter. It is a sad irony, then, that even though the objectivists resist paradigm, methodological hegemony by objectivists is the reality today in social sciences such as political science and economics. This is a doleful reminder that paradigms involve the very human power struggles of a disciplinary matrix as much as they do the practices of inquiry demonstrated in exemplars. Paradigms can be imposed socially even where they are most inappropriate intellectually.

Regardless of its roots in learning from examples, to talk of a new "paradigm" in the context of social science risks reinscribing the very foundationalism that a perestroikan-inspired phronetic social science seeks to challenge. To replace one paradigm with another simply encourages social scientists to privilege theory as some legislating and authorizing activity that it is not. Such foundationalism reflects a lingering commitment to universal rationality and fails to appreciate the contextualism that Toulmin and Flyvbjerg emphasize as central to understanding and contributing to social and political life.

A better response would be to approach phronetic social science as post-paradigmatic, or, as Flyvbjerg prefers, nonparadigmatic, research. Such a body of work would involve theory as something that grows out of the practices in specific contexts while still working to achieve critical distance on prevailing understandings of those social practices. This would be the beginning of research that could better help people challenge power.

In conclusion, I emphasize that phronetic social science is more than a dream; it already exists. It is just not organized, recognized, or named as such, existing here and there where scholars come to it on their own. It also has multiple sources of intellectual sustenance that have provided resources for challenging the orthodoxy of scientistic social science. One set of resources over the past few decades has come from what came to be called "interpretive social science" (see Scott and Keates 2001). Yet, there are others, as the "interpretive turn" in social science has been overtaken by the subsequent linguistic turn and a series of other related turns that followed, all contributing to the growing resistance to the hegemony of scientistic social science. Phronetic social science is but a pathway that comes from all these different turns. Yet, while the interpretive and subsequent turns helped provide resources for developing the phronetic research that already is among us; these prior turns do not by themselves constitute phronetic social science. A perestroikan-inspired phronetic social science involves taking more turns along the lines I have suggested in this chapter and perhaps taking other lines, as well. Yet, the future is not as predictable as the hegemons might suggest it is. Will the road ahead take more turns in a phronetic direction? That depends to a large extent on the plays of power, in the academy, the government, the think tanks, and anywhere else knowledge and power are being "disciplined."

## NOTES

1. The Perestroika listserv is replete with examples of dissertation advisers and journal editors who as a rule will not consider case studies. The archives of the listserv can be accessed by emailing perestroika_glasnost_warmhome@yahoo.com.

2. Thanks to Bonnie Honig for pointing out that, etymologically, paradigm from the Greek *paradeiknunai:* literally, "to show beside," from para, "alongside," and *deiknunai,* "to show," implying learning by imitating an example.

*2*

# The Perestroikan Challenge to Social Science

## *David D. Laitin*

The specter of an insurgency haunts political science. Under the leadership of a "Mr. Perestroika," a wide group of political scientists has abandoned the project of a scientific discipline.[1] It would be convenient to write off this quasi-coordinated attack on the scientific turn in the study of society, calling its proponents Luddites. Indeed, their abhorrence of all things mathematical—and their typical but useless conflation of statistical and formal reasoning—reveals a fear of the modern. It would be equally convenient to write off this attack for its lack of any manifesto offering an alternative view of the discipline. Mostly we hear a desire for pluralism, rather than a defense of best practices. But I think it would be prudent to respond, to defend what may well be a Sisyphean project in seeking a science of social life.

While there is no intellectual manifesto that lays down the gauntlet, a recently published book by Bent Flyvbjerg captures many of the core themes in Mr. Perestroika's insurgency (Flyvbjerg 2001). And thus this book offers an intellectual target for those who wish to confront the perestroikan challenge intellectually (White 2002). For in this clever, succinct, and readable book, Flyvbjerg portrays the quest for a *social* science as quixotic at best and self-defeating at worst. The social world, he argues, is sufficiently different from the natural world that any hopes for a Galilean conquest over the unknown in social science will forever remain unrealized. (Flyvbjerg equivocates throughout the book on the question of whether scientific work has any merit in the study of the social world. Compare Flyvbjerg 2001, 25, 76 49, 87.[2]) He does not provide evidence on the degree to which natural science research meets his standards. Social scientists, in order to sidestep the scorn that is regularly heaped on them by natural scientists who recognize the scientific limits to the study of humans, should cultivate their own turf by making reasonable judgments about the social world, based on a realistic view of power and sensitivity as to how that power is exerted. Relying on Aristotle's categorization, Flyvbjerg dubs this methodology phronesis. Social scientists can succeed doing phronesis, Flyvbjerg confidently asserts, because we write and read careful case studies that provide to us an expert's feel for how, in a particular context, our political interventions can bring social betterment.

This is a viewpoint to be taken seriously. Flyvbjerg has conducted well-conceived fieldwork in Denmark and has long been an astute commentator on urban planning and popular participation in social planning. Furthermore, *Making Social Science Matter* has received excellent notices from some of the leading social scientists in the world, including Clifford Geertz, Steven Lukes, and Pierre Bourdieu. Finally, the arguments in the book resonate with parallel points articulated by political science perestroikans, who have yet to be seriously confronted with intellectual arguments.

My response to Flyvbjerg and the challenge he presents to the scientific aspirations of many political scientists proceeds in stages. First, I challenge Flyvbjerg's stylized facts that purportedly show the failure of what he calls "epistemic" social science. Since Flyvbjerg presents these facts to motivate his study, it is important to establish that the premise of the book—constructed from these stylized facts—stands on weak foundations. Second, I challenge Flyvbjerg's portrayals of both context (which he claims is not subject to analysis) and science (for which he sets a standard that many research programs in the natural sciences could not meet). It is important to challenge these views because Flyvbjerg argues that the irreducibility of social context makes a predictive science of the social impossible. I can then show that Flyvbjerg's claims for the greater intellectual payoff for phronesis, because of his mistaken views on context and science, need to be radically circumscribed. Third, I discuss phronesis at work, first in a discussion of Flyvbjerg's use of that method in his field research on urban planning in Aalborg, Denmark, and then in a discussion of the work by Stanley Tambiah on ethnic war in Sri Lanka. In both cases, I argue, the work would have much greater scientific value if placed within what I have dubbed the "tripartite method of comparative research"—a method that integrates narrative (much of what Flyvbjerg calls phronesis), statistics, and formal modeling (Laitin 2002). Fourth, I discuss the contributions that phronesis makes in scientific explanation, showing why it has equal stature to statistics and formal modeling in the tripartite method. Finally, in the conclusion, and in defense of the tripartite method as a standard, I discuss (in reference to claims by one of Mr. Perestroika's defenders) the limits of methodological pluralism.

## The Premise of Flyvbjerg's Book

Flyvbjerg introduces his brief with three examples. Astonishingly, they all work to undermine his entire argument. The opening example is that of the now infamous contribution by the New York University physicist Alan Sokal to the journal *Social Text.* Sokal's "contribution" was a hoax. He purposefully submitted what he conceived of as postmodern gobbledygook. Yet it sailed through *Social Text*'s peer review as a serious critique of science. Flyvbjerg offers this example, and the controversy that occurred in the wake of Sokal's publication, as inter alia an "exposé of . . . social science." But why, the reader might ask, would social science get implicated in this scandal? *Social Text* has no pretensions to science. More important, in large part because of a cult of science in leading social science journals such as *American Political Science Review, Econometrica,* and *American Journal of Sociology,* it is doubtful that a physicist could get an article of that sort past peer reviewers. Reviewers would want to assure themselves that the data set was available and subject to review, the theory was clearly articulated, and the findings were linked closely to theory and data. Sokal chose *Social Text* precisely because members of its editorial board had ridiculed the notion of scientific objectivity.

The second example, immediately on the heels of the presentation of the Sokal hoax, concerns the study of human sexual practices conducted by scholars working at the National Opinion Research Center (NORC). Flyvbjerg delights in quoting *The Economist*'s humorous put-down of this study (and later on he uses an equally clever one-liner from *The Economist* to write off the entire profession of economics). Flyvbjerg also cites a more serious attack on the statistical methods employed in this study, written by a population geneticist, and a rather limp defense of those methods by the authors in response. This is evidence for Flyvbjerg that natural scientists hold social scientists in contempt. Social scientists, he concludes, should not even try to imitate the scientific method with fancy statistics and impressive regressions. Rather, if they sang a tune that they in fact could hold, they would no longer have opprobrium heaped on them by their natural science colleagues.

This example also works against Flyvbjerg's argument. The inference of low esteem toward social science in general drawn from a single review of a particular work in social science is unjustified. Making an inference from a single case, an ambiguous one at that, is logically unjustified. This suggests that Flyvbjerg has little concern for valid inference, something that should make supporters of his phronetic alternative nervous. His inference is not only invalid; it is wrong, and on two counts. First, Flyvbjerg ignores the intriguing collaborations between biologists and social scientific game theorists in the past two decades that have created new knowledge in fields closely related to the scientific critic of the NORC study (Axelrod and Hamilton 1981, 1390–96, political science and biology; Selten and Hammerstein 1994, 929–93, economics and biology; Boyd and Richerson 1985, anthropology and ecology). Natural scientists who have worked in productive collaboration with social scientists would hardly hold social scientists as a species in contempt, as did the reviewer of the NORC book.

His inference is wrong on a second count. The book appeared when the AIDS epidemic was first spreading. Many in the press were reporting linear and ghastly projections of the spread of the disease based on briefings from medical professionals. The NORC team, relying on its scientific finding that there are in America, especially among homosexuals, closed networks of sexual practice, predicted that the growth curve would flatten and that the disease would continue to eat away within segmented sexual communities. The NORC researchers could not offer a precise prediction of how many individuals would incur AIDS, but their research on sexual practice entailed an observable implication, which turned out to be true. This does not prove their methods to be impeccable. Indeed, one could well point to the methodological problem not only in the NORC study but also in the entire genre of studies that postulate causal sequences from cross-sectional survey data. But the NORC team's correct analysis that AIDS would not spread generally through the American population adds confidence that they were accurately portraying American sexual networks (also see Laumann et al. 1994, 546–47).[3] In sum, Flyvbjerg's use of the NORC example as evidence that natural scientists hold in ridicule all forms of scientific activity in the study of the social world is unconvincing.

Flyvbjerg's third example, a study of human learning conducted by Hubert Dreyfus and Stuart Dreyfus, serves as a leitmotif for the entire book. The Dreyfuses conducted an experiment in which subjects were asked to observe videotapes and then evaluate the competence of paramedics, made up of one expert and five novices who were all engaged in performing cardiopulmonary resuscitation (CPR) on victims of heart failure. The experimental subjects included people with three levels of expertise: experienced paramedics, students learning to become paramedics, and life-saving instructors. The experimental results showed that experienced paramedics, but not the other two sets of observers, could consistently and correctly pick out the expert practitioner of CPR. Those subjects who were novices, or so Flyvbjerg's preferred interpretation goes, were attuned to the question of who was best following the rules of CPR; meanwhile, the expert subjects were less interested in the rules. They were looking for the single practitioner who had an eye for context and knew which rules could be waived to save the largest number of victims.

One of the study's authors (Stuart Dreyfus) offered the following insight to make sense of the finding. He was a mathematician and a chess aficionado. For a long time, he believed that if he could solve all the necessary algorithms, he would become a master. To his chagrin, mathematical logic took him only so far. Those with an expert's "feel" for the chessboard were able to defeat him, and very often these people had no education in higher mathematics. Only those with a feel for the chessboard (often honed by playing "fast chess" rather than by studying algorithms), Stuart Dreyfus observed, could become masters. The lesson for social science that Flyvbjerg draws from the experiment and from the chess anecdote is that in the complex world of human beings, no algorithm will correctly predict action; rather, an expert's feel for the context will bring a better grasp of what is likely to occur. Only experts who have worked and lived in the social world (like chess players who have developed skills through practice) will be able to know how best, in the experimental case, to choose a paramedic if they are in need of one.

One could criticize the chess analogy (and by implication the inference) by pointing out that it is increasingly dated, as supercomputers are becoming chess masters with rule-based algorithms. But there are two far more disconcerting things about the use of the Dreyfuses' study as a justification for phronesis. First, there is another interpretation of this study, never considered, that undermines the thesis of the book. From what was presented (as admitted by Flyvbjerg (2001, 22), the Dreyfuses used a rather standard scientific procedure common in experimental psychology to make a discovery concerning human cognition. The experimenters learned from their controlled environment (certainly not a case study!) that there are different levels of competence in the human learning process, with implications for what it takes to become an expert. This seems to me to be an advertisement for the scientific method in gaining new psychological knowledge, rather than an invitation to jump the scientific ship. Second, there is overwhelming evidence from controlled experiments that statistical models outperform expert clinical intuitions in diagnosing human disease (Dawes, Faust, and Meehl 1989, 1668–74). Here is a case where natural scientists would put Flyvbjerg up for ridicule for not examining whether a finding he liked was sufficiently robust to work in other experimental settings.

In sum, looking at the Sokal example, the NORC sex study, and the Dreyfuses' study as compelling reasons to abjure the scientific method in social science, Flyvbjerg's attempt to create a sense of scientific failure through the use of telling examples is manifestly unsuccessful.

## Three Misunderstandings

Flyvbjerg is adamant that methodological admonitions urging students to study society scientifically are mired in misunderstandings about the social world. But he is guilty of some grievous misunderstandings himself.

### 1. What Is Context?

"Context" plays a leading role in many tracts that purport to show the limitations of scientific procedures for the study of society, and in Flyvbjerg's book as well (Flyvbjerg 2001, 9; also ch. 4 passim).[4] But Flyvbjerg never actually defines it. His method, we are told, is sensitive to context, whereas science is not. Humans are always sensitive to context, but not computers. Therefore, people are better judges of complex situations that are heavily influenced by context than are computers. This judgment rests on a grievous overstatement. *Context* comes to us from the Latin *contextus,* meaning a connection of words. In English, this has come to mean, among other related things, "the parts of discourse that surround a word or passage and throw light on its meaning" (*Webster's Ninth New Collegiate Dictionary*). If this is what *context* means, surely computers have been programmed to use surrounding words to throw light on a particular word's meaning. Search engines allow us, in our investigation of a particular concept, to specify words before and after this concept is used. This procedure helps throw light on a particular concept's meaning.

Of course, Flyvbjerg means more than word connections. Indeed, *con-textus* is closely related to the Latin *contexere,* "to weave." Here, context implies a skein of interwoven factors. But to say humans are good at capturing context is hardly a justification for phronesis. For one purpose of social science is to disentangle such skeins in order to trace the effects of its separate strands, or to examine the impact of particular interactions among strands. Appealing to context is merely to say that we have not yet discovered the various factors or the interaction of factors that produced outcomes of significance. Science *is* sensitive to context, if sensitivity means the desire to analyze it, to break it down to its separate strands, and to hypothesize how the woven strands influence the course of social events. Ultimately, one's hypotheses about the implications of various contextual strands will demand statistical verification with interaction terms and flexible functional forms. Appealing to context is therefore a copout; analyzing it and verifying our analytical judgments about it are what social scientists ought to be doing.

## 2. What Is Science?

Science for Flyvbjerg must meet an ideal, or else it is not science. It is portrayed as the activity that can "generate ultimate, unequivocally verified knowledge" yielding some "final truth" (Flyvbjerg 2001, 139). Hardly anyone in the natural sciences would hold such a view. Nor would mathematicians, who mostly rearrange symbols consistent with axioms rather than pursue a final truth. Most scientists see their findings as provisional, contingent, and subject to replication and rejection.

Oddly, of the several criteria for science elucidated in *Making Social Science Matter,* the only one Flyvbjerg insists that social scientists cannot achieve is that of prediction. Yet, this is the only criterion for which Flyvbjerg provides no "philosophy of science" citations. He just asserts it to be a necessary component of science.

This criterion is the most demanding of all, and many fields that are widely respected as scientific (e.g., population biology, evolution, and geology) would quickly fail this test. But if what is meant by prediction is the ability of scholars in the field to make reasonably good probability estimates of individual behavior under laboratory conditions or in well-defined activities (e.g., voting), then several branches of social science can meet such criteria. Social scientists, for example, have long been able to make reasonable predictions of how any individual will vote knowing a few facts about his or her socioeconomic background, age, and education.

Stating ideal criteria for science—and writing off those fields that do not meet these criteria as a breeding ground for phronesis—represents a bimodal approach to scientific categorization. It is better to evaluate research environments as a continuous variable, measuring the extent to which they approach commonly accepted scientific standards, with the notion that doing better in meeting such criteria dominates doing worse. Instead of some unreachable ideal as the criterion of science, I propose a notion of a scientific frame. To the extent to which a community of scholars is concerned about such things as uncertain (ex ante) conclusions, public procedures, careful measurement, rules of inference, and rewards for replication, that community has adopted a scientific frame.

I also propose that within the scientific frame, a tripartite methodology that includes narrative (the essential component to phronesis), formal, and statistical analyses is the best defense we have against error and the surest hope for valid inference. To the extent that a community has adopted a scientific frame and relies on a tripartite method, it will be in a better condition to make good judgments. The problem with good judgment that rests on only one leg of the tripartite method (exemplified in Flyvbjerg's rendition of phronesis) is that it is hard to know if one's judgment is wrong. The scientific frame buttressed with the tripartite method—as I will illustrate in a subsequent section—has ample procedures for figuring out if our best judgments are misplaced.

### 3. For What Is Phronesis Valuable?

Flyvbjerg is ambiguous about the goals to be maximized in social science. He seems to move the goal post. On one hand, he points to social scientists who seek to make valid causal inferences about the social world. He criticizes them for the inevitability of their failures. But in his alternative model, that of phronesis, his goal is to give students in professional schools useful knowledge, helping them to make a better world. Here I am sympathetic with Flyvbjerg's brief. For professional training of policy analysts and politicians, it seems useful to focus on normative questions (what kind of life do we want to lead?), experience to get a feel for the practical, and case studies (what kind of world did my predecessors face, and how well did they do?), with somewhat less emphasis on making valid causal inferences about how certain outcomes were reached. For Ph.D. training, the balance needs to be reversed. But the point here is that while Flyvbjerg's notion of phronesis may have some important role to play in the professionalization of social practitioners, it must be combined with statistical and formal analysis if the goal is valid social knowledge.

## *Phronesis at Work*

Flyvbjerg summarizes his politically engaged and ultimately successful research on city planning in Aalborg, Denmark, as an example of the potential for phronesis. He reports that a city-planning initiative in Aalborg was captured by downtown businessmen who had a vision of super-profits that would come with shoppers who arrived from long distances in their automobiles. They sacrificed the interests of local pedestrians and bicyclists, whose interests were subverted in the plan for roadways into the downtown center. Leaving the ivory tower of intellectual debate, Flyvbjerg confronted local power with phronetic knowledge, acquired through painstaking penetration of the particularities of a single city. Armed with a deep understanding of all backroom deals, his several public appearances parried the slander heaped on him. More important, he presented his data in a way that the public could appreciate. He was thus able to turn the tide away from business control over planning back to the interests of the pedestrians and bicyclists. The citizens of Aalborg were rewarded with democratic debate based on phronetic intervention and an outcome closer to their own preferences.

The smoking gun in Flyvbjerg's investigation was that the Chamber of Industry and Commerce in Aalborg had preferred access to the technical committee of the City Council. Through this preferred access, the chamber's point of view, in which the only route to commercial survival lay in attracting customers who arrived by car from far away, became the "rational" one in terms of how the future was to be determined. Flyvbjerg sees this as confirming the "basic Nietzschean insight [that] 'interpretation is itself a means of becoming master of something.'" Flyvbjerg concludes, now basing his notion of power on an extended analysis not only of Aristotle and Nietzsche but also of Habermas, Bourdieu, and Foucault, that "the interpretation which has the stronger power base [namely, that of the Chamber of Industry and Commerce] becomes Aalborg's truth" (Flyvbjerg 2001, 153).

There appears to be something tautological about this finding. The only way one knows the strength of the chamber's power base is the degree to which it was able to make its position hegemonic. This is hardly a finding about the effects of power on the setting of interpretive frames (but for a seemingly different account, see Flyvbjerg 1998a).[5] For that, we would need to know what resources translate most efficiently into the victory of hegemonic interpretations. We would further need to know the mechanisms (bribes, implicit or explicit threats to leave to other cities, campaign contributions) by which certain resources are expended to secure preferred interpretations. We would need to know how far people can be moved from their ideal points on a policy spectrum by power such as that held by the chamber. And if power is being exerted merely because those who are without it are afraid to defy those with it (and, therefore, the exertion of power is not directly observable), we would need to know about the off-the-path beliefs of those without power so that they would be induced into quiescence. Pointing out that power rules is hardly an explanation for its influence, and the two chapters on power give us little handle on its prospects and merits under different well-specified conditions.

To be sure, Flyvbjerg wants phronesis to answer a range of questions. The question of how power is used to create rationality is but one. He also wants social science to answer normative questions about what is desirable and what ought to be done. And he wants social science to help prepare professional students "to help them achieve real practical experience" (Flyvbjerg 2001, 145, 72). I have no quarrel at all with the promotion of normative and professional pursuits, but the promotion and quality of such pursuits stand outside the question of whether for a certain range of questions the scientific frame is appropriate for study of the social. Furthermore, in his discussion of power, Flyvbjerg trespasses onto the zone of science (seeking to identify the causes of the chamber's influence) without playing by its rules. It is phronesis inappropriately applied.

## The Danger of Isolated Phronesis

Nothing calls out more strongly for "social science that matters" than that of civil wars in the post–World War II world. In the course of the past half-century, there has been a slow, steady, incessant outbreak of new civil wars throughout the world. New wars break out at a faster rate than existing ones get settled, so that the number of active civil wars and the percentage of countries experiencing civil wars increased steadily from 1945 to 1999. In the past half-century, there have been more than 16 million deaths as a result of 122 distinct civil wars. Many of these wars have cost the lives of far more than one thousand people, the minimum necessary to be included in Michigan-inspired data sets (Fearon and Laitin 2003). In this category stands Sri Lanka, where more than sixty thousand people have been killed in a war in which Tamil separatists are pitted against the majority Sinhalese government. A social science that could help reduce the devastation of civil wars would matter a great deal.

Stanley Tambiah, a world authority on Buddhism, has sought to understand the sources of violence in Sri Lanka from a perspective that Flyvbjerg would clearly agree was phronetic. Tambiah was impelled to study this conflict from a deep normative desire to make his homeland once again an island of peace. He accumulated materials related to the conflict and wrote scholarly books on it and on a related set of deadly conflicts. But he was continuously engaged with authorities in Sri Lanka, with an international press that all too often systematically misrepresented the conflict, and with Sri Lankans around the world who were equally interested in ending a human tragedy. He examined the particular cultural and historical context of the dispute, and all his writings exhibit deep understanding of the local situation, a full recognition of the sources of local power, and a clear desire to alter the terrible curse of interethnic relations that seems Sri Lanka's fate.

Tambiah was at first revolted by but not engaged in Sri Lanka's troubles. In 1956, he brought a student team with him to investigate a peasant resettlement program in the country's Eastern Province. But the project was interrupted by the first ethnic riots to take place since the country achieved independence, in 1948. These riots occurred when an oppressive language law was being debated in parliament. The majority Sinhalese population had from the time of independence pressed for its language to become the medium of instruction, ultimately through the university curriculum. The language law of 1956, popularly known as the "Sinhala Only Act," promised to make Sinhalese the sole official language of the island within twenty-four hours. Tambiah, then teaching at the University of Ceylon, was immediately disenchanted and felt that he must emigrate. He felt he could not advance professionally if he were compelled to teach in Sinhalese (he is a native Tamil speaker, and English was the medium of instruction throughout his education). Furthermore, the quality of university education would, in his judgment, plummet were it to be cut off from Western scientific literature, a likely prospect were the medium of instruction to become Sinhalese. With ethnic tensions already evident on his home island, he moved his research site to Thailand (Tambiah, 1997, 8–10).

It was twenty-seven years later that he felt "compelled to take up the issues in Sri Lanka concerning ethnic conflict, ethnonationalism, and political violence" (Tambiah 1997, 14). A pogrom in 1983, leveled against the middle-class Tamil community in Colombo, in which ministers of the state were implicated, in his words, "fractured two halves of [his] identity as a Sri Lankan and as a Tamil." He wrote *Sri Lanka: Ethnic Fratricide and the Dismantling of Democracy* (1986) to find his "way out of a depression and to cope with a personal need to make some sense of that tragedy, which was the beginning of worse things to come" (Tambiah 1997, 26). In the preface to that book, he acknowledges that it is not a "distanced academic treatise" but more an "engaged political tract." His goal, he writes, is "not only to understand the Sri Lankan problem but also to change it; it intends to be a historical and sociological reading which necessarily suggests a course of political action" Tambiah 1986, ix). One might say that the 1983 pogrom moved Tambiah from epistemic to phronetic social science.

In his subsequent work on Sri Lanka, he was never far from contemporary politics, asking such phronetic questions (asked in Flyvbjerg 2001, 145) as where we are going and what should be done. He took his theoretical work on Buddhism (conducted in Thailand) to address a compelling concern to all those interested in a peaceful Sri Lanka: how could a religion that advocates nonviolence become the breeding ground for anti-Tamil pogroms? That his answer, published as *Buddhism Betrayed?* (Tambiah 1992), was banned in Sri Lanka (and its author accused of being a terrorist) showed that he was speaking truth to power (Tambiah 1997, 26–27).

Tambiah's accounts of the sources of the Sri Lankan civil war reflect deep concern and careful judgment. He weaves together the social, economic, religious, and political themes in a way that shows mastery of the material. He puts special emphasis on the "Sinhala Only Act." "That," he has noted, "is the beginning of the feeling among Tamils that they were discriminated against by the majority" (Tambiah 1997, 9). Tambiah recognizes that those Tamil youths, planning for professional employment and therefore most threatened by the language policy, were not themselves involved in the riots subsequent to the language act. The worst violence occurred in the peasant-populated settlement schemes in the Eastern Province. Tambiah therefore provides a holistic contextual account and writes that, "If one wonders what could be the relationship between the official language controversy and the ethnic violence . . . the answer is . . . the language issue was also becoming interwoven with the government's policy of peasant resettlement" (Tambiah 1992, 57, 47).

Sensitive to Flyvbjerg's phronetic concern that researchers address the issue in regard to any policy of "Who gains, and who loses, by which mechanisms of power?" (Flyvbjerg 2001, 145), Tambiah analyzes the winning coalition. Politicized Buddhists who espoused racialist doctrines calling for extermination of Tamils organized this coalition. These Buddhists were able to attract into their program rural elites, teachers, indigenous doctors, traders, merchants, and all those educated in Sinhalese who were threatened by the English-speaking elites in the capital. As for the 1983 riots in which up to two thousand people were killed, Tambiah writes, "those who stood to gain [the] most were, firstly, middle-level Sinhala entrepreneurs, businessmen, and white-collar workers, and secondly, the urban poor, mainly through looting" (Tambiah 1992, 20–27; Tambiah, 1996, 100).

Tambiah's analysis is fair minded and judicious. But what kind of truth comes from his phronetic engagement, one not combined with the statistical and formal methods? Consider first some statistical data that put a wrinkle in Tambiah's account. A cross-sectional analysis with "civil war" as the dependent variable shows that high levels of linguistic grievance are not predictors of civil war. In fact, controlling for GDP, in most model specifications there is a negative sign, suggesting that higher levels of linguistic grievance are associated with a lower susceptibility to civil war. Although the idea is counterintuitive, the statistical models open the possibility that the oppressive Sinhalese language laws might have ameliorated the violence (triggered by the settlement schemes) rather than exacerbated it (Laitin 1997, 97–137). (The subsequent discussion draws on that article, without use of quotation marks.)

The first-cut statistical test of the effects of interethnic oppression on the linguistic front raises a host of new questions, previously unasked.[6] Why, if Tamils were most threatened by the language policy, did the Sinhalese initiate most of the rioting in Colombo in both 1956 and 1958, with virtually no Tamil violence aimed at Sinhalese until 1975? Why should there have been post-language-law riots that were initiated by Sinhalese, inasmuch as they got the law they wanted? Why did the most horrifyingly fatal riots (those of 1981 and 1983) and the consequent full-scale Tamil rebellion occur after Tamil was accorded status nearly equal to that of Sinhalese in Sri Lankan law? Or, finally, why did the language issue disappear from public debate in inverse proportion to the level of escalation of violence on the island?

The tripartite scientific method helps to address these questions. The cross-sectional statistical data show that the holistic context of an interwoven linguistic and settlement grievance was not like two final straws on a camel's back. Rather, these two issues could well have had polar opposite impacts on the Tamil community (see Fearon and Laitin unpublished manuscript). To analyze why, it is useful to model linguistic grievances and to show what each party's best response would be to the probable action of others. From such a model, taking into account preferences of the parties over a range of possible outcomes, it turns out that those most aggrieved by the act were students and teachers. The aggrieved, given their payoff schedule, would gain more from bureaucratic bargaining than they would from guerrilla attacks. From this model, one can comprehend the logic by which the language laws temporarily concentrated Tamil opposition into the bureaucratic field and politicized rather than militarized the ethnic conflict.

This same model gains plausibility because it helps make sense of another conundrum, namely that while the Sinhala Only Act had broad public support, its implementation was almost nonexistent. In fact, Sinhala civil servants had every interest in undermining the implementation of a law that would diminish the value of the primary skill—competence in English—that had earned them their positions. These bureaucrats wrote careful annual reports on the efforts to implement Sinhala hegemony and in so doing perpetually delayed its fulfillment.

In this research, statistical results put previous narratives under critical scrutiny. A formal model captured the strategic core of the politics of language in Sri Lanka. Thus, through a combination of statistics and formal modeling, one is now compelled to rethink the relationship of the Sinhala Only Act to the Sri Lankan civil war. But explanation does not stop there. There is a third component to scientific explanation. Complementing the statistical and formal approaches is a return to narrative to see if the case would be illuminated, rather than obscured, by the statistical and formal models.[7] Suppose it were the case that a return to narrative showed again that language grievances drove Tamils into guerrilla camps and into violent confrontation with the state. This knowledge would compel the statistical analyst to specify anew the interaction terms that seemed important in the narrative. If this should turn out successful, the Sri Lankan narrative would have helped yield a more powerful general statistical model.

Similarly, formalists would be compelled to rethink the preferences of the actors or the structure of their interactions. Again, the goal would be for a general model of language grievance that could capture the effects of oppressive language laws for political action.

In this case, however, the statistical and formal models helped construct a new and more coherent narrative, one that has not (in my search through the literature) elsewhere been told. Facts that had been obscure in the Tambiah narrative can now be highlighted. For one, those educated Tamils who did not emigrate (as did Tambiah) mostly appealed their cases in the various governmental ministries to ensure their professional advance and the security of their civil service appointments. Second, as noted, the law was consistently subverted by Sinhalese government bureaucrats. More stunning is the fact that previous narratives ignored the crucial sequencing of the violence in 1956 in the face of the passage of the Sinhala Only Act. It was the Sinhalese who struck first in a violent manner, not the Tamils. A more coherent narrative (one which shows that the Tamils did not respond to the act with violence) can be told when there is knowledge that the coefficient relating language grievance to violence is negative! That this narrative has not yet been constructed is in part a result of the hegemonic view among experts that the language issue played at least some role in driving ethnic conflict into ethnic warfare.

The methodological lesson here is that serious social analysis requires a scientific frame, and this frame encompasses all three elements of the tripartite method. Sensitive observers saw oppression in the 1950s and civil war in the 1980s and naturally linked the two in a causal chain. In the absence of a data set that includes events in many countries, some facing linguistic oppression but most without, it is impossible to ascertain whether one particular factor was ameliorating or exacerbating. Tambiah imagined a positive coefficient linking levels of linguistic grievance to the likelihood of ethnic fratricide, and he therefore viewed Sri Lanka as a case that confirmed his theory of ethnic warfare. But if he had pictured a negative coefficient as his model, he would have been pushed to ask why Sri Lanka was the exception, having both language grievance and violence. The narrative demands of the question "How did the linguistic grievance play into the set of grievances that led to ethnic war?" are quite different from the one that asks, "Why, despite linguistic grievances, did Sri Lanka experience a civil war?" In some cases, a powerful narrative would force a respecification of statistical models that initially challenged the narrative's causal chain. Here, the statistical findings induced a narrative that shed new light on an old case.

As this example of civil war violence in Sri Lanka shows, it is the interaction of statistical, formal, and narrative work that fills the scientific frame. It helps illustrate why Flyvbjerg's attempt to separate out phronesis (as a kind of narrative) from its statistical and formal complements is radically incomplete and subject to uncontrolled bias. The stark distinction that Flyvbjerg draws between phronesis and the epistemic obscures the productive complementarity of narrative, statistics, and formal analysis in social science.

## The Tripartite Method in Practice

But what, it might be asked, especially by those who accept Flyvbjerg's plea for phronesis, is the positive scientific role for narrative within a tripartite method? Is my tripartite method merely giving lip service to narrative, while the technological giants of formal and statistical models wash away all its value? My answer is no. I see narrative as a co-equal to the statistical and formal elements of the tripartite method, playing three roles. First, narrative provides plausibility tests of all formal models, helping us to assess whether a game theoretic model actually represents a set of real-world cases. Connecting a plausible narrative with a formal model is a difficult and subtle task; doing it successfully adds plausibility to a formal model.

An exemplary use of this narrative tool is that by Robert Bates, who applied a reputation model (based on the chain-store paradox) to account for the dynamics of the rise and fall of the coffee cartel. It is often the case that formal models, absent narratives, lead researchers astray. The chain-store paradox is no exception. This formal model explains the rationality of large stores' cultivating reputations for underpricing new competition, even if it means selling at a loss until the upstart store goes bankrupt. The model can be appropriated elegantly to show how large countries that lead primary-product cartels can drive out of the international market those smaller countries that are seeking to lower prices to gain market share. In applying this model to the coffee cartel, Bates found that, although the model was internally consistent and powerful, he could not narrate the historical sequencing of the cartel on the basis of the moves of the reputation game. Brazil was insufficiently powerful to serve as chain-store leader. Thus, the narrative compelled him to rethink the strategic logic and to apply a different analytic tool. It turned out that a spatial model of coalition formation within the largest purchasing country (the United States)—in which a cold-war logic provided American support for high-priced imports—explained how a dispersed set of sellers could maintain an oligopoly price as long as they did and why it fell apart when the cold war waned. The narrative did not prove the reputation model wrong; rather, it showed that it was the inappropriate representation of the strategic situation that faced the coffee-exporting countries (Bates 1998; on the chain-store paradox see Selten 1978; Kreps and Wilson 1982). Elegant formal models standing alone are inadequate; they need to be supplemented by narrative to show that the real world is represented in the models. Thus, narrative adds plausibility to formal models.

The second role for narrative is to provide mechanisms to link independent and dependent variables in statistical analyses. It is quite common in social science to find explanatory power in macrovariables such as gross domestic product per capita, or democracy, or ethnic linguistic fractionization (a dispersion index that gives the probability that an individual randomly matched with another in his or her country will be of the same ethnic group). The problem is that such social facts as GDP are more like facilitating conditions than causal forces. They do not have the capacity to alter values on a dependent variable. It is therefore difficult to assess what it means for it to be causal for some outcome, such as democracy or civil war. As Elster has taught us, we need to link independent and dependent variables with mechanisms, basically showing how favorable conditions from a statistical sense translate into outcomes (Elster 1998; Pearl 2000).[8]

For example, Przeworski et al. show a statistical link between parliamentary rule and stable democracy (everything else held to mean value). This means that parliamentary democracies are more robust against economic shocks than are presidential systems (Przeworski et al. 2000). Random-matching techniques (Pearl 2000) allow us to avoid the unrealistic assumption that other independent variables have comparable values in parliamentary and presidential regimes. But this finding requires a mechanism to give it causal weight. This has led Przeworski (and other collaborators) to examine exogenous shocks, in a narrative mode, to figure out which of the scores of mechanisms listed in the literature are actually causal. One early conjecture was that in parliamentary systems, govern-

ments face no-confidence votes and are likely to fall. But here, the government, not the democracy, is challenged. Since presidents have fixed terms,
and there is no institution with the constitutional authority to vote the
president out of office for weak performance, in a presidential system an
exogenous shock is likely to invite the army to compel the president to
leave office. When this occurs, not only the government but also the
democratic regime falls. Here, the no-confidence weapon is the mechanism (found through narrative but then complemented with a formal
model and statistical tests) that gives the original statistical finding causal
weight. This conjecture remains provisional. While one of the papers to
emerge from this search for mechanisms emphasizes statistical tests and
formal proofs (Cheibub, Przeworski, and Saiegh 2004), the narrative mode
was the source of insight into mechanisms.

In providing plausibility to formal models and mechanisms for statistical models, it is sometimes the case that the role of narrative gets obscured
in the final presentation of scientific work. Consider an exemplary model
of the tripartite method, Randall Stone's *Lending Credibility* (2002). This
study assesses the impact of International Monetary Fund (IMF) condi-
tionality programs on economic performance in the post-Soviet states.
Numerous earlier studies found only mixed results. Sometimes the IMF
impact was positive and other times negative. Thus, the accepted view
developed that the IMF was no nostrum for structural maladjustment.
Through careful (one might say phronetic) investigations, Stone figured
out that the IMF succeeded only where its threats (to cut the country off
from further loans) were credible. For large countries of great strategic
value to the United States, however, such threats were not credible, as these
countries knew that they would be bailed out by the United States if they
defaulted. Stone therefore created a model of credibility that predicted
where the IMF would have success, and his statistical tests confirmed the
observable implications of the theory. As expected, strategically important
countries were punished more often, but their punishment periods were
shorter. Also, they were less likely to keep inflation under control and less
likely as well to attract foreign investment.

Stone's narratives helped him develop the formal model that was then put
to statistical test. The very success of the model meant, however, that there
were few surprises or new causal conjectures in the chapters that told narratives of particular countries that received IMF support. One might say that
the findings of the narrative were already eaten up by the formal model and
statistical tests. The four chapters narrating the model in the cases of Russia,

Ukraine, Poland, and Bulgaria therefore fell flat. This happened not because narrative was not important; rather, it happened because the findings from narratives fed into statistical model specifications in such a way that there was little new to add in the ultimate telling of the country-level stories.

Mechanisms, Stone's work illustrates, are in some cases no more than underspecified intervening variables. To the extent that a narrative provides the appropriate mechanism, it is incumbent on the researcher to specify the values of that mechanism and to run the statistical model again with a new variable. If the mechanism-turned-variable fails in a significance test, it should give us pause as to whether it really was the causal link between the independent and the dependent variables. But if it proves significant statistically, and it gets built into a formal model, adding it to the narrative will make it appear that the narrative is secondary. In fact, the narrative was the source for the correctly specified causal mechanism.

Suppose, however, that there are several mechanisms that link a set of values on right-hand-side variables to a specific value of a dependent variable. The favorable right-hand-side conditions might be thought of as opening a set of separate pathways toward the same value on the dependent variable. In such cases, all of the mechanisms could fail statistical tests even if properly specified because none could account for more than a small subset of the observations. I believe this is at least part of what Elster is suggesting with his view that mechanisms almost never reveal statistically significant relationships. A statistician might respond by saying that the mechanisms were not properly specified because the conditions under which they were conjectured to operate ("a small subset of the observations") were not adequately operationalized in the statistical model via interactions, nonlinearities, and so on. Even if there were not enough data for signal to overwhelm noise at conventional levels of statistical significance, Bayesians have developed methods to squeeze significance even when faced with "degrees of freedom" problems. But as pathways multiply, these techniques get increasingly tenuous. Under such conditions, narrative would need to stand alone, and rules of narrative coherence and completeness would help to decide whether the causal structure was as theorized. Here, narrative would be providing a more apparent value added than in the case where there was a single mechanism that linked right- and left-hand-side variables.

But even in the case where there is a single mechanism, one that holds up to statistical scrutiny, narrative plays a third role and this through the analysis of residuals. Never in social science is all variance explained, and even in powerful models, the amount that we are able to explain is often paltry. Narrative, by giving a more complete picture of a social process, fills in where statistical and formal models are incomplete. In the case of Stone's narratives, we learn in Poland that Finance Minister Leszek Balcerowicz was more committed to showing the credibility of Poland's reform to international capital than was the IMF. In the narrative, part of the causal weight goes to the charismatic and technical mastery of Balcerowicz over politicians on both the left and right sides of the political spectrum. We have few tools to model formally or to test statistically the role of charismatic leadership in the fostering of reform. Yet, in this case it may well have had causal weight, especially because Stone reveals that Poland was quite important strategically to the West, and this should have made its leaders more likely to defy the IMF and to inflate the currency (99). Examination of the residuals through narratives plants the seeds for future work that can better specify and model causal factors that carried weight in the narratives but were absent in the statistical and formal models.

There are thus three scientific roles entrusted to narrative in social science. First, they provide plausibility tests of formal models. Second, they provide mechanisms that link statistically significant facilitating conditions to outcomes. And third, through the plotting of residuals, they plant the seeds for future specifications of variables that have not yet been successfully modeled. In no sense is the phronetic part of the scientific enterprise a marginal one.

## Conclusion

The Aristotelian division between *episteme* and *phronesis,* as applied by Flyvbjerg, maps well onto recent methodological debates within political science, as evidenced in Mr. Perestroika's assault on the disciplinary hegemons, between rational choice and qualitative research. Like Flyvbjerg in regard to epistemic science, supporters of qualitative research equivocate about the long-term prospects of rational-choice modeling in the social sciences. But, at minimum, Mr. Perestroika's acolytes call for methodological pluralism (see Mearsheimer 2001). The approach taken to science in this article, while carrying no brief against pluralism, entails a caution against a pluralism that sees formal and statistical research as only two of a thousand flowers that should be permitted to bloom.

The caution is to insist that if theoretical logic or scientific evidence finds a theory or procedure to be fallacious, that procedure's flowerbed should no longer be cultivated within the discipline in which it was originally seeded. There can be no hope of cumulation if we insist that all methods, and all procedures, must be protected. A few examples of unjustified pluralism follow. Consider first the method of case selection in comparative politics. It was once considered by the community of comparativists a useful exercise to choose a set of cases that had the same interesting outcome (for example, modernization breakdowns) to learn what causes it. Subsequent work in the methods field called this procedure "selecting on the dependent variable" and showed why it will ultimately lead to faulty inferences about causation (Geddes 1990, 131–50).

Similarly, many statistically oriented scholars in the field of international relations relied on logistic regressions to analyze binary time-series data on whether there was an outbreak of war in a given year. This procedure was found to lead, at least in some cases, to invalid inferences. The authors who report the bias show that this problem can be corrected with a set of dummy variables that tap unmeasured state dependence in the data (e.g., the longer a spell of peace, the less likely a war, *ceteris paribus*) (Beck, Katz, and Tucker 1998). It would be a scientific travesty should one group of international-relations specialists demand that statistical modelers who do not correct for serial dependence have a right to continue as they were doing, simply because there is a long tradition in cross-sectional work that has in the past ignored problems of time dependence.

A final example: comparativists who do qualitative case studies have no claim to disciplinary recognition by virtue of the fact that examination of a single case is a time-honored procedure in their field. Theoretical work going back to Eckstein sets constraints on what a particular case can show (Eckstein 1975). More recent methodological work, exemplified in the text by King, Keohane, and Verba (1994), gives a road map on how a study of a single country can be transformed into a high-N research design, thereby increasing the study's scientific leverage. There can be no argument based on tradition justifying the minimization of leverage. New work in comparative politics must, if it is to gain respect in the wider discipline, adjust methodologically to take into account scientific advances. Pluralism without updating is not science.

This point is doubly important when fields get defined by positions in grand debates and protected by tradition. It would be a warping of the scientific frame if we were to build into the charter of any department of political science a requirement that there be an expert in "realism," or in "South Asia," or in "democracy," or in "qualitative methods." Of course, advertising for jobs by area of specialization is crucial, especially if a department seeks broad disciplinary coverage. But institutionalizing slots for particular specialties is a threat to scientific progress. Consider a document from seventeenth-century Spain in which the University of Barcelona appealed to the king's audience for the right to sidestep interference in its affairs by the Council of Castile, which had stipulated that the department of philosophy have three professors who held to Thomist views and three who did not (Case number 064 1681). Three centuries later, it appears quaint that a philosophy department should be divided along those lines. But the implications of such royal charters are dangerous. When any academic field consecrates a debate by giving interlocutors on both sides permanent representation, the result can only be resistance to innovation. A scientific frame would lead us to expect that certain fields will become defunct, certain debates dead, and certain methods antiquated. A pluralism that shelters defunct practitioners cannot be scientifically justified.

Flyvbjerg at his most generous is calling for pluralism but giving pride of place to an alternate methodology for the social sciences, going back to Aristotle's recommendations. But, rather than accepting an alternate methodology, this chapter asks that we all work inside a scientific frame. Within that frame, we ought to maximize inter alia openness of procedures, internal coherence of argument, good measurement of variables, increasing attempts to unravel context, assiduous concern for valid causal inferences, and rewards for replication. Along with formal and statistical analysis, narratively based case studies (as one element in the procedures Flyvbjerg recommends as phronesis) play a crucial role in filling in this frame.[9] Yet, there is nothing to be gained in advertising a program that does not insist on the best approximation to science as the data and our abilities allow.

NOTES

1. "Mr. Perestroika" is the pen name of an anonymous insurgent within the political science discipline. His movement began with an e-mail sent to friends and colleagues in October 2000, but it spread like a bush telegraph, precipitating a mass mobilization within the discipline against the practices of the American Political Science Association and its lead journal, the *American Political Science Review*. The ferment first received attention in an article in the *New York Times* (5 November 2000), followed by coverage in the *Chronicle for Higher Education* (17 November 2000). Movement members remain active in seeking to alter the discipline organizationally and intellectually.

2. On one hand, Flyvbjerg writes, "it is ... not meaningful to speak of 'theory' in the study of social phenomena, at least not in the sense that 'theory' is used in

natural science" (p. 25). On the other hand, he acknowledges the value of "attempts at formal generalization, for such attempts are essential and effective means of scientific development" (p. 76). Despite these occasional nods to the value of a social science (see also formulations on pp. 49 and 87), his major theme is that "we must drop the fruitless effotrts to emulate natural science's success in producing cumulative and predictive theory" (p. 166). He does not provide evidence on the degree to which natural science research meets his standards.

3. See a summary discussion on this matter at http://www.cdc.gov/mmwr/preview/mmwrhtml/00001277.htm. The team reported, while acknowledging validity problems due to the sensitivity of the questions, that "most Americans appear to be at relatively low risk of infection with HIV-1 and other STDs from sexual exposures." See also Laumann et al. (1994), 546–47.

4. "Context is central to understanding what social science is and can be" (p. 9). There are nineteen other references to this term in the index. Chapter 4 is called "Context Counts."

5. In fairness to Flyvbjerg, there is more explicit attention to mechanisms in his full study, *Rationality and Power: Democracy in Practice* (1998).

6. The results would be more compelling if the effect sizes were properly analyzed so that something could be said about substantive significance of the negative relationship between language oppression and violence. The point here, however, is not to infer a negative relationship supported by the data but to wonder why there was no strong positive relationship, as standard theories of grievance had led us to expect.

7. Many in the narrative tradition claim that narratives ought to be formalized. It may well be that game trees and narrative both are formal models but perform complementary tasks in scientific explanation. If this is the case, the terms referring to the tripartite agenda will require adjustment.

8. John Elster (1998, 45–73). Techniques to assess causal mechanisms without use of narrative include experiments and recently developed random-matching models in statistics. See Judea Pearl (2000) for explications of these techniques. I remain skeptical that either the experimental or the statistical innovations will supplant narrative in helping to uncover the causal mechanisms linking values on independent variables to values on dependent variables.

9. This argument applies to my promotion of the tripartite method. In response to a critic of their article cited earlier, Dawes, Faust, and Meehl point out that although the results are not conclusive, clinical predictions appear to be better if researchers rely on statistical models only and ignore clinical judgments by experts. See Benjamin Kleinmutz et al. (1990, 146–47). Should it be demonstrated that narrative judgments add no explanatory or predictive value in political science (which I doubt would occur), it would be in defiance of the scientific frame to continue insisting on the tripartite method.

# 3

# A Perestroikan Straw Man Answers Back
## David Laitin and Phronetic Political Science

## *Bent Flyvbjerg*

I am grateful to David Laitin (2003) and Stephen White (2002) for point-ing out that my book *Making Social Science Matter* (MSSM; Flyvbjerg 2001) captures many of the core themes in a perestroikan political science. I share the basic intent and argument of perestroikans and would be delighted if the book might help advance Perestroika in political science. However, where White provides a balanced review of the book, in the hands of Laitin I feel like the proverbial straw man.

I address three main issues in what follows. First, I show that Laitin misrepresents my work in the extreme. Second, I assess Laitin's proposed alternative to the methodology he claims I present in MSSM, his tripartite method, and "scientific frame." Third, I outline what I call phronetic social and political science, a methodology for the analysis of values and inter-ests aimed at praxis.

### Laitin's Misrepresentations

David Laitin's main move in developing both his critique and his alterna-tive is to distort my distinction in MSSM between phronetic and epistemic social science. Laitin equates phronetic disciplines with qualitative and narrative methods, whereas epistemic disciplines have formal modeling and statistics at their core, according to Laitin. He thus invokes the dualisms of qualitative versus quantitative methods, case study research versus large samples, and narrative versus formal modeling. This makes

Laitin's job easy in attacking soft political science and promoting his own hard methodology. But the dualisms Laitin calls upon are rhetorical devices that misrepresent what I say in MSSM.

In this chapter I present a number of examples to document this. For reasons of space, not all examples are included. However, because Laitin's misrepresentations and misuses of MSSM are so far-reaching, I want to refute the most important examples in some detail.

### Dominance or Balance for Qualitative Methods?

Laitin states, as one of the main assertions in the abstract to his article, "Bent Flyvbjerg makes the best case for a renewed dominance for qualitative and case study work throughout the social sciences" (Laitin 2003, 163).

In fact, I do not make the case for dominance for qualitative and case-study work. I make the case for balance and integration in several highly visible places in MSSM. The following is verbatim what I say about the case study and large samples:

> [My assessment of case study research] should not be interpreted as a rejection of research which focuses on large random samples or entire populations; for example, questionnaire surveys. This type of research is essential for the development of social science; for example, in understanding the degree to which certain phenomena are present in a given group or how they vary across cases. The advantage of large samples is breadth, while their problem is one of depth. For the case study, the situation is the reverse. Both approaches are necessary for a sound development of social science. (Flyvbjerg 2001, 87, from the summary of ch. 6 on case-study research, "The Power of Example"; see also 75, 79, and 83 for other examples)

Laitin continues his misrepresentations by criticizing perestroikans for having an "abhorrence of all things mathematical" (2003, 163). Following this line of argument he asserts, again mistakenly, "Social scientists, [Flyvbjerg] concludes, should not even try to imitate the scientific method with fancy statistics and impressive regressions" (2003, 165).

In MSSM I argue that social science probably cannot become scientific in the natural science sense, but I do not argue against statistics and regressions, as Laitin claims I do. In line with this misrepresentation, Laitin incorrectly presents my research on city politics and planning in Aalborg (Flyvbjerg 1998a)—which I use as an example of phronetic social science in MSSM—as if it were entirely qualitative (Laitin 2003, 17–71). Here is what I actually write in MSSM:

> In answering the question of who wins and who loses in the Aalborg Project, I carried out environmental and social impact audits using statistical and other quantitative analyses. This was necessary for relating process to outcome in the project. Here as elsewhere, the sharp separation often seen in the literature between qualitative and quantitative methods is a spurious one. (Flyvbjerg 2001, 196)

At a more fundamental level, Laitin misrepresents my conception of *phronesis* and narrative. Laitin (2003, 165, 169, 175) writes that I see *phronesis* as narrative. This is false, as is the following conclusion: "Flyv-bjerg's attempt to separate out *phronesis* (as a kind of narrative) from its statistical and formal complements is radically incomplete" (Laitin 2003, 175).

Compare this with what I actually write about *phronesis* and quantitative methods in MSSM:

> In my interpretation, phronetic social science is opposed to an either/or and stands for a both/and on the question of qualitative versus quantitative methods. Phronetic social science is problem-driven and not methodology-driven, in the sense that it employs those methods which for a given problematic best help answer the four value-rational questions [which stand at the core of phronetic social science; see discussion]. More often than not, a combination of qualitative and quantitative methods will do the task and do it best. (Flyvbjerg 2001, 196)

Thus, I do not separate *phronesis* from statistics or other social science tools. I argue for their integration. Nor do I see narrative and quantitative methods as opposites or as methods that stand outside each other. I integrate these as well, as documented by my empirical work, because it makes for better social and political science. In short, there is no factual basis for David Laitin's claim that I make a case for dominance for qualitative and case-study work throughout the social sciences.

## A Brief Example of Narrative Combining
## Qualitative and Quantitative Methods

Let me give a brief example of how I work with qualitative and quantitative methods and with narrative. Laitin (2003, 170) says that it was my "deep understanding of all backroom deals"—gained through in-depth qualitative research—that helped make planning in Aalborg more democratic. This is incorrect. What triggered change was my relating the backroom deals, once I had uncovered them, to street-level, everyday outcomes—established through statistical and other quantitative analyses. For instance, through statistical analyses of large samples and time-series data on traffic accidents, I established that the backroom deals had transformed a planned and politically approved reduction in traffic accidents of 30 to 40 percent into a statistically significant increase in accidents of about the same size.

I then integrated these qualitative and quantitative analyses into one narrative together with legal and ethical considerations on democracy. When published, this narrative created considerable commotion among politicians and the public, because it made it uncomfortably clear that more people were killed and injured in traffic because city officials had allowed the local chamber of industry and commerce an illegitimate influence on planning outcomes during the backroom deals. After this, it became impossible for officials to continue to practice the backroom setup for policy and planning. In this case it was the *combination* in one narrative of uncovering relations of power through qualitative analyses *and* linking power with outcomes through quantitative studies that helped make for more democracy.

This example is typical of my work and shows that I do not conclude against statistics and regressions, as Laitin claims. I see choice of method as dependent on the research problem at hand. Sometimes, quantitative methods best help answer the problem; sometimes, qualitative methods may do the job alone; and most often—if the problem is of practical-political import and the researchers want to make a difference with their research—a combination of quantitative and qualitative methods is most effective. MSSM explicitly reflects this position, as does my book *Rationality and Power: Democracy in Practice,* which is my main example of *phronesis* in MSSM. My most recent book, *Megaprojects and Risk: An Anatomy of Ambition,* and many of my articles also make extensive use of both quantitative and qualitative methods. (Flyvbjerg, Bruzelius, and

Rothengatter 2003; Flyvbjerg, Holm, and Buhl 2002) If Laitin wanted to criticize a purely qualitative researcher and use this to undermine Perestroika, as seems to have been his strategy, however misguided, he picked the wrong person.

## Social versus Natural Science

On the issue of social versus natural science, Laitin misrepresents MSSM like this: "The social world, [Flyvbjerg] argues, is sufficiently different from the natural world that any hopes for a Galilean conquest over the unknown in social science will forever remain unrealized" (Laitin 2003, 164).

Compare Laitin's statement with what I actually write and emphasize in MSSM, again in several highly visible places:

> It is worth reiterating that [the] plea for the importance of context [to social phenomena] is not an ultimate proof that social science can *never* be explanatory and predictive. It only makes it *probable* that this is so. (Flyvbjerg 2001, 46, emphasis in original; from the first paragraph in the conclusions to ch. 4, "Context Counts"; see also 4, 62, and 76)

Laitin (2003, 168) further claims that I do not define context in MSSM. In fact I use two chapters (chs. 3 and 4) to establish that context in social science is human beings' everyday background skills.

And the examples of misrepresentation go on. I will limit myself to only three more brief instances. First, Laitin (2003, 170–71) writes that I do not explain the influence of power in Aalborg. In fact, I present a historical explanation in terms of the *longue durée* in *Rationality and Power* similar to the type of explanation Robert Putnam (1993) and his associates use to explain power in Italian local government in *Making Democracy Work,* and I explicitly refer to *Rationality and Power* in MSSM (144–45) for the full story on this. Second, Laitin (2003, 168) says I do not provide any philosophy of science cites to support my claims regarding prediction as a criterion for science. In fact, the cites can be found on pages 38 and 175 in MSSM. Third, Laitin (2003, 167) claims that I "admit" that Hubert Dreyfus and Stuart Dreyfus used a standard scientific procedure to make a discovery concerning human cognition. Laitin even tries to lend credence to this claim by inserting a bogus endnote referring to where I am supposed to admit this (Laitin, 2003, 182, note 8). The problem for Laitin is that the two sources he quotes as evidence, both of which I authored or coauthored, do not even touch upon this issue, let alone "admit" to it. Moreover, one of the sources is in Danish, and I doubt Laitin has read this. Finally, it was not the Dreyfus brothers who made the discovery Laitin says they did, nor did they conduct the experiment or author the study that reported the experiment, as Laitin (2003, 166–67) wrongly claims. Laitin is as mistaken in the details of his article as he is on the larger issues.

### Possible Explanations for Laitin's Misrepresentations

The examples presented show that Laitin's misrepresentations regarding MSSM are extensive and concern the core of the book's argument. The examples document that Laitin has made up facts and results that are not in the book and presented them as if they were. The examples further show that Laitin has changed or omitted other facts and results so the research reported in MSSM is presented in Laitin's article in a highly inaccurate and biased manner.

Why would Laitin make himself guilty of such misrepresentations? I see two possible explanations; Laitin may have made his misrepresentations in error or deliberately. First, error would explain the misrepresentations if, for instance, Laitin had not really read MSSM but only sampled it carelessly. If you are a hegemon, as Laitin says he is, and *know* your methodology is correct, you do not have to read critiques carefully, and over time you are likely to develop a tin ear for such critiques. Error would also be a plausible explanation if Laitin had operated with overly simple distinctions in his analysis of MSSM that would make him all too ready to script MSSM and me into the preselected role of narrative, qualitative villain. My problem with this type of explanation is that I do not see a serious and experienced scholar making such mistakes. Making errors to a degree that would explain the misrepresentations documented here would imply a recklessness on Laitin's part that would be no less problematic and unethical than deliberate misrepresentation; it would violate basic scholarly canons of reasonable handling of information and debate.

Second, Laitin may have made his misrepresentations deliberately. Laitin claims he has read MSSM and is familiar with its content. If we take this claim at face value, we are led to assume that his misrepresentations are not results of error but are instead committed intentionally. My difficulty with this type of explanation is that I do not see an honest scholar demonstrating the type of manipulation and ill will against colleagues that deliberate misrepresentation entails.

Whichever explanation is correct, I do see how Laitin's misrepresentation of MSSM serves his purposes well for discrediting Perestroika and promoting his own methodology as science. In what follows, I argue, however, that even if Laitin were to succeed in undermining Perestroika and have his way with the "tripartite method" and "scientific frame," this would result in a political science that is no more scientific in the Kuhnian, natural-science sense than perestroikan or other political science. Furthermore, it would result in the type of stagnant social and political science that today relegates social science to the role of loser in the Science Wars. Let us see why.

## Problems with Laitin's Proposed Methodology

Laitin's tripartite method consists of integrating the well-known techniques of statistics, formal modeling, and narrative in political analyses (Laitin 2003, 163, 175–79). I agree with Laitin that all three elements can be useful in social science, depending on the questions social scientists want to answer. I also agree that the way Laitin proposes to combine the three elements may add rigor to formal modeling in places where this is currently lacking. I thus welcome Laitin's tripartite method as one way to improve validity in a specific type of social science research.

### How Approximate Is Laitin's "Approximation to Science"?

But Laitin's article is unclear regarding what type of science the tripartite method entails. In the context of the tripartite method, Laitin interestingly avoids talking about science as such and instead uses the fuzzy terms "scientific frame" (2003, 163, 169) and "approximation to science" (2003, 181). Does this mean that Laitin believes that the tripartite method will not, after all, produce results that are scientific in the natural science sense but only an "approximation"? If so, the obvious question is, how approximate? And which factors decide how approximate to science Laitin can get with his method? After Laitin's bombastic attacks on Perestroika and phronetic political science for not being sufficiently scientific, it is unsatisfactory and inconsistent that he does not answer these questions for his own proposed methodology.

Instead, Laitin leaves his reader with the vague notion of "scientific frame," which, when operationalized, appears to be something as noninnovative and noncontroversial as an ad hoc combination of three well-established social science research techniques. When deprived of his falsely based contrast with the phronetic alternative and his claim to hegemony for his own methodology, Laitin's scientific frame is so weak as to lack any real persuasiveness.

Laitin (2003, 176) says he sees narrative as a co-equal to the formal and statistical elements of the tripartite method. But he immediately contradicts himself by identifying three roles for narrative that subordinate and define this approach in relation to formal and statistical methods. Narrative, according to Laitin (2003, 176–79), should be used for, first, plausibility tests of formal game theoretic models; second, linking independent and dependent variables in statistical analyses; and third, analyses of residual variance in statistical models. I agree with Laitin that these three uses of narrative can be helpful in social science. I disagree that the three roles exhaust the work narrative can and should do. The history and philosophy of social science do not support Laitin in his narrow view of narrative. Were we to use narrative only in the ways Laitin proposes and refrain from all other uses, then a host of useful social science knowledge could no longer be produced or supported, including some of the most treasured classics.

## Does Laitin Have a Theory of Context and Judgment?

In presenting his case for formal modeling and statistics, Laitin appears to fall victim to a *pars pro toto* fallacy: if social science would use mathematical and statistical modeling like natural science, social science, too, would become scientific. But being scientistic does not amount to being scientific. Regardless of how much we let mathematical and statistical modeling dominate social and political science, they are unlikely to become science in the natural-science sense. This is so because the phenomena modeled are social and political and thus "answer back" in ways natural phenomena do not.

Here context enters the picture. As mentioned, I argue in MSSM that in social science the relevant context to social and political action is human beings' everyday background skills. Thus I do not see context as simply the singularity of each setting or as the distinctive historical and social paths taken to produce such a setting, even if both may be important to an understanding of specific social and political phenomena. I further argue that background skills are central in deciding what counts as the relevant objects and events whose regularities social and political theory try to explain and predict. I finally argue that human skills are based on judgment that cannot be understood in terms of features and rules. Therefore, a "hard" theory of context is seemingly impossible. But if context decides what counts as relevant objects and events and if context cannot be formalized in terms of features and rules, then social theory cannot be complete and predictive in the manner of much natural-science theory, which does not have the problem with self-interpretive objects of study.

This leads me to conclude that social science is neither "normal" nor "revolutionary" in the Kuhnian sense. Nor is it pre-or post-paradigmatic as, respectively, Hubert Dreyfus (1991) and Sanford Schram (2003) argue, because no paradigmatic phase has preceded the current situation or is likely to follow. Kuhn's concepts regarding paradigms were developed to fit natural science, and they confuse rather than clarify when imported into social science. In my analysis, social science is *nonparadigmatic* and is neither relatively cumulative nor relatively stable. In comparison, although natural science may not be as rational nor as cumulative as believed earlier, it still shows a type of stability and progress not found in social science.

Many quantitative political scientists see economics as an ideal to follow because it is the hardest and thus seemingly most scientific of the social sciences. Commentators talk about "economics envy" among political scientists (Stewart 2003). Such envy is misguided, for not even economics has succeeded in avoiding context and becoming cumulative and stable, as I argue in MSSM. Economists have been defined, jokingly but perceptively, as "experts who will know tomorrow why the things they predicted yesterday did not happen today." Furthermore, it seems that the more "scientific" academic economics attempts to become, the less impact academic economists have on practical affairs. This is a main complaint of Perestroika's companion movement in economics, The Post-autistic Economics Network (2004). As pointed out by Esther-Mirjam Sent (2002), Wall Street firms prefer to hire physicists because they have a real as opposed to fake natural-science background. Academic economists have had little to no role to play in the final decisions concerning the North American Free Trade Agreement. And though the spectrum auction has been claimed as a victory for game theory, a closer look at the developments reveals that the story is a bit more complex, according to Sent. Quantitative political scientists should make pause before insisting on emulating academic economics.

Against my argument that social science cannot avoid context, Laitin claims that appealing to context is merely to say that we have not yet discovered the various factors or the interaction of factors that produced outcomes of significance. Appealing to context when arguing that social science can probably never be explanatory and predictive in the manner of natural science is therefore a "copout," according to Laitin (2003, 168).

To this I reply that so far, all attempts have failed to analyze context in social science as merely very complex sets of rules or factors. And I wonder whether Laitin has found a way around this problem, as he seems to indicate. If he has, he should publish the evidence, because this would be a real discovery and would, indeed, open up the possibility that social science could have the type of theoretical explanation and prediction that today we find only in parts of natural science.

The political philosopher Alessandro Ferrara (1989) has rightly pointed out that we need a theory of judgment in order to avoid contextualism and that such a theory does not exist as yet. In MSSM I argue that the reason we still lack a theory of judgment, and therefore cannot bring closure to context, is that judgment cannot be brought into a theoretical formula. When Laitin says that appealing to context is a copout, he invites the burden of proof either to provide a theory of judgment or to argue that Ferrara is wrong in saying we need such a theory in order to avoid appeals to context.

In MSSM (46–47) I further argue that we cannot, in principle, rule out that context, skills, and judgment may be studied in terms of elements that would make social science explanatory and predictive in the manner of natural science. But for this to happen, we would need a vocabulary in social science that picks out elements that are completely different from those abstracted from our everyday activities. The elements would have to remain invariant through changes in background practices. No one has yet found such elements, and the logical possibility that some day they may be discovered has little practical use. This possibility is merely in principle and cannot be used to conclude that the social sciences are pre-paradigmatic owing to historical coincidence, to social science being young, or to a high degree of complexity in the social world (Dreyfus 1991).

One could reasonably ask whether, if no one can specify judgment in such a way as to produce uniformly accurate predictions, more modest and less successful efforts at dealing with judgment are useless, as in, for instance, accounts of bounded rationality, and whether that means that we cannot distinguish better from worse instances of judgment. The answer is no on both counts. Such efforts may be useful. But they are not science in the natural science sense; they have to rely on validity claims of the kind described in the section on phronetic political science.

Thus, Laitin appears to be wrong when he claims that we can have a successful science of context and of political and other social behavior. To demonstrate that he is right, Laitin would, in my analysis, need to meet the burden of either providing a theory of judgment or an argument that such a theory is not needed to avoid appeals to context.

### Laitin's Leap of Faith

As an aside, given Laitin's strong endorsement of statistics as part of his method, I was surprised to see that he shows limited understanding of what one can and cannot do with statistics. It's a general tenet of statistics that one cannot infer causally from statistical pattern to individual outcome. Only propensities, or expectations, can be given. Thus Laitin (2003, 173) goes further than statistics supports when, in his exemplification of the tripartite model, he argues that statistical models open the possibility that oppressive Sinhalese language laws in Sri Lanka might have ameliorated violence rather than exacerbated it. The statistical models Laitin refers to do not, and logically cannot, explain the individual case of the Sinhalese language laws. They can only give predictions, useful before the results are known. In several places, Laitin (2003, 173–74, 175) goes too far in implying that a negative causality exists between levels of linguistic grievance and levels of violence, where only negative correlation has been documented. In sum, it seems that Laitin does not fully appreciate that statistics is useful for giving stochastic predictions and general tendencies, not reasons.

Laitin (2003, 179–80) ends his article by stating that over time we must expect certain fields within social science to become defunct, certain debates to die, and certain methods to become antiquated. Again, I agree with Laitin, but he ignores the possibility that this might also apply to his scientific frame and tripartite method. When Laitin (2003, 180, emphasis added) indiscriminately asks "that *we all* work inside a scientific frame" and encourages us to ignore "alternate methodology," he is placing the scientific frame outside the open-minded, skeptical ethos of the scientific ideal he claims to speak for. This is not consistent, in my analysis.

Laitin here makes a peculiar leap of faith for one approach over others. And it is a leap into thin air that "we all" better not take, if my argument is correct that the scientific frame, understood as the "approximation" to natural science that Laitin (2003, 181) appears to endorse, has no more chance than other types of social science of becoming stable and cumulative.

Thus, I do not agree that the tripartite method is or can be a general methodology of social and political science, as Laitin seems to think. Nor will it make social science scientific in the natural science sense any more than existing social science methodology. Finally, the tripartite method is not *phronesis,* as also argued by Schram (2004); *phronesis* is problem driven, and the simple identity Laitin sets between narrative and *phronesis* is mistaken. We will see later what *phronesis* is beyond Laitin.

David Laitin is mistaken if he thinks Perestroika is about fear among perestroikans of formal and statistical analysis. Perestroika is about fear of domination and stagnation. And Laitin's article is good evidence that such fear is well founded when he claims hegemony for his proposed methodology. This type of claim confirms the suspicion of many perestroikans that anti-perestroikans are interested not in an open discussion of political science and its potential but instead in promoting a dogmatic version of *the* correct interpretation of what political science is, namely rational-choice theory and statistics. Perestroikans appear to have a sound sense that trouble lies ahead when someone suggests "we all" do the same thing in social science. Perhaps this occurs because, as good social scientists, they understand that social systems, including social science, thrive on diversity.

## Phronetic Political Science

Social and political science will remain weak vis-à-vis natural science so long as people insist on comparing both types of science in terms of their epistemic qualities. Such a comparison is misleading, however. The two types of science have their respective strengths and weaknesses along fundamentally different dimensions. The social sciences are strongest where the natural sciences are weakest: just as the social sciences have not contributed much to explanatory and predictive theory in the natural science sense, neither have the natural sciences contributed to the reflexive analysis and discussion of values and interests, which is the prerequisite for an enlightened political, economic, and cultural development in any society and which should be at the core of social science if we want to transcend the malaise of the Science Wars.

## What Is *Phronesis?*

A contemporary interpretation of the Aristotelian concept of *phronesis,* variously translated as "prudence" or "practical wisdom," may effectively help us develop social and political science as reflexive analysis of values and interests aimed at praxis. In Aristotle's (1976, 1140a24–b12, 1144b33–45a11) words, *phronesis* is an intellectual virtue that is "reasoned, and capable of action with regard to things that are good or bad for man." *Phronesis* concerns values and goes beyond analytical, scientific knowledge (*episteme*) and technical knowledge or know-how (*techne*), and it involves judgments and decisions made in the manner of a virtuoso social actor. *Phronesis* is so commonly involved in political and administrative practices that any attempts to reduce political science to *episteme* or *techne* or to comprehend them in those terms are misguided.

Aristotle was explicit in his regard of *phronesis* as the most important of the three intellectual virtues: *episteme, techne,* and *phronesis. Phronesis* is most important because it is that activity by which instrumental rationality is balanced by value-rationality, to use the terms of Max Weber, and because, according to Aristotle and Weber, such balancing is crucial to the sustained happiness of the citizens in any society. A curious fact can be observed, however. Whereas *episteme* is found in the modern words "epistemology" and "epistemic," and *techne* in "technology" and "technical," it is indicative of the degree to which scientific and instrumental rationality dominate modern thinking and language that we no longer have a word containing a variant of the root term for the one intellectual virtue, *phronesis,* that Aristotle and other founders of the Western tradition saw as a necessary condition of successful social and political organization. We need to redress the imbalance among the intellectual virtues. The goal is to help restore social and political science to its classical position as a practical, intellectual activity aimed at clarifying the problems, risks, and possibilities we face as humans and societies and at contributing to social and political praxis.

The term "epistemic science" derives from the intellectual virtue that Aristotle calls *episteme,* which is generally translated as "science" or "scientific knowledge."[1] Aristotle defines *episteme* in this manner (round parentheses in original, brackets added, here and elsewhere):

[S]cientific knowledge is a demonstrative state, (i.e., a state of mind capable of demonstrating what it knows) . . . i.e., a person has scientific knowledge when his belief is conditioned in a certain way, and the first principles are known to him; because if they are not better known to him than the conclusion drawn from them, he will have knowledge only incidentally.—This may serve as a description of scientific knowledge. (Aristotle 1976, 1139b18–36)

*Episteme* concerns universals and the production of knowledge that is invariable in time and space and achieved with the aid of analytical rationality. *Episteme* corresponds to the modern scientific ideal as expressed in natural science. In Socrates and Plato, and subsequently in the Enlightenment tradition, this scientific ideal became dominant. The ideal has come close to being the only legitimate view of what constitutes genuine science, such that even intellectual activities like political and other social sciences, which are not and probably never can be scientific in the epistemic sense, have found themselves compelled to strive for and legitimate themselves in terms of this Enlightenment ideal. Epistemic political science makes claims to universality and generic truths about politics. Epistemic political science is the mainstream of political science.

Whereas *episteme* resembles our ideal modern scientific project, *techne* and *phronesis* denote two contrasting roles of intellectual work. *Techne* can be translated into English as "art" in the sense of "craft"; a craftsperson is also an *art*isan. For Aristotle, both *techne* and *phronesis* are connected with the concept of truth, as is *episteme*. Aristotle says the following regarding *techne:*

> [S]ince (e.g.) building is an art [*techne*] and is essentially a reasoned productive state, and since there is no art that is not a state of this kind, and no state of this kind that is not an art, it follows that art is the same as a productive state that is truly reasoned. Every art is concerned with bringing something into being, and the practice of an art is the study of how to bring into being something that is capable either of being or of not being. . . . For it is not with things that are or come to be *of necessity* that art is concerned [this is the domain of *episteme*] nor with natural objects (because these have their origin in themselves). . . . Art . . . operate[s] in the sphere of the variable. (Aristotle 1976, 1140a1–23)

*Techne* is thus craft and art, and as an activity it is concrete, variable, and context dependent. The objective of *techne* is application of technical knowledge and skills according to a pragmatic instrumental rationality, what Michel Foucault (1984a, 255) calls "a practical rationality governed by a conscious goal." Political science practiced as *techne* would be a type of consulting aimed at better politics by means of instrumental rationality, where "better" is defined in terms of the values and goals of those who employ the consultants, sometimes in negotiation with the latter.

Whereas *episteme* concerns theoretical *know-why* and *techne* denotes technical *know-how, phronesis* emphasizes practical knowledge and practical ethics. *Phronesis* is often translated as "prudence" or "practical common sense." Let us again examine what Aristotle has to say:

> We may grasp the nature of prudence [*phronesis*] if we consider what sort of people we call prudent. Well, it is thought to be the mark of a prudent man to be able to deliberate rightly about what is good and advantageous. . . . But nobody deliberates about things that are invariable. . . . So . . . prudence cannot be a science or art; not science [*episteme*] because what can be done is a variable (it may be done in different ways, or not done at all), and not art [*techne*] because action and production are generically different. For production aims at an end other than itself; but this is impossible in the case of action, because the end is merely doing *well.* What remains, then, is that it is a true state, reasoned, and capable of action with regard to things that are good or bad for man. . . . We consider that this quality belongs to those who understand the management of households or states. (Aristotle 1976, 1140a24–b12, emphasis in original)

The person who possesses practical wisdom (*phronimos*) has knowledge of how to manage in each particular circumstance that cannot be equated with or reduced to knowledge of general truths about managing. *Phronesis* is a sense or a tacit skill for doing the ethically practical, rather than a kind of science. For Plato, rational humans are moved by the cosmic order; for Aristotle, they are moved by a sense of the proper order among the ends we pursue. This sense cannot be articulated in terms of theoretical axioms but is grasped by *phronesis* (Taylor 1989, 125, 148).

One might get the impression in Aristotle's original description of *phronesis* that *phronesis* and the choices it involves are always good. This is not necessarily the case. Choices must be deemed good or bad in relation to certain values and interests in order for good and bad to have meaning. Phronetic political science is concerned with deliberation about such values and interests.

In sum, the three intellectual virtues *episteme, techne,* and *phronesis* can be characterized as follows:

> *Episteme:* Scientific knowledge. Universal, invariable, context indepen-dent. Based on general analytical rationality. The original concept is known today by the terms "epistemology" and "epistemic." Political science prac-ticed as *episteme* is concerned with uncovering universal truths or laws about politics.
>
> *Techne:* Craft/art. Pragmatic, variable, context dependent. Oriented toward production. Based on practical instrumental rationality governed by a conscious goal. The original concept appears today in terms such as "tech-nique," "technical," and "technology." Political science practiced as *techne* is consulting aimed at better politics by means of instrumental rationality—a type of social engineering—where "better" is defined in terms of the values and goals of those who employ the consultants, sometimes in negotiation with the latter.
>
> *Phronesis:* Ethics. Deliberation about values with reference to praxis. Pragmatic, variable, context dependent. Oriented toward action. Based on practical value rationality. The original concept has no analogous contem-porary term. Political science practiced as *phronesis* is concerned with delib-eration about (including questioning of) values and interests aimed at praxis.

Aristotle found that every well-functioning society was dependent on the effective functioning of all three intellectual virtues—*episteme, techne,* and *phronesis.* At the same time, however, Aristotle (1976, 1144b33–45a11) emphasized the crucial importance of *phronesis,* "for the possession of the single virtue of prudence [*phronesis*] will carry with it the possession of them all."[2] *Phronesis* is most important, from an Aristotelian point of view, because it is that intellectual virtue that may ensure the ethical employ-ment of science (*episteme*) and technology (*techne*). Because *phronesis* today is marginalized in the intellectual scheme of things, scientific and technological development take place without the ethical checks and bal-ances that Aristotle and, later, Max Weber saw as all important.

## Priority of the Particular

*Phronesis* concerns the analysis of values—"things that are good or bad for humans"—as a point of departure for action. *Phronesis* is that intellectual activity most relevant to praxis. It focuses on what is variable, on that which cannot be encapsulated by universal rules, on specific cases. *Phronesis* requires an interaction between the general and the concrete; it requires consideration, judgment, and choice (Ruderman 1997). More than anything else, *phronesis* requires *experience*. About the importance of specific experience, Aristotle says,

> [P]rudence [*phronesis*] is not concerned with universals only; it must also take cognizance of particulars, because it is concerned with conduct, and conduct has its sphere in particular circumstances. That is why some people who do not possess theoretical knowledge are more effective in action (especially if they are experienced) than others who do possess it. For example, suppose that someone knows that light flesh foods are digestible and wholesome, but does not know what kinds are light; he will be less likely to produce health than one who knows that chicken is wholesome. But prudence is practical, and therefore it must have both kinds of knowledge, or especially the latter. (Aristotle 1976, 1141b8–27)

Here, again, Aristotle is stressing that in the practical administration of human affairs (in this case the administration of health, which was a central concern for the ancient Greeks), knowledge of the rules ("light flesh foods are digestible and wholesome") is inferior to knowledge of real cases ("chicken is wholesome"). Some of the best schools of business administration, like Harvard Business School, have understood the importance of cases over rules and emphasize case-based and practical teaching. The rules are not the game, in business or in politics. Such business schools may be called Aristotelian, whereas schools that stress theory and rules may be called Platonic. We could do with more Aristotelian schools of political science.

Some interpretations of Aristotle's intellectual virtues leave doubt as to whether *phronesis* and *techne* are distinct categories, or whether *phronesis* is just a higher form of *techne* or know-how (Dreyfus and Dreyfus 1990; 1991, 102–7). Aristotle is clear on this point, however. Even if both *phronesis* and *techne* involve skill and judgment, one type of intellectual virtue cannot be reduced to the other; *phronesis* is about value judgment, not about producing things. Similarly, in other parts of the literature one finds attempts at conflating *phronesis* and *episteme* in the sense of making *phronesis* epistemic. But insofar as *phronesis* operates via a practical rationality based on judgment and experience, it can be made scientific in an epistemic sense only through the development of a theory of judgment and experience. And such a theory does not and probably cannot exist, as argued earlier. Aristotle warns us directly against the type of reductionism that conflates *phronesis* and *episteme.*

With his thoughts on the intellectual virtues, Aristotle emphasizes properties of intellectual work, which are central to the production of knowledge in the study of political phenomena. The particular and the situationally dependent are emphasized over the universal and over rules. The concrete and the practical are emphasized over the theoretical (Devereux 1986). It is what Martha Nussbaum (1990, 66) calls the "priority of the particular" in Aristotle's thinking. Aristotle practices what he preaches by providing a specific example of his argument, light flesh foods versus chicken. He understands the "power of example." The example concerns the administration of human health and has as its point of departure something both concrete and fundamental concerning human functioning. This is typical of many classical philosophers.

Despite their importance, the concrete, the practical, and the ethical have been neglected by modern science. Today one would be open to ridicule if one sought to support an argument using an example like that of Aristotle's chicken. The sciences are supposed to concern themselves precisely with the explication of universals, and even if it is wrong the conventional wisdom is that one cannot generalize from a particular case (Flyvbjerg 2004b). Moreover, the ultimate goal of scientific activity is supposedly the production of theory. Aristotle is here clearly anti-Socratic and anti-Platonic. And if modern theoretical science is built upon any body of thought, it is that of Socrates and Plato. We are dealing with a profound disagreement here.

For political scientists it is worth noting that Aristotle links *phronesis* directly with political science:

> Political science and prudence [*phronesis*] are the same state of mind [They are not identical, however. *Phronesis* is also found at the level of the household and the individual]. . . . Prudence concerning the state has two aspects: one, which is controlling and directive, is legislative science; the other . . . deals with particular circumstances . . . [and] is practical and deliberative. (Aristotle 1976, 1141b8–b27)

Two things should be highlighted here. The first is Aristotle's (1976) assertion that political science, as a consequence of the emphasis on the particular, on context, and on experience, cannot be practiced as *episteme*. To be a knowledgeable researcher in an epistemic sense is not enough when it concerns political science because, "although [people] develop ability in geometry and mathematics and become wise in such matters, they are not thought to develop prudence [*phronesis*]" (1142a12–29). Aristotle explains that a well-functioning political science based on *phronesis* is imperative for a well-functioning society, inasmuch as "it is impossible to secure one's own good independently of . . . political science" (1141b27–42a12).

Second, Aristotle emphasizes in his concept of *phronesis* both the collective (the state) and the particular, rules and circumstance, directives and deliberation, sovereign power and individual power. Since Aristotle, however, an unfortunate division has developed in philosophy and in the social and political sciences, of two separate traditions, each representing one of the two sides stressed by Aristotle. One tradition, the dominant one, has developed from Plato via Hobbes and Kant to Jürgen Habermas and other rationalist thinkers, emphasizing the first of the two sides, that is, rules and rational control. The other, partly Aristotelian and partly sophist in origin, has developed via Machiavelli to Nietzsche, and to Michel Foucault in some interpretations, emphasizing particular circumstances and practical deliberation. Today the two traditions tend to live separate lives, apart from occasional, typically rhetorical attacks from thinkers within one tradition on thinkers within the other. Aristotle insisted, however, that what is interesting, for understanding and for praxis, is what happens where the two now largely separate sides intersect—where rules meet particular circumstance—and that this point of intersection is the locus of appropriate phronetic political science.

## Power and *Phronesis*

Aristotle never elaborated his conception of *phronesis* to include explicit considerations of power. Hans-Georg Gadamer's (1974) authoritative and contemporary conception of *phronesis* also overlooks issues of power. Yet, as Richard Bernstein (1989, 217) has pointed out, if we are to think about what can be done to the problems, possibilities, and risks of our time, we must advance from the original conception of *phronesis* to one explicitly including power. Unfortunately, Bernstein himself has not integrated his work on *phronesis* with issues of power. But conflict and power are phenomena constitutive of modern social and political inquiry. Thus social and political science can be complete only if they deal with issues of power. I have therefore made an attempt to develop the classic concept of *phronesis* to a more contemporary one, which accounts for power, by tracing the Aristotelian roots in the thinking of Machiavelli, Nietzsche, and Foucault (Flyvbjerg 2001, chs. 7 and 8).

Besides focusing on values—"what is good and bad for humans," which is the classical Aristotelian focus—a contemporary reading of *phronesis* must also pose questions about power and outcomes:

"Who gains, and who loses?"

"Through what kinds of power relations?"

"What possibilities are available to change existing power relations?"

"Is it desirable to do so?"

"What are the power relations among those who ask the questions?"

Phronetic political science poses these questions with the intention of avoiding the voluntarism and idealism typical of so much ethical thinking. The main question is not only the Weberian "Who governs?" posed by Robert Dahl and most other students of power. It is also the Nietzschean question: what "governmental rationalities" are at work when those who govern govern? With these questions and with the classical focus on values, phronetic political scientists relate explicitly to a primary context of values and power. Combining the best of a Nietzschean-Foucauldian interpretation of power with the best of a Weberian-Dahlian one, the analysis of power is guided by a conception of power that can be characterized by six features:

1. Power is seen as productive and positive, and not only as restrictive and negative.

2. Power is viewed as a dense net of omnipresent relations and not only as being localized in "centers" and institutions or as an entity one can "possess."

3. The concept of power is seen as ultradynamic; power is not merely something one appropriates; it is also something one reappropriates and exercises in a constant back-and-forth movement within the relationships of strength, tactics, and strategies inside which one exists.

4. Knowledge and power, truth and power, rationality and power are analytically inseparable from each other; power produces knowledge, and knowledge produces power.

5. The central question is *how* power is exercised, and not merely *who* has power and *why* they have it; the focus is on process in addition to structure.
6. Power is studied with a point of departure in small questions, "flat and empirical," not only, nor even primarily, with a point of departure in "big questions" (Foucault 1982, 217). God is in the detail, as far as power is concerned.

Analyses of political and administrative power following this format cannot be equated with a general analytics of every possible power relation in politics and administration. Other approaches and other interpretations are possible. The format can, however, serve as a possible and productive point of departure for dealing with questions of power in doing contemporary *phronesis*.

### Core Questions of Phronetic Political Science

The principal objective for a phronetic political science is to perform analyses and derive interpretations of the status of values and interests in politics and administration aimed at praxis. The point of departure for contemporary phronetic research can be summarized in the following four value-rational questions, which must be answered for specific, substantive problematics:

1. Where are we going?
2. Who gains and who loses, and by which mechanisms of power?
3. Is this development desirable?
4. What, if anything, should we do about it?

Examples of substantive problematics could be politics for peace in the Middle East, fair elections in the United States, livable downtowns, or fewer toxins in drinking water. Phronetic political scientists realize there is no global and unified "we" in relation to which the four questions can be given a final answer. What is a "gain" and a "loss" often depend on the perspective taken, and one person's gain may be another's loss. Phronetic political scientists are highly aware of the importance of perspective and see no neutral ground, no "view from nowhere," for their work. The "we" may be a group of political scientists or, more typically, a group that includes other political actors, as well. Phronetic political scientists are well aware that different groups typically have different world views and different interests and that there exists no general principle by which all differences can be resolved. Thus, *phronesis* gives us both a way to analyze relations of power and evaluate their results in relation to specific groups and interests.

The four value-rational questions may be addressed, and research developed, using different methodology. As said, *phronesis* is problem driven, not methodology driven. Thus, the most important issue is not the individual methodology involved, even if methodological questions may have some significance. It is more important to get the result right—to arrive at social and political sciences that effectively deal with deliberation, judgment, and praxis in relation to the four value-rational questions, rather than being stranded with social and political sciences that vainly attempt to emulate natural science.

Asking value-rational questions does not imply a belief in linearity and continuous progress. The phronetic political scientist knows enough about power to understand that progress is often complex, ephemeral, and hard won and that setbacks are an inevitable part of political and administrative life. It should also be stressed that no one has enough wisdom and experience to give complete answers to the four questions, whatever those answers might be. Such wisdom and experience should not be expected from political scientists, who are on average probably no more astute or ethical than anyone else. What should be expected, however, is attempts from phronetic political scientists to develop their partial answers to the questions. Such answers would be input to the ongoing dialogue about the problems, possibilities, and risks that politics face and how things may be done differently.

Focusing on values, phronetic political scientists are forced to face the perhaps most basic value-question of all, that of foundationalism versus relativism—that is, the view that there are central values that can be rationally and universally grounded versus the view that one set of values is as good as another. Phronetic political scientists reject both of these positions and replace them with contextualism or situational ethics. Distancing themselves from foundationalism does not leave phronetic political scientists normless, however. They take their point of departure in their attitude to the situation being studied. They seek to ensure that such an attitude is based not on idiosyncratic morality or personal preferences but on a common view among a specific reference group to which the political scientists refer. For phronetic political scientists, the socially and historically conditioned context—and not the universal grounding that is desired by certain scholars, but not yet achieved—constitutes the most effective bulwark against relativism and nihilism. Phronetic political scientists realize that, as researchers, they have only sociality and history as a foundation, that these represent the only solid ground under their feet; and that this sociohistorical foundation is fully adequate for their work as political scientists.

As regards validity, phronetic political science, like any other social science, is based on interpretation and is open for testing in relation to other interpretations and other research. Thus, the results of phronetic political science may be confirmed, revised, or rejected according to the most rigorous standards of social science, and such results are open for testing in relation to other interpretations. This does not mean that one interpretation can be just as good as the next, which would be the case for relativism, for each interpretation must be based on validity claims. It does mean, however, that phronetic political science will be as prepared to defend such claims as any other research. Phronetic political scientists also oppose the view that any one among a number of interpretations lacks value because it is "merely" an interpretation. As emphasized by Alexander Nehamas (1985, 63), the key point is the establishment of a *better* option, where "better" is defined according to sets of validity claims. If a new interpretation appears to better explain a given phenomenon, that new interpretation will replace the old one—until it, too, is replaced by a new and yet better interpretation. This is typically a continuing process, not one that terminates with the discovery of "the right answer." Such is the procedure that a community of political scientists would follow in working together to put certain interpretations of political life ahead of others. The procedure does not describe an interpretive or relativistic approach. Rather, it sets forth the basic ground rules for any social and political inquiry, inasmuch as social science and philosophy have not yet identified criteria by which an ultimate interpretation and a final grounding of values and facts can be made.

## Phronetic Research Is Dialogical

Phronetic political science is dialogical in the sense that it incorporates and, if successful, is itself incorporated into a polyphony of voices, with no one voice, including that of the researcher, claiming final authority. The goal of phronetic political science is to produce input to the ongoing dialogue and praxis in politics and administration, rather than to generate ultimate, unequivocally verified knowledge about the nature of these phenomena. This goal accords with Aristotle's maxim that in questions of praxis, one ought to trust more in the public sphere than in science. Dialogue is not limited to the relationship between researchers and the people they study. The relevant dialogue for a particular piece of research typically involves more than these two parties—in principle, anyone interested in and affected by the subject under study. Such parties may be dialoguing independent of researchers until the latter make a successful attempt at entering into the dialogue with their research. In other instances, there may be no ongoing dialogue initially, the dialogue being sparked by the work of phronetic researchers.

Thus, phronetic political science explicitly sees itself as not having a privileged position from which the final truth can be told and further discussion arrested. We cannot think of an "eye turned in no particular direction," as Nietzsche (1969) says. "There is *only* a perspective seeing, *only* a perspective 'knowing;' and the *more* affects we allow to speak about one thing, the *more* eyes, different eyes, we can use to observe one thing, the more complete will our 'concept' of this thing, our 'objectivity,' be" (119, §3.12, emphasis in original). Hence, "objectivity" in phronetic political science is not "contemplation without interest" but employment of "a *variety* of perspectives and affective interpretations in the service of knowledge" (119, §3.12, emphasis in original; see also Nietzsche 1968b, 287, §530).

The significance of any given interpretation in a dialogue will depend on the extent to which the validity claims of the interpreter are accepted, and this acceptance typically occurs in competition with other validity claims and other interpretations. The discourses in which the results of phronetic political science are used have, in this sense, no special status, but are subordinated to the same conditions as any other dialogical discourse. If and when the arguments of researchers carry special weight it would likely derive not from researchers having access to a special type of validity claim, but from researchers having spent more time on and being better trained at establishing validity than have other actors. We are talking about a difference in degree, not in kind. To the phronetic researcher, this is the reality of social and political science, although some researchers act as if validity claims can and should be given final grounding. The burden of proof is on them. By substituting *phronesis* for *episteme,* phronetic political scientists avoid this burden, impossible as it seems to lift.

Some people may fear that the dialogue at the center of phronetic political science, rather than evolving into the desired polyphony of voices, will all too easily degenerate into a shouting match, a cacophony of voices, in which the loudest carries the day. In phronetic political science, the means of prevention is no different from that of other research: only to the extent that the validity claims of phronetic political scientists are accepted will the results of their research be accepted in the dialogue. Phronetic political scientists thus recognize a human privilege and a basic condition: meaningful dialogue in context. "Dialogue" comes from the Greek *dialogos,* where *dia* means "between" and *logos* means "reason." In contrast to the analytical and instrumental rationality, which lie at the cores of both *episteme* and *techne,* the practical rationality of *phronesis* is based on a socially conditioned, intersubjective "between-reason."

## Examples of Phronetic Political Science

A first step in moving toward phronetic social and political sciences is for social and political scientists to explicate the different roles of their research as *episteme, techne,* and *phronesis.* Today, social and political scientists seldom clarify which of these three roles they are practicing. The entire enterprise is simply called "science" or "research," even though we are dealing with quite different activities. It is often the case that these activities are rationalized as *episteme,* even though they are actually *techne* or *phronesis.* As argued previously, it is not in their role of *episteme* that one can argue for the value of social and political science. Nevertheless, by emphasizing the three roles, and especially by reintroducing *phronesis,* we see there are other possibilities. The oft-seen image of impotent social sciences versus potent natural sciences is misleading and derives, as mentioned, from their being compared in terms of their epistemic qualities. If we instead compare the two types of science in terms of their phronetic qualities, we get the opposite result: strong social science and weak natural science. The importance of *phronesis* renders the attempts of social and political science to become "real" epistemic science doubly unfortunate; such efforts draw attention and resources away from those areas where social and political science could make an impact and into areas where they do not obtain, never have obtained, and probably never will obtain any significance as Kuhnian normal and predictive sciences.

The result of phronetic political science is a pragmatically governed interpretation of the studied political and administrative practices. The interpretation does not require the researcher to agree with the other actors' everyday understanding; nor does it require the discovery of some deep, inner meaning of the practices. Phronetic political science is in this way interpretive, but it is neither everyday nor deep hermeneutics. Phronetic political science is also not about, nor does it try to develop, theory or universal method. Thus, phronetic political science is an analytical project, but not a theoretical or methodological one.

The following examples serve as brief representations of an emerging body of political science that contains elements of *phronesis* as interpreted earlier. It is interesting to note, however, that contemporary political science does not have quite the conspicuous figures doing *phronesis*-like research that we find in other social sciences, for instance, sociology with Pierre Bourdieu and Robert Bellah and philosophy and the history of ideas with Michel Foucault and Ian Hacking, among others (see more examples from various fields in Flyvbjerg 2001, 162–65). Even though the thinkers of prudence par excellence, Aristotle and Machiavelli, are central to the intellectual history of political science, today their influence is limited in the discipline. For reasons that must remain unexplored here, the mainstream in contemporary political science does not place at its core the questioning of values and power that was central to classical political science and is central to phronetic political science. Outside the mainstream, however, work is being carried out that shares many of the characteristics of phronetic social science, just as certain works inside the mainstream have phronetic qualities.

Outside the mainstream, we find Wendy Brown (1995), Barbara Cruikshank (1999), Éric Darier (1998), Mitchell Dean and Barry Hindess (1998), François Ewald (1986, 1996), and Hindess (1996). Schram (2004) similarly mentions work by James Scott, Cynthia Enloe, Frances Fox Piven, and Richard A. Cloward and others as examples of Perestroika. Common to these works is a focus on the micropractices of power, power as seen from the bottom up, instead of political science's conventional focus on sovereign power, that is, power as seen from the top down.

Inside the mainstream, a study like Robert Putnam et al.'s (1993) *Making Democracy Work*, which is presented by the authors as a fairly conventional although exceptionally rigorous work of hypothetico-deductive political science, has turned out to have important phronetic effects regarding our understanding of where we are going with civil society and what to do about it (Flyvbjerg 1998b, 208). With this work—and with *Bowling Alone, Better Together,* and the founding of the Saguaro Seminar, which brings together practitioners and scholars to develop actionable ideas to strengthen civil society—Putnam has effectively addressed the four value-rational questions at the core of *phronesis* and linked them with praxis (Putnam 2001; Putnam and Feldstein 2003). Putnam may be using conventional methods, but he puts them to uses that are highly unconventional, in the sense that few other contemporary political scientists work as attentively with the research/praxis problematic as do Putnam and his associates. This underscores the point made earlier, that phronetic social science can be practiced in different ways using different methodologies, so long as the four value-rational questions are addressed effectively and the public has use for the answers in their deliberations about praxis.

Examples of phronetic research also exist from more specialized fields such as the politics of policing (Harcourt 2001; Donzelot 1979), poverty and welfare (Dean 1991; Procacci 1993), sexual politics (Bartky 1990; Minson 1993), and the politics of psychology (Rose 1985, 1996). My own attempts at developing phronetic research have been aimed at understanding democracy and its institutions, and especially how power and rationality interact inside these institutions to shape urban politics and planning (Flyvbjerg 1998a; Flyvbjerg, Bruzelius, and Rothengatter 2003). More examples of relevant research may be found in Dean (1999, 3–5) and Flyvbjerg (2001, 162–65).

A main task of phronetic political science is to provide concrete examples and detailed narratives of the ways in which power and values work in politics and administration and with what consequences and to suggest how power and values could be changed to work with other consequences. Insofar as political and administrative situations become clear, they are clarified by detailed stories of who is doing what to whom. Such clarification is a principal concern for phronetic political science and provides the main link to praxis.

## Conclusions

On the basis of the analysis and discussion in this chapter, I conclude the following:

- David Laitin misrepresents my work on phronetic social and political science to a degree where he violates basic scholarly canons of reasonable handling of information and debate.

- When deprived of his false contrast with the phronetic alternative and his claim to hegemony, Laitin's proposed tripartite method and scientific frame represent a noncontroversial and noninnovative ad hoc combination of three well-known research techniques: statistics, formal analysis, and narrative.
- Laitin's claim that political science may become normal, predictive science in the natural science sense is unfounded. It presupposes a theory of human judgment that no one, so far, has been able to develop. Moreover, it is unlikely that such a theory can be developed, because human judgment appears not to be rule based, whereas theory requires rules.
- If political scientists were to follow Laitin's call for emulating natural science and for hegemony for his tripartite method and scientific frame, this would contribute to the type of stagnation in political science that perestroikans try to get beyond.
- Phronetic political scientists substitute *phronesis* for *episteme* and thereby avoid the trap of emulating natural science. Instead, they arrive at social science that is strong where natural science is weak, that is, in the reflexive analysis and discussion of values and interests aimed at praxis, which is the prerequisite for an enlightened political, economic, and cultural development in any society.

Two scenarios may be outlined for the future of social and political science. In the first scenario, scientism, understood as the tendency to believe that science holds a reliable method of reaching the truth about the nature of things, continues to dominate thinking in social and political science. The relative success of natural science inspires this kind of belief. Explanatory and predictive theory is regarded as the pinnacle of scientific endeavor in this scenario. But scientism in social science will continue to fail for the reasons outlined earlier and fully developed in Flyvbjerg (2001). Consequently, social science will increasingly degenerate as a scholarly activity.

The second scenario replaces scientism with *phronesis*. In this scenario, the purpose of social and political science is not to develop epistemic theory but to contribute to society's practical rationality in elucidating where we are, in whose interest this is, where we want to go, and what is desirable according to different sets of values and interests. The goal of the phronetic approach becomes one of contributing to society's capacity for value-rational deliberation and action. The contribution may be a combination of concrete empirical analyses and practical philosophical-ethical considerations; "fieldwork in philosophy," as Pierre Bourdieu called his version of phronetic social science. In this scenario, social and political scientists actively ensure that their work is relevant to praxis. The aim is to make the line between research and the world direct and consequential, in order for research to have an impact.

Today, the dominant streak in social and political science continues to evolve along the first scenario, that of scientism. This is clearly David Laitin's setting. But scientism in social science is self-defeating, because the reality of social science so evidently does not live up to the ideals of scientism and natural science. Therefore, it is the second scenario, that of *phronesis*, that is more fertile, and worth working for, which is what I have tried to do in Flyvbjerg (2001) and my other work.

David Laitin appears to be wrong when he claims epistemic science can be successful in political science if we just get it right, which, according to Laitin, means that we would all follow his method. Steven Weinberg (2001, 97), winner of the Nobel Prize in physics and an astute observer of what makes for success in science, seems right when he observes that "it has been an essential element in the success of science to distinguish those problems that are and are not illuminated by taking human beings into account." As soon as human beings are taken into account, human skills and human judgment enter the picture, and the possibility of epistemic science appears to take leave. Phronetic science is still an option, however. This is an option a natural scientist like Weinberg does not, and needs not, consider in the role as natural scientist.[3] But it is something to which social scientists should pay close attention if they want success in what they do. On this background, it is encouraging to see that a growing number of political scientists are endorsing Perestroika with its challenge to the dominance of scientism in political science and its support for *phronesis*-like approaches.

If we want more *phronesis* in social and political science, we need to do three things. First, we must drop all pretense, however indirect, of emulating the relative success of the natural sciences in producing cumulative and predictive theory, for their approach simply does not work in social and political science. Second, we must address problems that matter to groups in the local, national, and global communities in which we live, and we must do it in ways that matter; we must focus on issues of context, values, and power, as advocated by great social scientists from Aristotle to Machiavelli to Max Weber. Finally, we must effectively and dialogically communicate the results of our research to our fellow citizens and carefully listen to their feedback. If we do this—focus on specific values and interests in the context of particular power relations—we may successfully transform social and political science into an activity performed in public for social and political publics, sometimes to clarify, sometimes to intervene, sometimes to generate new perspectives, and always to serve as eyes and ears in ongoing efforts to understand the present and deliberate about the future. We may, in short, arrive at social and political sciences that matter.

The author would like to thank Erik Albæk, Irene Christiansen, John Dryzek, Ido Oren, Tim Richardson, Sanford Schram, Georg Sørensen, Stephen White, Alan Wolfe, and the editors of *Politics & Society* for valuable comments on an earlier draft of this article.

### NOTES

1. In the short space of this chapter, it is not possible to provide a full account of Aristotle's considerations about the intellectual virtues of *episteme, techne,* and *phronesis.* Instead, I have focused upon the bare essentials. A complete account would further elaborate the relations among *episteme, techne,* and *phronesis* and the relationship of all three to *empeiria.* It would also expand on the relationship of phronetic judgments to rules, on what it means to succeed or to fail in the exercise of *phronesis,* and on the conditions that must be fulfilled if *phronesis* is to be acquired. For further discussion of these questions and of the implications of Aristotle's thinking for contemporary social science, see my discussion with Hubert Dreyfus and Stuart Dreyfus in Dreyfus and Dreyfus (1991: 101ff.). See also Bernstein (1985), Heller (1990), Lord and O'Connor (1991 eds.), Macintyre (1984), and Taylor (1995).

2. For Aristotle, man [*sic*] has a double identity. For the "human person," that is, man in politics and ethics, *phronesis* is the most important intellectual virtue. Insofar as man can transcend the purely human, contemplation assumes the highest place. Aristotle (1976, 1145a6ff., 1177a12ff.).

3. Natural scientists may well consider, and be practitioners of, *phronesis* if they take on the role of what has been called "concerned scientists," that is, scientists with a concern for the effects of science on, for instance, nuclear, biological, environmental, and social risks. The Danish physicist Niels Bohr was an early example of a scientist of this type, as was Albert Einstein.

# 4

# A Statistician Strikes Out

## In Defense of Genuine Methodological Diversity

### Patrick Thaddeus Jackson

> Allan Roth, the team statistician . . . recorded every pitch of every game on a sheet of graph paper and tabulated his data in a cross complexity of techniques. . . . Rickey had hired Roth to supply information to the manager. If Shuba never hit lefthanders' curves, then sit him down against Ken Raffensberger [a left-handed pitcher who threw curveballs]. Dressen [the manager] regarded Roth and his bodies of facts as threats. "I got my own way of figurin'," he said. Dressen soared on intuition and probably feared that figures might wither his expertise. (Kahn 1972, 126–27)

There is an old argument in professional baseball about the best way to manage a team to victory. On one side of this debate stand the traditionalists, trusting to their instincts in making decisions about which players to draft and retain and which to put in the game at key moments. On the other side stand the aficionados of "sabermetrics," the highly technical practice of breaking every aspect of a player's performance down into quantifiable components, and making management decisions on the basis of numerical projections and analyses. Each of these two positions leads to very different ways of evaluating players, with traditionalists emphasizing subjective judgments about a player's potential and sabermetricians focusing on measured past performance (Lewis 2003, 30–32). The jury remains out on which of these approaches is the superior one, although the sabermetric approach seems to be gaining popularity with a number of teams.

Many recent discussions of "methodological diversity" presume that the debate within political science is, in essence, the same as the debate within baseball: numbers or gut instincts? The putatively pluralistic answer offered by scholars like David Laitin (2003) and Gary King, Robert Keohane, and Sidney Verba (King, Keohane, and Verba 1994) turns out, on closer examination, to be not particularly pluralistic at all. King, Keohane, and Verba suggest that there is no essential difference between "qualitative" and "quantitative" research and that therefore all scholars "cannot afford to ignore sources of bias and inefficiency created by methodologically unreflective research designs" (King, Keohane, and Verba 1994, 229). For Laitin, case narratives based on practical experience with a situation can serve to test formal models, provide causal mechanisms, and plot residuals in preparation for future formalization (Laitin 2003, 179). Likewise, statistics and formal modeling have their assigned tasks in the social scientific enterprise; this "tripartite methodology . . . is the best defense we have against error and the surest hope for valid inference" (ibid., 169). Hence, underlying any surface-level diversity of particular kinds of research is a single, unitary, and uncontestable logic of inquiry.

In statements such as these, we see the partisans of a particular mode of social inquiry—a *statistical-comparative* mode, in which all valid inference is exhausted by the search for cross-case correlations—stepping to the plate and taking critical swings against an emergent alternative position based on dialogue and diversity. These critical swings appear to be calls for tolerance and multiplicity, but, upon closer examination, they outline a Procrustean bed into which more interpretive and relational modes of social inquiry—to say nothing of "critical" or *phronetic* notions of social science (Flyvbjerg 2001)—fit uneasily, if at all. This faux diversity rests on three subordinate positions:

1. the assertion, usually never demonstrated, that all social inquiry has or should have the same goals;
2. the notion that social life is a closed system within which constant conjunctions between independent and dependent variables obtain; and
3. the devaluing of open dialogue in favor of closed consensus in the matter of knowledge construction.

All three of these positions depend on a misrepresentation of the current political science debate—which is actually quite different from, and more far-reaching than, the baseball debate about numbers versus gut instincts. As such, these three swings miss the mark.

## Methods and Methodologies

In baseball, as in other organized sports, there is only one goal for a manager: winning games. Even teams that are "rebuilding," or are dumping their high-priced veteran players in favor of lower-salaried rookies, have the objective of winning baseball games at some point in the future firmly in mind. Statistical-comparative methodologists presume that what is true of baseball is equally true of political science, with "valid inference" standing in place of a winning record as the sole arbiter of a successful effort (King, Keohane, and Verba 1994, 34; Laitin 2003, 166). This presumption underpins their professed tolerance for multiple methods in the study of social reality, in that many different techniques (including quantitative statistics, formal modeling, and narrative) are welcome to contribute to the analysis of social life *only if* they accept and contribute to this single goal (King, Keohane, and Verba 1994, 56, 75; Laitin 2003, 181, 179). So everyone can play, as long as all participants agree in advance to play by the same rules.

But these rules, centering on the disclosure of cross-case correlations between independent and dependent variables, leave only a sharply limited space for nonstatistical techniques. For example, Laitin's apparently tolerant tripartite scientific method relies on formal models primarily as a way to generate falsifiable hypotheses, which hardly exhausts the modeling enterprise. As for narrative, Laitin reduces its role to, in effect, the provision of local color for spare formal analyses and the factual presentation of how independent and dependent variables are linked, along with the description of unexplained variance in preparation for future systematic analysis (Laitin 2003, 177–79).

Partisans of the statistical-comparative approach also have a difficult time appreciating nonstatistical modes of inquiry in their own terms. For example, Laitin propounds a highly selective reading of Bent Flyvbjerg's call for a more phronetic social science as being merely a call for sustained case narratives, rather than a call for social science to contribute "to the reflexive analysis and discussion of values and interests" (Flyvbjerg 2001,

3). Laitin seems to regard the goal of disclosing cross-case correlations to be self-evidently equivalent to the notion of "valid inference" and devotes no space in his article to *justifying* this goal; hence, it is not surprising that he devotes no space to engaging different specifications of the goals of social inquiry. Similarly, King, Keohane, and Verba's discussion of Clifford Geertz's anthropological point that one cannot understand the meaning of an action without immersing oneself in the local situation (Geertz 1973, 6–7) reduces the issues involved to the question of whether particular social actions are correlated in a systematic fashion (King, Keohane, and Verba 1994, 38–40). Again, there is little or no *justification* provided for this position.

But, unlike in baseball, not everyone in political science actually has the same goals. To continue the metaphor, some people are less interested in managing a team to victory by looking for the predictors of overall team success than they are in studying how the social structure of baseball—the rules that are, by necessity, taken for granted by managers engaged in the act of managing a team—came to be the way that they are (Gould 2003; Markovits and Hellerman 2001). Others are more interested in tracing the links between baseball and other elements of public culture (Seidel 1988). These are different kinds of questions. Looking for well-verified correlations between factors, explaining how domains of social life congeal and disperse, and tracing meaningful relations according to an abstract specification of what is important about a situation are *qualitatively different* analytical exercises. All are empirical (rather than normative) questions, and all demand a relatively rigorous application of theoretical precepts to masses of information; in this broader (Weberian) sense, they are all "scientific" questions (Weber 1949). These three questions should not be shoehorned into a single conception of social inquiry.

I have not chosen these three questions at random. Each is an example of the kind of question that would be asked by Laitin's three components of science if we considered these three as *methodologies* rather than simply as *methods*. The distinction is critical: methods are techniques for gathering and gaining access to bits of data, whereas methodologies are "grounded . . . in the history of political or social scientific thought and/or in related epistemological-ontological assumptions taken up in the philosophy of (social) science and embedded in the research process" (Schwartz-Shea and Yanow 2002, 459–60; see also Shotter 1993). As such, methodological considerations are more basic than questions of method, "for once a methodology is adopted, the choice of methods becomes merely a tactical matter" (Waltz 1979, 13). In a sense, methodology (often called simply "theory" in older works) *constructs* an analytical world out of the veritable infinity of data characteristic of any particular situation, by grounding "a frame of reference that fixes the order and relevance of the facts" in specific ontological and epistemological considerations. In David Easton's pithy formulation, "A fact is a particular ordering of reality in terms of a theoretical interest," and methodological considerations are never absent from concrete empirical research (Easton [1953] 1971, 53).

Although never absent, methodological considerations can be more or less explicit; in Laitin's statement, the methodology is almost completely implicit and, as such, is asserted rather than demonstrated. But from his criticism of Tambiah's account of the Sri Lankan civil war (Laitin 2003, 173–75) it is apparent that Laitin's preferred methodology is a *statistical-comparative* one that seeks to identify independent variables that are efficient predictors of outcomes across cases. This seemingly innocuous position actually supervenes on a variety of contentious metaphysical assumptions, including the stability of entities and the uniformity of causal effects, that Andrew Abbott has gathered up under the heading of "general linear reality" (Abbott 1988).

But there are other alternatives. For example, take the second component of Laitin's tripartite approach to science: formal modeling. What many methodologists fail to take seriously is that models are quintessentially *interpretive* in character, participating in a rather different exercise than that advanced by statistical-comparative methodology. Models sort data into relevant categories, with relevance specified by the model itself, and provide a baseline from which to render phenomena comprehensible. Empirical findings cannot "falsify" the model, which is ideal-typical rather than descriptive; instead, discrepant information provides an opportunity to further calibrate the model, so that the former discrepancies become newly comprehensible (Hardin 1995, 91–100).[1] Also, the truth criterion for a formal model is its logical soundness, and not the correspondence between its theoretical terms and the empirical world. Hence, a model can be logically true but practically useless—a situation that does not arise when operating in a statistical-comparative methodology (Waltz 1979, 71–72).

Seen in this way, the use of a model has more in common with the act of interpreting a text than it does with the act of testing a hypothesis. The point is to make connections plain and comprehensible, rather than to look for law-like patterns of correlation. This is particularly true of models that make presumptions about the contents of individual minds, such as the rational-choice accounts of human behavior often implicitly equated with "formal models" (e.g., Laitin 2003, 176–78). Such models have an unfalsifiable hermeneutic core, a "model of man" that guides and grounds the effort to explicate a plethora of concrete situations; this core can never be subjected to falsification in the course of an investigation, since it serves as the centerpiece of the analytical apparatus generating the findings in the first place (Moon 1975). But the same is true of all forms of modeling, including systems models that make no presumptions about the contents of individual minds: the exercise of applying a model to a case or set of cases is a particularly disciplined form of interpretation rather than an exercise in falsification.

Likewise, Laitin's third component—narrative—can be easily understood as a methodology, rather than as a method. Setting aside for a moment the merely descriptive aspects of Laitin's notion of narrative, we are left with a focus on causal mechanisms. But Laitin's declaration that to focus on mechanisms means to "link independent and dependent variables . . . basically showing how favorable conditions from a statistical sense translate into outcomes" (Laitin 2003, 176–77) ignores a substantial body of recent *relational* work on mechanisms that proceeds in a very different direction. The central thrust of this work is that causal mechanisms are qualitatively different from intervening variables that link inputs and outcomes but exercise their impact in unique configurations. The goal of relational analysis is to show how a number of robust mechanisms come together in a particular case so as to produce a unique outcome. What replicates across cases, then, is *not* a systematic correlation between inputs and outputs but particular causal mechanisms like brokerage and certification (McAdam, Tarrow, and Tilly 2001, 29–34, 142–48; see also Tilly 1995). The role of narrative when it comes to these mechanisms is not simply to trace linkages between factors but also to demonstrate how concrete outcomes are produced through concatenations of these mechanisms and processes. Methodologically, this is a relational approach to the study of social life, privileging mechanisms and processes rather than the putatively rational decisions of self-propelled actors or the homogenous effects of independent causal factors (Emirbayer 1997; Jackson and Nexon 2002; Tilly 2002, 73–75).

By suggesting that Laitin's three "methods" are better thought of as three divergent methodologies, I do not mean to dismiss any of the three as prima facie invalid; nor do I mean to suggest that Laitin's effort to sub-

sume interpretive and relational techniques under a statistical-comparative methodology is necessarily inappropriate. But it is incumbent on
Laitin to *argue for* his preferred methodology, instead of simply *assuming*
its transcendental validity and recommending that a "procedure's
flowerbed should no longer be cultivated within the discipline in which it
was originally seeded" if it does not advance his preferred goals (Laitin
2003, 179). This is a familiar strategy among partisans of statistical-comparative methodology, who frequently declare their methodological orientation instead of arguing for it—as though that orientation were simply
and self-evidently equivalent to "social science" per se (King, Keohane, and
Verba 1994, 7).

Where statistical-comparative partisans value only a diversity of *methods,* we could instead prize *methodological* diversity. In order to really
address this issue, statistical-comparative partisans would have to begin by
acknowledging that not every social researcher wants to develop winning
strategies for a baseball team.

## Open and Closed Systems

In a standard nine-inning baseball game, a team must send men to the
plate a minimum of 25 times.[2] Each team plays 162 games during the regular season, for a minimum total of 4,050 plate appearances per season.
And there are 30 major league baseball teams, so that an annual season
generates a minimum of 121,500 plate appearances—a "large n" by almost
anyone's standards. But what makes baseball an ideal situation for statistical-comparative analysis is not merely that a lot of data are generated, or
even that the data are readily quantifiable into on-base percentages and
batting averages and the like; many parts of social life generate such volumes of numerical data. Rather, what makes baseball amenable to statistical-comparative analysis is that the data are generated by repeated actions
that take place within a very stable system of rules that set boundaries on
acceptable play but do not uniquely determine outcomes. Baseball's numbers are *meaningful,* and have been so for over a century—ever since the
pitcher's mound was moved back to its present distance from home plate
(Gould 2003, 152–53). Baseball thus constitutes an arena in which major
factors are effectively fixed and small variations among players, ballparks,
and strategies of play can be effectively correlated with measurable outcomes.

In other words, baseball approximates a closed system: a system of action that is relatively isolated from external influences and features essential individuals interacting in restricted ways (Bhaskar 1975, 75–78). Present in situations like those in a laboratory, a closed system permits the formulation and testing of statistical-comparative hypotheses with relative ease, as the relevant boundary conditions are truly parametric and experimenters can consequently work to isolate the impact of minute variations while holding most other factors constant.

But it remains an open question whether social life *as a whole* constitutes a closed system. Most philosophers of science and social theorists who have taken up the issue argue that it is better to think of social life as an open system, within which causation is not always marked by systematic cross-case correlation. As such, generalization cannot take place at the level of systematic connections between inputs and outputs, but must take place elsewhere—either at the level of causal mechanisms and processes or at the level of innate dispositional essences of entities (Bhaskar 1998; Giddens 1986; Wendt 1999). If social life is not as approximately closed as baseball is, then statistical-comparative techniques may not be the most appropriate ones for investigating it.

In fact, although baseball, like most organized sports, is deliberately produced as an approximately closed system through the actions of a bureaucracy dedicated to preserving the integrity of the game, this closure remains only approximate. Economic, environmental, and pharmacological factors continually intervene to change the game in various ways over time. The perpetuation of the sport as a relatively closed system of action—like the perpetuation of any set of social boundaries—takes (practical, discursive) work (Neumann 1999, 35–37; Tilly 1998, 67–70). It might be a useful *pragmatic* assumption to simply posit the game as a closed system, particularly if one is trying to solve a particular set of problems and manage a team to victory, but this assumption should not be reified into a description of how the system "really is" (Easton [1953] 1971, 128–29, 291–92; Parsons 1954, 216–17). In addition, such a methodological commitment closes off several avenues of inquiry—in particular, a critical examination of the rules that govern the game and of the processes and mechanisms that came together so as to produce the particular arrangement of rules presently in force. Whether these trade-offs are justified is a complex matter, worthy of extended discussion rather than dismissal through silence.

In particular, any case for methodologically presuming that social life constitutes a closed system needs to confront two related issues. First of all, precisely isolating the boundaries of a social system is empirically problematic, even for relatively closed systems like organized baseball. Commentators continue to debate whether alterations in the height of the pitcher's mound and the size of the strike zone, or the introduction of a "wild card" playoff spot, have irrevocably altered the game (Boswell 2004; Gould 2003, 304–10). Recently implemented revenue-sharing measures hope to address the imbalances between rich, large-market teams and their poorer, small-market brethren (Pennington 2003). It is far from simple to adjudicate just how significant these changes are. The basic conceptual problem is that "'obeying a rule' is a practice," as is determining whether some particular rule is essential to an activity or not; the best that can be done is to advance an argument based on a sense of what the game is all about (Wittgenstein 1999, §202, 562–68). Formal specifications of rules never exhaust the activity that they supposedly govern, which means that there is always room to contest any particular specification of the rules—even for baseball (Flyvbjerg 2001, 42–45).

The problem becomes even more acute when we consider social arrangements in which the rules of the game are themselves an object of contestation. The play of the game of baseball does not directly involve revisions of the rules, but many other areas of social life—legislative and judicial processes, social movement activism, international diplomacy, and the like—*do* directly involve such an ongoing contestation of the rules. In fact, I would venture to say that most of the phenomena of interest to social scientists involve this kind of practical endogeneity, where the activities under investigation have at least the potential to modify the boundaries of the phenomenon. But this does not mean that there can be no systematic study of these phenomena. Nor does it mean that there can be no causal conclusions about these phenomena, unless we follow Laitin and other statistical-comparative partisans in restricting causality and the "zone of science" to the search for invariant laws in a closed system (Laitin 2003, 171).

As before, my purpose is not to simply dismiss the statistical-comparative position. To the contrary, I would like to see it spelled out more explicitly. I think that someone could do the field a great service by making explicit arguments on behalf of considering social life as a whole to be a closed system in which constant conjunctions of variables obtain on a regular basis. Among other things, such arguments would serve as useful foils for those of us who disagree.

## Dialogue Versus Synthesis

Indeed, it is this absence of explicit arguments that constitutes the greatest failing of statistical-comparative partisans: they generally neglect to provide *grounds* for their positions. Instead, we are confronted with a plethora of assertions about the character of "science" and implicit presumptions about the nature of social reality that calls for such a science. This is a very unfortunate way to respond to calls for open dialogue about these basic issues—calls such as that consistently issued by the "Perestroika" movement within American political science. There is, by design, no perestroikan "manifesto offering an alternative view of the discipline" (Laitin 2003, 163), because the perestroikan alternative is (in my reading, at least) based on dialogue, rather than consensus. The alternative to the present dominance in the field of statistical-comparative methodology is not the dominance of some rival methodology but instead a sustained dialogue about the social world among practitioners of rival methodologies

The need for such a dialogue, as far as I am concerned, rests on what Max Weber identified many years ago as the "irresolvable conflict" between "different value-orderings of the world" (Weber [1917/1919] 1994, 16–17). Different practitioners of social inquiry necessarily approach the world with very different value-orderings and regard different aspects of particular phenomena as being of interest. But Weber's solution is not to declare some methodologies and their encoded value-orientations categorically invalid; instead, his solution is to demand that each researcher make her or his presuppositions explicit and that each researcher implement her or his project in a rigorous, logically consistent manner (Weber 1949, 80–84). Weber argues that this will produce insights that can be appreciated even if cultural values (and their associated methodologies) change (Weber 1949, 58–59). But what it will *not* lead to is a fieldwide consensus on fundamental value-orderings, because systematic empirical enquiry cannot itself definitively answer questions about such things (Weber [1917/1919] 1994, 19–20).

Obviously, appreciating the insights generated by a different set of value-orderings is made much easier if authors explicitly spell out what their value-orderings *are*. In practice, particular authors cast their lots with particular methodologies, at least for the purpose of particular projects; nothing in my Weberian stance militates against that. A commitment to dialogue at the level of the field should not be mistaken for a demand that every scholar deploy multiple methodologies in a single piece of empirical research. Indeed, the field is probably well served by individual (and perhaps even departmental) methodological specialization—as long as a sustained dialogue with scholars and scholarship stemming from different methodological traditions accompanies this specialization. Laitin's caricature of an engaged pluralism (Lapid 2003) as involving the protection of "defunct practitioners" from challenges misstates the case; the purpose of a dialogue is not to entrench the participants further into their separate camps but to encourage discussion of issues from multiple perspectives (Laitin 2003, 180). Faced with these two alternatives—the statistical-comparative resolution of these fundamental philosophical issues by fiat and the call for sustained dialogue about those issues advanced by many in the Perestroika movement—we should ask ourselves: which path points towards the kind of social science that we want?[3]

## The Post-Game Wrap-Up

David Laitin has staked out and presented a postion shared by many in contemporary social science: that all methods of inquiry should take their places in the division of labor established by a firm commitment to a stastistical comparative methodology. In this way, they can all trangulate on the essential character of social reality and help us to better understand and affect it. Laitin is certainly one of the most sophisticated practitioners of this kind of social science; his empirical work provides numerous examples of one way of making case narratives, formal models and statistical hypothesis-testing work together. But in this particular trip to the plate, Laitin has failed to reach base safely. He swings through the first pitch tossed by many advocates of methodological diversity—the notion that there are diverse goals of social inquiry—by simply presuming that every social theorist has the same aims. He fouls off the second pitch—the notion that social life is, or might be, an open system—by failing to confront the issue squarely. And he misses the third pitch—the call for dialogue, rather than a too-hasty synthesis—by trying to refute a straw-man argument about the protection of defuct perspectives. Hence:

> there is no joy in Stats-ville—
> mighty Laitin has struck out.[4]

Thanks to Brian Caterino, Elizabeth Dahl, Peter Howard, Daniel Nexon, Kiran Pervez, Joe Soss, Sherrill Stroschein, and Charles Tilly for helpful comments and suggestions on an earlier draft.

NOTES

1. In this light, the position that disconfirming or discrepant evidence should lead to a reformulated model, which is sometimes claimed as an innovative methodological position (e.g., Bates et al. 1998, 16), appears less radical and more conventional—at least, more conventional for a *methodology* of modeling, rather than for a *method* of modeling serving as an adjunct to a statistical-comparative methodology.

2. A team can send only twenty-five men to the plate during a game if (a) they are the home team; (b) the visiting team faces only three batters per inning for a total of seven innings and faces four batters—only one of whom scores—during one and only one inning; and (c) the home team holds the visiting team scoreless for nine innings. [A team can face only three batters per inning either by (i) retiring the side in order or (ii) retiring the side in such a way that no one scores and no one is left on base, which would involve a combination of double and triple plays, successful pick-off attempts, and runners caught when attempting to steal a base.] As this is tremendously unlikely to happen even once during the regular season, actual plate appearance numbers are, obviously, much higher, raising the population size even more. Thanks to Charles Tilly and Peter Howard for reminding me of these issues.

3. For an exploration of how these issues are played out on the curricular level in political science Ph.D. departments in the United States, and an argument that instituting a philosophy of social science requirement would go a long way towards producing a condition of engaged pluralism, see Schwartz-Shea 2003.

4. Adapted from "Casey at the Bat," by Ernest L. Thayer. In the poem Casey lets the first two pitches go by without taking a swing, while Laitin does swing at all three. But it's still a swinging strikeout, like that of the mythical Casey.

# 5

# Reflections on Doing
# Phronetic Social Science
## A Case Study

*Corey S. Shdaimah and Roland W. Stahl*

In 2003, the Women's Community Revitalization Project (WCRP), a community-based organization in Philadelphia, received a grant from the William Penn Foundation to study and advocate around home repair and home maintenance issues of concern to low-income homeowners. WCRP used these funds to augment its advocacy efforts in Philadelphia. In accordance with the terms of the grant, WCRP solicited proposals from researchers at academic institutions to study the home maintenance and repair problems of low-income homeowners in the city. The authors of this chapter were part of the three-person academic research team chosen by WCRP.

The goal of the study was to develop a solid understanding of the home repair and home maintenance needs of low-income homeowners, including the root causes of these needs, to establish which city programs were ostensibly designed to meet these needs, to assess whether in fact they did meet these needs, and to estimate what programs or resources would be necessary to meet those needs that currently go unmet. The multimethod study relied on a combination of statistical analysis, an extensive review of program literature, and in-depth interviews with policymakers, administrators, advocates, and homeowners.

In this chapter, we use the collaboration between WCRP and the academic research team as an example of "phronetic research" as defined by Bent Flyvbjerg (2001) in *Making Social Science Matter* (MSSM). Our analysis shares Flyvbjerg's assumption that making social science matter is a laudable goal. As Flyvbjerg states, "the principle objective for social science with a phronetic approach is to carry out analyses and interpretations of the status of values and interests in society aimed at social commentary and social action, i.e. praxis" (Flyvbjerg 2001, 60). This is congruent with the founding vision of social science, and Flyvbjerg frames his argument as a return to the roots of social science rather than a radical departure into the unknown: "The goal [*phronesis*] is to help restore social science to its classical position as a practical, intellectual activity aimed at clarifying the problems, risks, and possibilities we face as humans and societies, and at contributing to social and political praxis" (Flyvbjerg 2001, 4).

Applying a phronetic framework to our research has enabled us to examine a number of tensions that social science researchers frequently face but rarely articulate (see Schram 2004; Shapiro 2002; and Smith 2002). We focus in particular on Flyvbjerg's claim that in order for the work of social science researchers to be relevant to the communities in and with which they work, social scientists should not pretend that value questions can be ignored when doing factual research. Indeed, we argue that social scientists should in fact go further to consciously and explicitly develop the value premises of the social phenomena they study.

For Flyvbjerg, the value premises of social science research can be developed only if social scientists take into account the particular sociopolitical and cultural context in which they work. An important consequence of this approach to social science is that scientists can no longer credibly claim that they are above the fray of political interests as suggested by the methodological canon (Laitin, this volume). Rather, Flyvbjerg maintains that social scientists must acknowledge the interests of and actively enter into dialogue with other stakeholders concerned with particular social phenomena or problems: "the phronetic researcher becomes a part of the phenomena studied" (Flyvbjerg 2001, 132).

Applying phronetic principles thus raises questions about the relationship between social scientists and the public sphere. Moreover, explicitly addressing value questions increases study participants' and other stakeholders' engagement with the work of the social scientist. Initiating such interest is an integral component of Flyvbjerg's "social science that matters" (Flyvbjerg 2001, 166). Our study is particularly well suited to reflect on the relationship between researchers and the public sphere because it was organized in close collaboration and communication with relevant stakeholders.[1] This arrangement engendered a charged and dynamic research environment, and it brought into sharp relief the challenges of phronetic research, providing fertile ground for exploring phronetic research in action.

We address the relevancy of values and interests in the context of our study by discussing at length what we refer to as the "homeownership dream." In recent years, policymakers in the United States have emphasized that owning a home is the most promising (and largely exclusive) solution to low-income housing problems. Policymakers and pundits claim that owning a home strengthens the economic and sociocultural well-being of low-income homeowners, as well as their communities at large, both in the short term and in the more long-term goal of assets-building (see, for example, Retsinas and Belsky 2002). The findings of this study, reported in Shdaimah, Stahl, and Schram (2004), however, raise questions about the efficacy and the discursive rationale of this strategy. First, our findings indicate that homeownership does not always lead to an increase in the sociomaterial well-being of low-income homeowners. This is true for low-income homeowners who can usually afford only old and dilapidated homes, especially in the urban centers of the Northeast such as Philadelphia. Moreover, analysis of the homeownership discourse suggests that in touting the dream of owning a home as the best strategy for low-income individuals and their communities, there might be interests and values at stake other than the economic well-being of low-income homeowners. We argue that homeownership as the central focus of low-income housing policy fits hand-in-glove with the call for personal responsibility that dominates U.S. social policy debates generally, as represented by the writing of influential conservative scholars such as Charles Murray and Lawrence Mead and the political rhetoric exemplified by the debate around the 1996 Personal Responsibility and Work Opportunity Reconciliation Act, commonly know as "Welfare Reform." The emphasis on homeownership is increasingly the primary way, together with wage labor, to demonstrate that one is personally responsible and deserving of the status of first-class citizenship (Feldman 2004). Yet, as has been argued by progressive social-policy scholars such as Sanford Schram (2002) and Martin Gilens (1999), "personal responsibility" is often used as a politically palatable placeholder for attempts to cut social programs. Unfortunately, for low-income families, homeownership is a hollow status where one has the nominal right to first-class citizenship but reaps none of the economic gains associated therewith.

The application of phronetic principles presented a number of hurdles to our collaboration with our partners at WCRP. For example, our critical analysis of the homeownership dream proved inconsistent with some of WCRP's basic assumptions regarding low-income housing policy. While advocates understandably focus on the immediate social and economic advantages of homeowning for low-income families, our findings pointed to some of the potential disadvantages of low-income homeownership. By examining low-income homeownership from a broader perspective, we exposed tensions between WCRP's immediate and long-term goals, which in turn caused tensions between WCRP and the academic research team.

On the other hand, we experienced the benefits of a collaborative approach to social science that enables both researchers and political actors to learn from each others' perspective of a social problem. While advocates are challenged to think more about the long-term consequences of advocating for better homeownership supports, researchers are challenged to think more strategically about raising issues that problematize the emphasis on homeownership in public discourse. We believe that this mutual learning process has considerably strengthened the relevance of our study to WCRP and to all stakeholders in the policy process.

In the first section of this essay, we address some theoretical implications of applying phronetic principles to the collaboration between researchers and the public sphere. The subsequent section uses the homeownership dream as a lens to examine our collaborative phronetic research project. We consider how the doubts about the benefits of low-income homeownership emerged from previously unchallenged assumptions; why their emergence raised difficult questions regarding the need to proceed carefully in making it the central focus of low-income housing policy; and how our critique played out in debates with our partners at WCRP. In the final section, we suggest how to understand the tensions created by "making social science matter" and advocate the importance of phronetic research as a fruitful tool for social scientists and for other stakeholders *because* of these tensions.

## Social Scientists and the Public Sphere

Flyvbjerg's claim that social scientists must consider value issues if they want their endeavors to matter raises fundamental questions about the role of social scientists as different from other stakeholders in a research project. On a general level, this issue harkens back to the fact-versus-value debate that has haunted the social sciences from their inception. Max

Weber, for example, in his famous essay on "science as a vocation," postulates that:

> Science today is a "vocation" organized in special disciplines in the service
> of self-clarification and knowledge of interrelated facts. It is not the gift of
> grace of seers and prophets dispensing sacred values and revelations, nor
> does it partake of the contemplation of sages and philosophers about the
> meaning of the universe. (1918/1946)

Weber maintains that the distinction between factual and value questions can be made with sufficient clarity. Weber does not say that philosophy and theology do not raise significant questions. He rather states that they are not *scientific* questions. Weber goes further than stating merely that the two *can* be distinguished by exhorting that their integration has no place in (and likely interferes with) the scientific endeavor; value questions cannot be settled by reference to empirical evidence, and factual problems cannot be decided using normative considerations.

Given the long and embattled history of the fact-versus-value debate, it is not surprising that phronetic research is considered misguided by some social scientists who view the integration of values as necessarily leading to the abandonment of the imagined value-free objectivity that lies at the very heart of modern science (Laitin, this volume). Social scientists sought to erect clear boundaries between themselves as scientists and political actors in order to contain potential conflicts of interest and to establish "neutral" criteria for adjudicating the credibility of fact claims. According to this school of thought, social scientists cannot purport to present the facts, *and only the facts,* if they engage in value issues. This is true in terms of social scientists' own values and interests, as well as because of the potential impact of values and interests of relevant stakeholders on social science research.

Flyvbjerg counters this line of thinking in MSSM by pointing out that the value-free objectivity that positivist social science aspires to is a myth, or has at least not proven to be attainable thus far: "Phronetic researchers can see no neutral ground, no view from nowhere for their work" (Flyvbjerg 2001, 61; see also Toulmin 2001). In fact, it is today widely accepted among social scientists that complete neutrality is unattainable, even among those who continue to view it as an aspiration (Campbell 1975). Values do not disappear if we pretend they do not exist but rather persist unexamined. Ignoring values only limits the scope of any intellectual or political enterprise by precluding reflection, hence limiting the possibility of reasoned choices.

In MSSM, Flyvbjerg shows in great detail that phenomena that are studied by social scientists are always embedded in particular contexts and that these phenomena "talk back" (Flyvbjerg, this volume). Social science is affected by its subject matter and vise versa. This cyclical process means that social science inevitably involves the values implicit in social phenomena being studied. For instance, studies of low-income homeownership inevitably are affected by the value given to homeownership in the particular social context being studied. The distinction between facts and values is therefore better seen as a theoretical construct rather than an aspect of social reality. As useful as the fact/value distinction is for a variety of analytical purposes, social scientists should not forget that facts and values are inextricably intertwined in the real world. Hence, Flyvbjerg argues, we cannot study social phenomena without considering what they *mean* both to us as social scientists and to the people being studied and other stakeholders.

As a consequence, Flyvbjerg argues, phronetic researchers who attempt to integrate values into social science research must become part of public debates.

> Phronetic researchers seek to transcend [the] problem of relevance by anchoring their research in the context studied and thereby ensuring a hermeneutic "fusion of horizons." This applies both to contemporary and historical studies. For contemporary studies one gets close to the phenomenon or group whom one studies during data collections, and remains close during the phases of data analysis, feedback, and publication of results. Combined with [a] focus on relations of values and power, this strategy typically creates interest by outside parties, and even outside stakeholders, in the research. These parties will test and evaluate the research in various ways. The researchers will consciously expose themselves to reactions from their surroundings—both positive and negative—and may derive benefit from the learning effect, which is built into this strategy. (Flyvbjerg 2001, 132)

Flyvbjerg asks us to recognize that research is always influenced by stakeholders who operate in a given context. His argument is, of course, rather provocative to those engaged in more conventional approaches to social science. Social scientists have traditionally ignored stakeholders, often claiming that scientific research should strive to neutralize any effect they might have on the subject of study in order to produce objective research (Flyvbjerg 2001, 166), even as they fail to acknowledge "invisible" stakeholders, such as those who publish our articles and fund our studies. Instead, argues Flyvbjerg, researchers should test their arguments publicly, *in dialogue* with stakeholders involved with and interested in a particular study. Collaboration between stakeholders and researchers is necessary to provide a critical forum in which to determine the morality and relevance of projects and to assess findings and possible courses of action. Social scientists who try to answer Flyvbjerg's "so what" problem (Flyvbjerg 2001, 132) by taking part in such a public discussion must ask: what is the relevant public or forum *to which* my work matters?

This approach to practicing social science necessarily leads to questions about the specific role of social scientists in public debates. What remains distinctive about the contributions of social scientists to the public debate once we give up our claim to an objective standing in these debates? In our view, social scientists play a distinct role, one that persists even when the myth of objectivity is conceded. The distinct contribution of the social scientist to public debates follows not from some kind of special standing, but rather from what they *add* to public debates. As we demonstrate in our discussion of the homeownership dream, the particular contribution of social scientists is the ability to "complicate" debates about specific social problems, practices, and discourses, both by looking closely at the relevant empirical facts *and* by asking what these facts mean. Clifford Geertz captures this goal succinctly in his discussion of the science of interpretive anthropology when he states that it "is a science whose "progress is marked less by a perfection of consensus than by a refinement of debate. What gets better is the precision with which we vex each other" (Geertz 1973, 28–29).

We preserved our distinct role as social scientists in the WCRP project by explicitly investigating what our advocate-partners assumed they "already knew" (i.e., the underlying value of homeownership) about low-income housing policy and the home repair problem in particular. As we found out soon enough, our approach brought forth results that were, to a certain extent, contrary to the expectations of our collaborators. The people we worked with at WCRP had a clear goal for the study from the outset, which was to secure increased funding for homeowners to repair and maintain their homes. Their interest was to find solutions to the problem *as they defined it.* The disparity of expectations should come as no surprise; it is exactly what social scientists should expect. Stakeholders will have particular expectations in terms of the findings of a study, especially if they are political actors such as the WCRP advocates. Their expectations will depend upon their particular views of the phenomenon or problem studied.

Our study was well suited to reflect upon the relationship between scientists and political actors. Collaborative research blurs the boundaries between advocates in their role as political actors and social scientists as researchers engaged in the production of knowledge. A participatory phronetic approach increased our openness to the perceptions of our partners at WCRP, which provided us with important information and insights. Our different but related perspectives broadened their thinking as well as ours and elicited in-depth understandings of the problem, ultimately expanding the scope of what WCRP looked at as relevant to the issue under study. In our view, one of the core ideas of phronetic social science is to critically examine the various perspectives and to do so explicitly and openly. This type of dialogue over the meaning and use of the results, which respects the perspectives of researchers and of other stakeholders, ensures that the findings of studies will matter to those concerned with a particular problem.

In the next section, we further examine the differences in the role of the advocate and the researcher as a source of tension in the context of our research. We summarize the findings of our study as they relate to the homeownership dream, focusing on our critical assessment of the discourse that frames debates about low-income housing policies and how that led to tensions between researchers and advocates in our project. Yet, as we hope to show, our study demonstrates that collaboration between scientists and political actors who acknowledge their distinctive roles produces social science that matters.

### Values in Context: The Homeownership Dream Revisited

Homeownership has long occupied an important place in the American Dream. Living in one's own home symbolizes individual freedom and responsibility for one's life. A broad consensus exists that homeownership will strengthen American society in the long-term (Shlay 2004). Homeownership promotes neighborhood involvement, strengthens schools, and builds up healthy communities for families and children. People who live

in their own homes tend to be better off economically, if for no other reason than owning a home represents an efficient way to invest one's money
(Retsinas and Belsky 2002).

Federal housing policies have resulted in steadily rising homeownership
rates over the last several decades, particularly among middle class Americans (Addams-Miller 2002; Denton 2001; Feldman 2004; and Retsinas and
Belsky 2002). Homeownership has also increased among low-income families, especially since the 1990s. The fast-paced economic growth of the
1990s in concert with favorable federal housing policy has encouraged and
helped low-income people to become homeowners at record rates.
Despite such growth, there remains a relative lag in homeownership
among racial minorities and low-income families (Retsinas and Belsky
2002). Public policies have yet to close the gap between what the very poor
can pay for housing and what actual housing costs. Notwithstanding this
"affordability gap," low-income homeownership seems here to stay as a
public-policy priority for the foreseeable future (Hillier and Cullhane
2003).

Whether owning a home is always beneficial to low-income homeowners remains to be seen (Shlay 2004; Denton 2001). In particular, there are
relatively few studies that have looked specifically at how low-income
homeowners deal with the financial burdens that accompany owning a
home (Reid 2004). In addition to mortgage payments, our study indicates
that maintenance and repair costs present a significant burden for low-
income homeowners. Home maintenance and repair problems are commonly exacerbated by the fact that people with low incomes for the most
part own older, lower-end housing stock. Not surprisingly, older housing
stock is much more prone to serious and expensive maintenance and
repair problems than houses built over the past few decades. Thus, hous-
ing-policy experts and advocates increasingly assert that low-income
homeownership policies must take into account maintenance and home
repair costs. Along with other low-income housing advocates, WCRP
insists that government programs increase assistance to homeowners who
cannot afford the basic repair jobs necessary to preserve their housing at a
level that satisfies even the most minimal licensing and inspection regula-
tions.

While the condition of the housing stock makes it less expensive and
therefore brings homeownership within the reach of many low-income
homeowners, low home values also mean that homeownership is not necessarily the route to building equity that is often put forth as one of the

advantages to homeownership (Denton 2001; Reid 2004; and Shlay 2004). Our interviews with homeowners and advocates revealed that in the absence of public support for maintenance and repair costs, ownership of old and low-quality housing stock places burdens on low-income homeowners that often exceed potential benefits of owning a house. In short, we found that while the homeownership ideal may reflect the empirical reality of middle- and upper-income families (Rohe, Shannon, and McCarthy 2002), the predominant political discourse is inconsistent with the empirical reality of low-income homeownership.

The promotion of low-income homeownership as an assets-approach to redress poverty has potential problems that go beyond empirical inconsistencies. A careful analysis of the homeownership dream discourse suggests that it rests on market-based and therefore individualistic assumptions that also structure other current social policy debates such as discussions about assets development for the poor (Schram 2006). Consider as an example the following statement in which President George W. Bush asserts:

> Homeownership lies at the heart of the American Dream. It is a key to upward mobility for low- and middle-income Americans. It is an anchor for families and a source of stability for communities. It serves as the foundation of many people's financial security. And it is a source of pride for people who have worked hard to provide for their families. . . . It makes a lot more sense to help people buy homes than to subsidize rental payments forever. (2001)

This statement is suffused with notions of personal responsibility and the fear that families might become or remain "dependent" on the government.

As we have found in our study, one of the major problems of a market-driven approach to housing policies is that it puts the responsibility for failure on the individual homeowner, rather than on the policies (and political interests) that drive low-income homeownership. Homeowners who fail to keep up with costs associated with homeownership, and who eventually either have to sell or abandon their homes, are seen not as the victims of systemic problems but rather as "those poor who have not yet learned the lesson of personal responsibility." Yet, given the findings of our study, it is not at all surprising that low-income homeowners often fail in their attempt to become successful homeowners (see also Reid 2004). As the mere fact of homeownership will not catapult poor people into the middle class, is not surprising that low-income homeowners are set up to fail in their attempt at upward socioeconomic mobility.

## Doing Social Science That Matters

Our collaboration with WCRP enabled us to study the repair and maintenance problems of low-income homeowners in Philadelphia in depth. We carried out an exploratory study about the extent and source of the maintenance and repair problems for low-income homeowners in Philadelphia, as well as the relevant public policies and programs. We conducted a statistical analysis to provide basic descriptive information about the socioeconomic status of low-income homeowners in the city of Philadelphia more generally and the extent of maintenance problems more particularly. We also conducted extensive interviews with key informants inside and outside the city government such as policymakers, researchers, administrators, and advocates working for local and state lobby and community groups. In addition to our own research efforts, our colleagues at WCRP conducted more than one hundred interviews with low-income homeowners in the three focus neighborhoods, which we reviewed. WCRP and a number of other community groups used these interviews as an advocacy tool in their efforts to lobby City Council and City agencies, as well as to gain narrative information about maintenance and repair problems of low-income homeowners.

At the same time, the extensive collaboration with community groups involved in low-income homeownership (chiefly WCRP) enabled us to develop and implement our study in a way that ensured that the research processes and findings of our research would be of practical relevance to the advocacy efforts of our partners.[2] To guarantee ongoing input by our partners at WCRP, we held periodic meetings of the entire project team. These meetings served to build a working relationship and trust between the academic researchers and the other members of the team. As part of our collaborative approach to the project, we included both empirical findings and our critical analysis of the homeownership dream, as outlined in the previous section, in our interim reports and raised them in our project meetings with our partners at WCRP. In particular, we asked them to think about our findings and the way it challenged their own assumptions and advocacy strategies related to low-income housing policy. It quickly became clear that this was a difficult topic, and it in fact brought out the tensions between the academic research team and WCRP in their different roles as researchers and advocates.

A major focus of our debates revolved around our critical appraisal of the (low-income) homeownership dream upon which WCRP bases its advocacy strategies. Specifically, our partners balked at the idea of stressing this finding in the final report. They noted that it could be detrimental to their advocacy efforts, which focus on increased funding for home repair and home maintenance programs rather than on alternative housing policies or even more complex efforts to address major structural issues (education, health, labor policies), as implied in our critique of the homeownership dream. WCRP argued that when developing new policy proposals, it must consider various constraints, such as limited funding and political feasibility. In particular, our partners pointed out that their strategy formulation must consider the problems particular to current debates around low-income housing policy in the city of Philadelphia. For example, the city has recently embarked on the Neighborhood Transformation Initiative (NTI), a major citywide project to be implemented over a decade, that largely focuses on the demolition of dilapidated housing and clearing blocks for market-rate residential and commercial development. At this time, much of NTI is focused on attracting middle- and upper-class families into the city. How much new affordable housing for low-income families will be built as part of this initiative remains uncertain. Therefore, our partners at WCRP argued, it is critical in the short run to focus advocacy efforts on expanding and revising Philadelphia's low-income home repair programs. In fact, advocacy efforts over the past few years have resulted in a rechanneling of some NTI funds from their demolition focus into some of the city's home repair programs, although this is a proverbial drop in the bucket in terms of both the percentage of NTI monies and how far they have gone to address home repair needs.

Nevertheless, we believe that in order to avoid yet again reinforcing notions of individual responsibility (and its flip side, individual failure) over solidarity, as discussed in the previous section, researchers and advocates must also critically assess the values, interests, and power processes that frame particular public-policy discourses. This poses a conflict between long- and short-term needs and between strategic contingency and more fundamental critique. It is what Schram (2002) refers to as the "dilemma of accessibility." The dilemma of accessibility refers to the perception that in order to have one's interpretations and recommendations remain politically feasible, one must work within the existing terms of the debate. Yet, doing so risks buying into the very terms that should be challenged: "Limiting arguments to those that are politically salable . . . can risk diluting the critical edge of scholarship so that it is of little value in challenging the existing state of affairs" (Schram 2002, 26).

Collaboration between social scientists and advocates can help resolve or mitigate the dilemma of accessibility by pooling the contributions of each. In examining the discourse and problematizing the terms of the debate, social scientists can expose the discursive fallacies and pitfalls that advocates are understandably hesitant to examine due to perceived strategic constraints. In the case of low-income homeownership policies, this means raising critical questions about policies that usually focus on the individual *homeowner* rather than on the structural problem of *poverty* and are as such largely based on illusions of choice. Advocates, for their part, can help keep social scientists grounded in political realities and navigate the policy process. Together, advocates and social scientists in their respective roles can work together to ensure that all make reasoned choices in the policy arena and that none fall into the trap of limiting our imagination and understanding to those set by others.

Our collaboration with WCRP and the discussion of homeownership ideology has highlighted some of the potential and risk in engaging in phronetic social science. While our study was commissioned by WCRP and thus to a large extent shaped by their goals, neither all the research questions nor the study methods were dictated by WCRP. Further, WCRP has not limited our use of the data and our conclusions to influence policy as we see fit. This is a result, in large part, of the mutual respect we hold for each others' different roles in the policy arena. The debates around WCRP's strategies and perceived constraints refined and expanded our understanding of low-income housing policies and politics in Philadelphia. We believe that the interpretive parts of our report have helped WCRP gain a more critical understanding of low-income homeownership in general. It is also likely that WCRP will in fact consider the broader implications of our findings, whether or not it chooses to consider them in its immediate advocacy efforts.

Despite the friendly nature of the discussions and the different possibilities of using the knowledge we have produced collaboratively, unresolved tensions remain. Should WCRP choose to deemphasize our interpretations in their work, this raises questions about whether the report will help promote consideration of the long-run consequences of the group's advocacy efforts. On the other hand, if our interpretations are given serious consideration, this might undermine WCRP's short-run advocacy efforts. Further, if either part of the team allows consideration of the other's position in a way that overly constrains our respective roles and imagination, there is the risk of losing the unique contribution of our respective professional roles in the joint enterprise. We do not believe that these are tensions that can or even should be fully resolved. Compromises may indeed always be necessary for the collaboration to produce research that can contribute to effective advocacy. And the more that social science matters, the more likely these tensions are to emerge and to plague engaged researchers. The resolution of these dilemmas will always be contingent and context dependent, and we believe that an open discussion of them is preferable for the richer and more honest dialogue they produce.

Researching the homeownership dream raised tensions regarding the identities of researchers and advocates, tensions between short-term and long-term strategy, the problem of working with the prevailing categories of homeownership policy, and even the questions regarding the consequences of supporting low-income homeownership. On the one side, our research indicated that better supporting low-income homeownership could reduce homelessness; on the other side, our research also indicated that overemphasis on homeownership could lead to further neglect of those who do not own their own homes, thereby making more economically fragile families even more vulnerable to becoming homeless. It is not our intent to offer a specific solution to these tensions at this point. Rather, we have used this case study to demonstrate the kind of collaboration and debates between advocates and researchers that produce and are produced by social science that matters. Scientists increase understanding of a problem by providing rigorous description of the problem and by analyzing the values that frame the perception of the problem and its solution. Advocates, for their part, force scientists to consider political and socioeconomic realities on the ground. This helps scientists to remain connected with the specific social problem they study. It is this type of collaboration that will produce social science that matters even as it engenders some of the dilemmas we have highlighted here.

## Conclusion

The contours of our discussions with our partners at WCRP illustrate the fertile exchange that takes place when researchers and advocates collaborate. For researchers, this requires acknowledging the importance of specific strategic issues without having them dictate our exploration and understanding of issues and grappling with them head on. This allows social scientists to make their unique contribution, which is the production and interpretation of knowledge that may not be predicted or immediately beneficial to advocacy agendas. On the other hand, the consideration of values that accompanies serious engagement with political actors ensures that social science is relevant. Political actors have explicit agendas, and their clarity in advocating these agendas and navigating strategic and political hurdles is precisely what enables them to act in complicated and contingent arenas that are often not amenable to the more careful and nuanced analysis that social scientists seek and insist upon. They can and will make different use of social science findings for different purposes, but certainly their efforts will be enhanced by the engagement and their imagination and understanding stretched in ways that contribute to advocacy efforts (Shlay and Whitman, 2004).

While phronetic research calls for engaging in social science that matters through entering the policy fray, it is not necessary to abdicate our roles as researchers and social scientists in the process. In order for social science to matter, it is not enough to be relevant. Instead, social science must be relevant in a way that ensures its unique contribution to debates about social issues. This means insisting on those aspects of social science that make it different from advocacy. Collaboration is not about melding identities; rather, it is an attempt to pool the unique contributions that members of a collaborative team can make. As much as political actors can (we hope) learn from critical social science, so must social scientists be prepared to listen to particular contextual considerations on the ground. This is surely a very different model of social science from the one that is most often taught or practiced in the academy today. While not without its own tensions and dilemmas, it is an alternative social science worth pursuing.

Both authors contributed equally to this chapter and the project on which it is based. The authors thank Sandy Schram, Bent Flyvbjerg, Frances Fox

Piven, Bill Reynolds, Laurie Hart, and members of Bryn Mawr College's Graduate Idea Forum for commenting on the chapter.

NOTES

1. Specifically, this project was designed as Participatory Action Research. We leave for future discussion the exact relationship between PAR and phronetic research (see also Flyvbjerg 2001, 137).

2. We use the collaboration between researchers and our partners at WCRP as an example of phronetic research. In a more extensive discussion of the project, we would extend this debate to other relevant stakeholders, such as low-income homeowners, policymakers, administrators, and other advocacy groups. We have interviewed representatives of each of these groups as part of our study.

# Part II

# Phronesis Reconsidered

# 6

## Social Science in Society

### *Theodore Schatzki*

The observation is a familiar one: out of the desires to count as science and to garner the prestige and support enjoyed by science, social inquiry has long sought to emulate the latter's methods, aims, and theories. It has not, however, come close to matching the predictive, explanatory, and control successes of the natural sciences. For decades, investigators and commentators have divided on how to explain or react to this failure. Standard responses include the claim that the social sciences are at a less mature stage on the road to objectivity and truth and the thesis that differences in the subject matters of the social and natural disciplines underlie a fundamental cleavage in their character, methods, and aims. Concerned with the intellectual and public standing of the social sciences in the wake of the "science wars" and the Sokal affair, Bent Flyvbjerg (2001) defends a more consequential reaction: these disciplines should cease understanding themselves primarily as a form of general knowledge and, instead, think of themselves as working toward the realization of the good society. Although this self-conception does not proscribe the pursuit of general or theoretical knowledge, in prioritizing successful praxis it frees social investigators to try out diverse methods and epistemologies. Even more important, in orienting social investigation toward the realization of the good society, it promises to save this division of knowledge from the self-inflicted obliteration threatening it from its failed attempt to equal the natural sciences. Flyvbjerg labels this understanding of social inquiry "phronetic social science."

Defending and fostering phronetic social science requires argumentation on several fronts. A credible explanation for the failures of scientistic social inquiry must be provided. A persuasive account of phronetic investigation must be in the offing. Students of social affairs must be moved to affirm a practical undertaking with its ethical orientation. Flyvbjerg's book addresses the first two needs. To satisfy the first, Flyvbjerg promulgates, in Part I, Hubert Dreyfus's arguments against predictive theory in the social sciences. To satisfy the second, Flyvbjerg presents, in Part II, a sensible Foucaultian version of phronetic social inquiry. Flyvbjerg says little about the third issue. His silence suggests that he hopes that the failure of scientistic social inquiry will embolden social investigators to adopt a phronetic identity.

I affirm Flyvbjerg's thesis that social science should be phronetic. My general evaluation of his book is that it importantly rearticulates this occasionally heard claim and states a reasonable case for it. The text, moreover, contains a number of salutary arguments and passages about which I will say nothing. One is the superlative chapter 6, on case studies, which powerfully defends their importance and epistemological cogency. Others are a nuanced and perceptive account of Foucault, which spans several chapters, and the accessible summary, in chapter 2, of the Dreyfus's account of skill acquisition. But, although I affirm the timeliness and need for the book, I believe that its critique is misdirected and possibly besides the point and that it offers a needlessly narrow picture of phronetic social science, which is not likely to be as successful in promoting phronetic work as a more capacious delimitation would. Section I of this chapter examines the soundness and significance of the argument Flyvbjerg directs at predictive theory. Section II considers the general nature and bounds of phronetic social investigation.

## The Critique of Predictive Theory in Social Investigation

The attempt to emulate natural science shapes many dimensions of social inquiry, both empirical and theoretical. Flyvbjerg's critique of this impulse targets its theoretical dimension, in particular, the attempt to construct predictive theories. His criticism is basically a restatement of Hubert Dreyfus's arguments (1982) for the dismal prospects of this endeavor

According to Dreyfus, an ideal modern scientific theory has six characteristics. It is (1) explicit, (2) universal, (3) abstract, (4) discrete, (5) systematic, and (6) complete and predictive. "Explicit" means that the theory's content is exhaustively specified by the propositions that make it up. "Universal" means that the theory applies to all times and places. "Discrete" means that it is formulated with context-free elements alone (i.e., with elements that "do not refer to human interests, traditions, institutions etc." [38–39]). "Systematic" means that its elements are systematically related by laws or rules. "Complete," finally, means that the theory specifies every element pertinent to, and all the effects of the specified elements on, the domain of study. This means that, given proper information (initial conditions), the theory offers reliable predictions. Flyvbjerg adds that this last criterion is "the hallmark of [contemporary] epistemic sciences" (39).

Just how widespread in the social disciplines is the search for theory as just defined? Flyvbjerg writes as if it dominates social inquiry, but I wonder whether this is still true (assuming that it once was). Consider the sixth criterion. A prima facie case can be made that economics, and also political science, seeks predictive theory. Can this claim be upheld, however, vis-à-vis geography, sociology, and anthropology? What about urban studies and religious studies? I have the strong impression that predictive theory, though still alive, is no longer the dominant telos in these disciplines. Many investigators continue to pursue *explanatory* theories, but not prediction. Others continue to predict, but not on the basis of theories as defined (instead, on the basis of empirical patterns and trends). It may even be true that most practitioners in the named disciplines aim at explanatory theories or nontheoretical predictions. Theory-based prediction, however, is no longer the goal.

Explanation and prediction are clearly pulling apart in contemporary social research. While the pursuit of explanation (e.g., factor analysis), maybe explanatory theory, too, remains king, the provision of predictions now often takes the form of forecasts that are self-consciously offered without guarantee to politicians, administrators, and the interested public. It follows that any argument that targets predictive theory has decreasing relevance to at least many social disciplines (note that Dreyfus's argument dates from the early 1980s).

I concede, however, that my impression might be wrong. So let us turn to Dreyfus's argument. Flyvbjerg writes that "the study of society, insofar as it attempts to follow natural science, must . . . abstract [context-independent] elements from the context-dependent activities of human beings in order to subsequently explain and predict those activities in terms of formal relations . . . between the abstracted elements" (39). "Abstraction" means extraction. It is Dreyfus's view that science proceeds by extracting (decontextualizing) elements of the everyday world and inserting (recontextualizing) them in theories conceived of as networks of extracted elements. In the case of social science, the reality from which elements are abstracted is purposive human activity-proceeding-in-a-world of meaningful entities. Two arguments against the likelihood of predictive theories follow from this account of theory.

The first argument rests on the observation that "what human beings pick out as objects and events [in their activities] need not coincide with the elements over which the theory ranges" (40). The reason for this divergence is that which objects and events people pick out is tied to the situations in which they act, and theories leave out such contexts in working with context-independent elements. "Therefore, predictions, though often correct, will not be reliable. Indeed, these predictions will work only as long as the elements [of the] theory happen to coincide with what the human beings falling under the theory pick out and relate in their everyday activities" (40).

This argument contends that predictions can be reliable only if they cite entities that "coincide with," or more weakly, correlate with or are tied to the entities that actors pick out and relate in their activities. The demands that this thesis places on theoretical concepts parallel the so-called condition of adequacy for social scientific concepts formulated by Alfred Schutz (1962) and Peter Winch (1958). To emphasize continuity with their discussions, I formulate the following considerations in the linguistic, as opposed to material, mode.

Dreyfus's argument is persuasive vis-à-vis abstractions qua extractions. It does not hold, however, for types of social-scientific theoretical concepts that Dreyfus does not seriously consider, for example, postulations and constructions. A postulation (e.g., repression, id) is a hypothetical causal concept, whereas a construction (e.g., liquidity preference, preference ranking) is a technical concept that is such that what there is in the world to its holding of people is, to talk with Dreyfus, their performing particular actions, on the basis of certain skills, in particular situations, with such-and-such understanding of what they are doing. Concepts of these two types should not be jettisoned for predictive purposes merely because they fail to track the concepts people use in coping with their situations and carrying out their activities. Social scientists introduce postulations and constructions on one or more of the following presumptions: (1) that the concepts people use in coping do not pick out everything about their activities and situations that is relevant to how they act; (2) that people's activities and interactions over time exhibit patterns that cannot be captured with their own concepts; and (3) that what there is in the world to a

concept that is not one of the actors' holding of those actors is their performing certain actions and using certain concepts in picking out and
relating entities and events. If Dreyfus's argument is applied to all theoretical concepts, it simply rules out the possibility—a priori—that concepts
that are designed not to track those of actors can support reliable predictions about human activity. If, in fact, theoretical concepts such as repression and liquidity preference do not support reliable predictions, this is
not because of the mismatch Dreyfus emphasizes but because of the
nature of human activity and whatever is actually responsible for the
course of human action. After all, it would be misguided to exclude the
possibility of reliable scientific predictions of young children's behavior
*simply* because investigators' concepts do not correspond to those of children. In general, the only responsibility theoretical schemes have to the
concepts people use in coping (or: the objects and events people pick out
and relate in their everyday activities) is to be capable of referring to them
and of registering the differential role they play vis-à-vis activity (cf. Giddens 1993, 152). As things are, I believe that reliable predictions of human
activity are impossible in any language. The reason for this, however, is
that human activity is indeterminate.

The second argument based on Dreyfus's account of theory responds to
an imagined defense of the possibility of predictive laws. This defense contends (1) that a social science such as economics takes as given what people consider to be money, property, profit maximization, and so on, and
(2) that economists "thereafter seeks out laws, which relate these socially
defined concepts to each other" (44). It follows from these theses that, if
what people take money, property, and the like to be remains constant,
that is to say, if the practices by which people take certain things and not
others to be money and so on are stable, predictive economic laws are in
principle possible. Of course, it also follows from these theses that the possibility that these practices might change threatens the claims of predictive
economic theory to universality and to completeness, thus its status as scientific theory. These claims, the defense continues, can nonetheless be
secured by either (1) harnessing an auxiliary theory (meeting the stated
specifications) that predicts changes in the practices involved or, more
plausibly, (2) adding these background practices and understandings to
the theory as conditions that must obtain for the predictive laws to hold.
In this way, the possibility of universal prediction can be vindicated.

In response, Flyvbjerg writes that "The problem for social sciences is
that the background conditions change without the researcher being able

to state in advance which aspects one should hold constant in order for predictions to continue to operate" (45). I find this argument too terse to be intelligible without further explication, which Flyvbjerg does not provide. Dreyfus, in any event, has a stronger objection than the one gestured at here, namely that these background practices and understandings *cannot* be added to the theory as limiting conditions because they cannot be translated into context-independent elements such as rules and propositions. The more plausible option, in other words, is impossible. What's more, it can be added, stability in more than people's understandings of money, property, profit, and so on alone is a limiting condition of the applicability of economic laws—people's understandings of, for example, desire and of the pursuit of ends also have to be stable, indeed, perhaps much of their understanding of human beings.

Notice that this argument, like both the defense it opposes and the first argument, presumes that social-scientific concepts are abstractions qua extractions. This may or may not be true of the particular example. Regardless, however, of whether profit maximization is an extraction or, like liquidity preference and preference ranking, a construction, not all theoretical concepts in social science are extractions. Hence, the second argument is incomplete. Dreyfus's arguments require further reflection on the long-standing issue of the proper relations between actors' and investigators' concepts (or: between the events and objects picked out and related by actors and by theories).

In the imagined defense of predictive theory, the desiderata of universality and completeness motivate the desire to incorporate background practices and understandings into theories in the form of rules and propositions. A defender of theory who is not wedded to reliable predictions or closure could recast theories in some form such as the following: wherever the practices by which people understand money, property, profit maximization, and so forth are pretty similar to ours (where "we" are modern Western peoples), an economic system of type X (say, free-market capitalism) exists, and the definitions, descriptions, generalities, and laws that specify the nature, composition, and workings—form a theory—of such systems apply to their lives. The theory is a lens through which an investigator can conceive of and examine other people's practices without necessarily seeking to predict—or even explain—their activities. The question of whether others' practices are "pretty similar" to our own can be referred to detailed examinations of particular cases. This recasting loosens the conditions under which generalities hold and excuses theories from translating practices and understandings into propositions. Although theory is still subject to limiting conditions, the point of theory no longer requires that the conditions be ones of stasis-sameness or be fully specified. The facts that many people's practices pertaining to money, property, and profit are "pretty similar" to our own, and that research can uncover whether people's practices are such, makes this a sensible tack. In understanding, moreover, that her technical terms and laws depend on a variable and not fully specified context of background practices, the defender of theory also, in a sense, abandons context dependence.

I sketch this reconception because today, I believe, many social investigators would accept something like it. They no longer expect the scope of generalizations, laws, trends, and general descriptions to be fully and determinately formulated, let alone to include all peoples at all times (however far back those times are supposed to go). They might happily acknowledge that such general considerations hold only of people who, to put the point conventionally, experience similar types of motivations, situations, and institutions. If I am right about this, then Dreyfus's account of theory is too narrow to capture the sort of theory to which many contemporary social scientists aspire, including modelers. Not only have most researchers jettisoned the hope of reliable prediction, but many accept a degree of looseness about when their schemes, models, and theories apply (also, that the elements of their theories presuppose practices, motivations, situations, and institutions). In short, social science has already largely abandoned the attempt to emulate natural science—at least when the natural sciences are understood to be generators of predictive theory as specified earlier.

Sometimes Flyvbjerg reduces the argument against predictive theories to a quick and dirty conflict: "while context is central for defining what counts as an action, context must nonetheless be excluded in a theory in order for it to be a theory at all" (42, see 47). Recall the economics example used to illustrate the second argument against theory. The contexts that economic theory necessarily excludes are the everyday situations that determine the meanings of the concepts (or: the being of the elements) that the theory presupposes and—tries—to work with (i.e., money, profit). These contexts are excluded in the sense that the theory makes no mention of them. Pace Flyvbjerg's just cited formulation, however, such exclusion does not conflict with the context dependence of the concepts (or entities) involved; a theory does not need to describe the contexts in which its terms have meanings in order to use them. The only theories that such a conflict endangers are those whose object is skilled human activity as such (what Dreyfus calls "theories of human capacities"). Theories that *presuppose* skilled human activity need not worry. As the Dreyfuses have famously argued (see Flyvbjerg 2001, ch. 2), the skills people use in coping with objects and events are context dependent. This implies that skills cannot be adequately reconstructed out of context-independent elements such as rules. Because, therefore, theories marshal context-independent elements, any theoretical account of skilled human activity as such is doomed to failure.

This conclusion, however, is compatible with the context dependency of skills being part of a "theory" of human activity (a phenomenological one in this instance). A theory of human activity can also discuss and elucidate the practice contexts in which terms (entities) in general, and its own terms (elements) in particular, have meaning (are such and such). Most Wittgensteinian accounts of meaning constitute examples. Similarly, Dreyfus's skills and Bourdieu's habitus (which Flyvbjerg invokes) are theoretical concepts that pick out part of the context in which terms have meaning (entities are such and such). Dreyfus and Bourdieu also describe general features of the contexts in which skills and habitus form.

Of course, the accounts that Dreyfus, Bourdieu, and Wittgensteinians proffer of meaning and activity are not theories of the predictive type. It is important to insist that they are theories nonetheless. They clearly exhibit Dreyfus's second and third features (they do not exhibit the first feature, explicitness, because nothing does). They also boast the fourth feature, since they use the concepts of skill, habitus, practice, field, and context context-independently. These accounts, further, form wholes whose systemicity is due, not to rules or laws, but to linguistic formulations. Finally, some of these accounts (e.g., Bourdieu's) aim to be explanatory. Consequently, the fact that theories do not mention the contexts in which their terms have meanings (their elements have being) does not imply the impossibility of general theories ("systematic accounts," if that sounds better) of meaning and activity that invoke and elucidate the contexts of these phenomena. Unfortunately, Flyvbjerg does not discus this—or any other further—sort of theory. In restricting the expression "theory" to predictive theory (39), and focusing Part I on the issue of whether predictive theory is possible in social inquiry, he neglects other sorts of theory that might enter social investigation.

This oversight is doubly unfortunate. First, it closes down discussion of the role theory might play in phronetic social science. Knowledge of social affairs is crucial in phronetic research, and such knowledge is often tied to such theories as typologies, models, ontologies, and conceptual frameworks. Second, Flyvbjerg concludes Part I with the question of what should replace the conventional search for predictive theory. Phronetic social science is the heir apparent. This answer neglects the possibility that social inquiry might yield theory-informed knowledge not based on predictive theory. The either-or, or rather, both-and (49) of predictive theory and phronetic social science somehow misrepresents the options.

Finally, I want to comment on the compulsion Flyvbjerg feels to challenge predictive theory in the name of phronetic social science. The value that researchers place on prediction reflects not just the urge to emulate natural science but also the desire to contribute to a better world. Flyvbjerg writes, moreover, as if the futility of social science prediction is self-evident. Assuming this is true, all but the most benighted investigators must appreciate its bareness. Those enamored of natural science who reply that the complexity of social affairs is the obstacle and better predictive theory the solution are not likely to be moved by a priori arguments against the possibility of such theory. Since this predictive failure is self-evident, moreover, social scientists concerned with improving the human lot are presumably open to other ways of achieving this: they should *already* be primed for Part II of Flyvbjerg's book. The upshot is that intellectual need alone counsels explaining the failure of predictive theory *as a set-up* for proposing phronetic social science as alternative. Of course, if the poverty of social scientific prediction is not self-evident, Flyvbjerg's end might be best served by documenting this. Then the described motivation could kick in.

## Phronetic Social Science

Part II of Flyvbjerg's book describes his alternative to predictive theory: phronetic social science. Because Flyvbjerg calls this alternative "phronetic," it is best to recall basic features of Aristotle's *phronesis* so that the full scope of what might count as phronetic inquiry can be appreciated. According to Aristotle, *phronesis* is a intellectual feature of praxis. It is a feature of activity because it is insightful deliberation about what to do, and it is intellectual because it is insightful deliberation. "*Phronesis* is a state grasping the truth, involving reason, concerned with action about what is good or bad for a human being" (Aristotle 1976, 1140b4–5). As this quotation indicates, *phronesis* ascertains the action that is good for the person deliberating (more precisely, the action that helps constitute that person's living well). Insightful deliberation, moreover, requires knowledge of both the general and the particular: "Nor is *phronesis* about universals only. It must also come to know particulars, since it is concerned with action and action is about particulars" (1141b15–6). In sum, *phronesis* is (1) insightful deliberation (2) about what to do that (3) ascertains which actions constitute the actor's good on the basis of (4) knowledge of general matters and (5) familiarity with particular phenomena.

In dubbing a portion of social science "phronetic," Flyvbjerg ascribes two additional features to *phronesis*. The first is that *phronesis* must deal with power. The second is that the entity who insightfully deliberates is no longer an individual person, but the citizens of a democracy as a collective. *Phronesis* is a political process in which citizens publicly deliberate about and decide on ends and policies. The issue of how social science can matter once again is the issue of how social science can matter to a democracy. Correlatively, Flyvbjerg's call for phronetic social science is, in the end, a call for social science to be part of or relevant to this public democratic process.

Flyvbjerg defines phronetic social science in several ways. What is common to most of the definitions is something that prima facie does not characterize natural science or predictive theory: orientation toward political-ethical values. This orientation is embodied in the fact that *phronesis* is deliberation about the good. In this vein, Flyvbjerg defines phronetic social science as social inquiry that aims to answer four so-called "value-questions." Three of these are these: Where are we going?, Is it desirable?, and What should be done? (162, 60). Notice that *phronesis*, as a feature of practice, is concerned, above all or strictly, with the third question. The first two are pertinent insofar as they throw light on the third. Curiously, Flyvbjerg is unclear whether a piece of research, in order to be phronetic, must answer the third question, for example, propose reforms, policies, laws, or collective actions. Does research count as phronetic if it answers the first two questions (or the first) alone and is injected, by the researcher or by others, into public deliberation? Flyvbjerg suggests different answers to this question. He occasionally writes that phronetic social science answers all the questions (162; footnote 7 on 196). At other points, he indicates that "the goal of phronetic research is to produce input to the ongoing social dialogue and praxis in a society" (139; cf. 61), thereby suggesting a more capacious delimitation. I will assume the wider interpretation, in part because it maximizes the breadth and, thus, promise of the phronetic enterprise and in part because of political considerations with which I will conclude.

Flyvbjerg also writes (60) that "the principal objective for social science with a phronetic approach is to carry out analyses and interpretations of the status of values and interests in society aimed at social commentary and social action, i.e., praxis." These lines occur in a section titled "Where natural science is weak and social science is strong." I agree that social science is better than natural science is at carrying out the "reflexive analysis of goals, values, and interests that is a precondition for an enlightened development in any society" (53). I note, however, that Flyvbjerg nowhere mentions the humanities in this context. The humanities not only have something to offer this analysis but arguably have executed it better than the social sciences have. Since the aims of Flyvbjerg's book concern the social disciplines alone, his neglect of the humanities is forgivable. Still, some of the guidelines for phronetic research enunciated in chapter 9 are familiar from humanistic contexts; more generally, the sketch in that chapter of phronetic social science exemplifies the sort of humanistic social research (and social scientific humanistic research) that, today, befuddles the separation of these divisions of knowledge. A more comprehensive account of phronetic social science than Flyvbjerg's must consider contemporary hybrid humanistic-social scientific research.

Indeed, the bounds of what can justifiably be called phronetic social inquiry are wide. Combining the five features of Aristotelian *phronesis* discussed earlier with Flyvbjerg's general characterizations of phronetic investigation reveals that the following seven tasks are bound up with this sort of work:

1. Choosing problems or issues that the research addresses or is oriented toward
2. Articulating and pondering ends and values that bear on these issues
3. Ascertaining particular realities pertinent to these issues and studying other particulars parallel or similar to these
4. Applying general considerations to the issues and particular realities involved
5. Judging realities in light of ends and values
6. Advocating courses of action for dealing with the selected issues
7. Publishing and publicizing the research.

Must, however, a research project carry out all seven tasks to qualify as phronetic? Any issue-oriented project will perform tasks (1) and (3), and it is hard to imagine one that did not also tackle (4). Task (7) is also essential. Whether a project must carry out any or all of the remaining three tasks is tied to how narrow or catholic the epithet "phronetic" is interpreted. On the narrow reading, (5) and (6) are central to phronetic work, whereas on the catholic reading not just these two tasks, but even (4) might be optional. On the latter reading, a research project counts as phronetic simply if it produces "input into ongoing social dialogue and praxis"—and just about any nonevaluative and nonprescriptive analysis of social affairs could, if launched into the public sphere, constitute such input. It would not even be necessary, in principle, to choose an issue (task [1]). Simply publishing a catalogue of facts, say, about underage U.S. children could serve as input. In actuality, of course, the key differences are between projects pursuing description, understanding, and explanation ([1], [3], and [4]), those pursuing these plus evaluation ([5]), and those pursuing these plus prescription ([6]).

What about task (2), articulating and commenting on values and ends? When democratic public deliberation is conceptualized as *phronesis*, it is crucial that such activity occur—somewhere. Indeed, at one point Flyvbjerg characterizes *phronesis* as "the analysis of value . . . as a point of departure for praxis" (57). Is this a task for social science? For philosophy? For any interested person, thus not just academics, but also essayists, editorialists, jurists, writers, politicians, and concerned citizens at large? I return shortly to one answer to this sort of question.

Someone might ask about the point of specifying the boundaries of phronetic social investigation. There may be no point to drawing the line in any particular place. The point of raising the *issue* of what qualifies as phronetic is to suggest that the phronetic is a broad arena. Indeed, it falls to the advantage of the overall phronetic enterprise that as many types of social research as possible be included in it. Not only do a wide range of investigators want to think of themselves as helping to make society better, but a researcher who furthers social dialogue and praxis might have intellectual reasons to abjure one or another task (e.g., [2] or [6]). I do not see the point of restricting the term "phronetic" to those projects that address all seven tasks. To do this is to conflate the important and valid point that social science must offer input into (or "effectively deal with" [129]) social dialogue and praxis with the claim that social science should be practiced *as phronesis* (ibid). It is *society* that must be phronetic—with all the help social inquiry can offer it.

Consider, in this context, the research of Foucault's that Flyvbjerg takes as paradigmatic. Notoriously, Foucault neither analyzes values nor advocates courses of action. Take the latter refusal. Although Foucault chooses research topics in light of contemporary local struggles that he finds pressing (the prisoner movement, in the case of *Discipline and Punish*), he does not propose strategies, solutions, or blueprints to the groups struggling. He hopes, instead, that his research will prove useful to them, for example, in revealing how such and such situations came about and what about them can be changed. Like many contemporary theorists, Foucault assigns the question of what should be done to the people entangled in the power constellations his research documents (cf. 103). Any prescription by the researcher is a violation of the liberty, autonomy, and growth of others. If, like Foucault, a researcher believes that she qua researcher should refrain from prescription, she can advocate change only, say, qua citizen or qua affected party. Prescription, for her, is not a component of social *science.* For researchers of this conviction, consequently, the expression "phronetic social science" harbors a tension: whereas *phronesis* is essentially oriented toward selecting action, the social researcher enjoins herself not to do this.

Consider a further dimension of phronetic social research: bringing general considerations to bear both on the issue at hand and the particulars relevant to it. I use the vague expression "general considerations" deliberately, to encompass generalizations, trends, laws, models, ontologies, definitions, typologies—anything that embraces multiple particulars. This understanding of general considerations allows predictive theory in principle to be a component of phronetic social inquiry—not just a pursuit different from phronetic research that can profitably pursued alongside the latter (the import of the "both-and" formulation on 49). I affirm Flyvbjerg's point (e.g., 84, 86) that studying particulars (case studies) crucially fosters a social scientist's ability to conduct research (and to make political-ethical judgments). Still, to put the point intuitively and familiarly: to the extent that advocating actions is the goal, it pays to draw on general schemes that identify relevant causes and maybe also predict what will happen if certain courses are pursued—even if the predictions are known to be uncertain and are often wrong (within a tolerable degree of error; consider, in this context, the value of economic forecasting despite its inaccuracy). After all, one of the three "value questions" mentioned earlier that Flyvbjerg wants phronetic work to address is nonnormative in character: where are we going? (Taken literally, this question almost demands a prediction.) Because predictive theories, ontological frameworks, typologies, and other general considerations contribute to the acquisition of knowledge, any of them might contribute to answering this question. This is not to advocate predictive theory in particular but to suggest that, since predictive theory exists, it might as well be utilized as best it can to better society. If, moreover, it is in fact useful for this purpose, it should be encouraged, to an extent commensurate with its usefulness in this regard relative to that of epistemically different styles of research. My point here is well illustrated by Jürgen Habermas's (1971) conception of critical theory in the 1960s and 1970s.

This point fills out why, as I wrote in the previous section, the juxtaposition of predictive theory and phronetic social inquiry somehow misrepresents the basic existential choice social scientists face in doing research. The choice is not between predictive theory (or the emulation of natural science) and phronetic work but between pursuing knowledge for the sake of knowledge, alternatively, for the sake of understanding the world and doing research in the hope of making the world a better place. Predictive, like any other sort of, theory or research can be pursued for either end, just as social research, journalism, teaching, politics, activism, and many other callings can be pursued for the sake of the social good. In this context, it is worth recalling that Plato, the great proponent of *episteme*, maintained that the ultimate point of theory is the proper and good conduct of life.

Phronetic social investigation is a vast arena. In chapter 9, by contrast, Flyvbjerg tenders a list of methodological guidelines that considerably narrows which investigations qualify. The guidelines, for example, make no mention of theory. The would-be *phronimos* is advised to place power at the core of the analysis, to get close to reality, to focus on small things, to look at practice before discourse, to study cases and contexts, to interpret (in Geertz's words, to offer "thick descriptions" of [133]) the phenomena examined, to write narratives, to join agency and structure, and to dialogue with a polyphony of voices. The reader will recognize this list as a hodgepodge of mostly familiar methodological injunctions defended by opponents of mainstream social scientific explanation and theory (e.g., interpretists, phenomenologists, postmoderns). The reader might also notice that, together, these guidelines constitute a reasonable representation of the method used in Flyvbjerg's paradigm: Foucault's works on power. Why, however, should phronetic social investigation hew so closely to the work of just one of its illustrious practitioners? (Or, why should the expression "phronetic social science" be reserved for this sort of research? cf. 140.) The circle is closed in chapter 10 where Flyvbjerg illustrates these guidelines (very nicely, it should be added) by describing a research project on transportation reform that he himself carried out and input-ed into public dialogue.

It turns out, however, that, pace Flyvbjerg's occasional proclamation, these guidelines do not constitute *the* phronetic method. They are guidelines that Flyvbjerg developed for his *own* research (162; many of them also hold of a further example of phronetic research Flyvbjerg rightly admires: Bellah et al.'s *Habits of the Heart* [1996], 62–65). Flyvbjerg concedes that there are alternative phronetic methods and other ways of practicing phronetic social science (162, 129). One wonders, once again, just how flexible the guidelines are—can any and all of them be forsaken? What about, in particular, the suggestion that power be placed at the core of the analysis? I mentioned that there is a fourth question that phronetic research aims to answer. It is this: who gains, and who loses, by which mechanisms of power? This question makes the study of power intrinsic to phronetic work. The necessity of power follows from its pervasiveness in social life, a fact into which Flyvbjerg credits Machiavelli, Nietzsche, and Foucault with great insight. Through a critique of Habermas in chapter 7, Flyvbjerg argues that social-political thought is problematic without a conception of power and that in order for the public sphere to contribute to democracy, it must be linked to conflict and power (110; cf. 155). Flyvbjerg also advocates Foucault's conception of power and indicates that it is the conception most needed for phronetic work, though he occasionally notes that traditional notions of power can add something. Flyvbjerg also champions Foucault's genealogical approach (to power) and incorporates it into his methodological guidelines.

I will not address the particulars of Flyvbjerg's arguments about power and method. I will simply point out that, for Flyvbjerg, Foucault's work not only serves as an example of phronetic research but also constitutes the framework in which such research proceeds. In this regard, Flyvbjerg's characterization of phronetic social science resembles Lawrence Grossberg's (1997) Foucaultian characterization of cultural studies. Although I am a devotee of Foucault, I find this use of him to be overly, and unnecessarily, constraining. Power is a crucial aspect of social life that social research must constantly examine. But so, too, for instance, is gender. Others would claim that social-political thinking is problematic without an account of identity, or of culture, or of rationality, or of the nature-technology-society constellation. Still others would claim this of space. And so on. Why should power, from among these notions-phenomena, be singled out and made constitutive for phronetic work? Moreover, Foucault's claim that power is everywhere indicates that his notion of a net of force relations is an ontology: a specification of basic aspects of sociality. Given the multiplicity of alternative ontologies and the aim of phronetic research, it is inadvisable to lash such research to a particular ontology. What about the contrast between lifeworld and system or the notion of homologous fields of practice, to cite the ontologies of two thinkers that Flyvbjerg criticizes or draws on, respectively? Phronetic research might have to study power. It might also, however, have to deal with other matters and in fact profit from the use of multiple ontological frameworks. Moreover, vis-à-vis power, it would have been better if Flyvbjerg had addressed, not Habermas, but theorists such as Carl Schmitt (1996) and Chantal Mouffe (e.g., 1993), who, like Foucault, espy power everywhere in the sociopolitical realm but work with different, including more traditional, notions of it.

One further oversight must be mentioned in this context. At the end of Part I, Flyvbjerg dismisses critical theory with the remark that it "has long been preoccupied with Habermas's attempt to formulate a normative discourse theory and its consequences for politics and jurisprudence" (48). This claim holds at best of that strand of "critical theory" that Habermas has directly schooled (and which centers around Northwestern University and the Johann Wolfgang Goethe University in Frankfurt). It is decidedly not true of other heirs to the Frankfurt tradition, such as Douglas Kellner, Lukes, and Ben Agger. Indeed, the Frankfurt school counts as an early entry in the phronetic pantheon. Members of the Institute sought to combine theory and empirical work with a practical interest in emancipation, which they pursued largely through the avenue of critique but also through the advocacy of particular solutions and strategies. Flyvbjerg claims that few researchers have conceptualized or pursued phronetic work. This remark must be tempered by acknowledgement of the Frankfurt school tradition in critical theory. (And it must be withdrawn if policy studies qualify as phronetic research.)

## Conclusion

All in all, Flyvbjerg's book is a helpful restatement and a timely reminder of the desirability of a phronetic orientation in social research. Both its critique of mainstream social scientific theory and its depiction of phronetic research, however, are narrow and incomplete. I conclude with a cautionary note. Flyvbjerg begins with the contemporary science wars and the Sokal hoax. He worries that these events have damaged the image of social inquiry both in the academy and before the educated public and that further damage is inevitable if social investigators continue trying to emulate the natural sciences. Phronetic social science, by making social research relevant to society, is the way to skirt this peril. At the same time, Flyvbjerg's claim that phronetic research answers four "value-questions," in particular the two genuine value-questions among them (Is it desirable? and What should be done?), effectively politicizes social inquiry. As any student of science knows, one of the virtues that has been routinely extolled for scientistic social science is its (alleged) value-freedom, its retreat from engagement in or advocacy of political matters in an objective pursuit of the truth. The phronetic conception returns social science to society and its politics, to concern itself with society's improvement, to advocate steps in this direction, and to enter public dialogue and praxis. One wonders which holds the greater "danger" for the future of social science: continued, partly misguided emulation of natural science or engagement with sociopolitical issues. I suppose it depends on the character of a society, the quality of its public sphere, the disposition of its people, the objectivity of researchers, and whose side of an issue a given piece of research advocates. Familiar concerns about the sources of research funding offer a glimpse into this constellation.

# 7

# Power and Interpretation

## *Brian Caterino*

In *Making Social Science Matter,* Bent Flyvbjerg employs two distinctive approaches to practical reason: a mutual understanding approach derived from neo-Aristotelian and interpretive views and a Nietzschean (power-interpretive) approach. Unearthing the relationship between these approaches is central to understanding the tensions in his account of power. I argue that Flyvbjerg's account of the relation between these two elements of practical reason is inconsistent. At times Flyvbjerg treats the two accounts as complementary (Flyvbjerg 2001, 59, 110–12), but in the end, he subordinates the mutual understanding account to the Nietzschean one. This subordination hides a difficulty in Flyvbjerg's analysis of power. Flyvbjerg overestimates the capacity of strategic power to define and disclose reality. He fails therefore to present a compelling account of power and domination.

Unlike many critics who argue that interpretive approaches separate understanding and power, I argue that mutual-understanding approaches are not power-free. These approaches identify an independent source of power, *communicative power,* which binds participants to one another. Communicative power has a world-disclosing power and a reality-defining capacity that strategic power lacks. Forms of strategic power can hegemonically direct or restrict this power but cannot create it. The power-interpretive reading must draw on the binding power of mutual understanding to defend its own account. However weakly, mutual understanding retains its independent power to challenge domination.

## The Mutual-Understanding Model

Flyvbjerg discusses the mutual-understanding model in MSSM via the contemporary revival of Aristotelian thought. Neo-Aristotelians have returned to an approach to politics, ethics, and the human sciences that rests on the priority of practical reason over theoretical reason (Macintyre 1997; Beiner 1983). Not simply the subject who knows but the acting subject who judges is the locus of analysis. "Practice," Hans Georg Gadamer writes, "consists of choosing, of deciding for something and against something else, and in doing this a practical reflection is effective" (Gadamer 1983, 81). Practical knowledge is judgment or *phronesis*, the wise discernment of the right thing to do in the situation. For Aristotle, of course, *phronesis* was practical in a second sense. It was a form of judgment without preestablished rules. Flyvbjerg adopts Aristotle's understanding of *phronesis* as a practical capacity for wise and prudent action (Flyvbjerg 2001, 56–57). Social inquiry is always concerned with questions of the good life.

Flyvbjerg's conception of practical reason follows the neo-Aristotelian critique of modern reason (Arendt 1958; Habermas 1973). Theory, for the ancients, represented a realm of permanent unchanging truths through which they could contemplate the order of the universe, while praxis referred to a realm of changeable and epistemically uncertain knowledge only known through involvement in social life. Modern philosophy retained the emphasis on objective knowledge but replaced the contemplative model with a subjective conception of knowledge rooted in the mastery of nature: one could know only what one could make. Technical mastery displaced *phronesis*. Here, though, modern philosophy detaches technical mastery from the ancient sense of *techné* as know-how or practical making (production). Practical reason abandons its focus on the good life and becomes a form of social engineering. Practice is applied social science.

While Flyvbjerg accepts those elements of the post-positivist critique of natural science that question value and context freedom, he also holds that natural science is cumulative. Natural science has elements of stability and progress that are lacking in the social sciences. The "key concepts" of natural scientific inquiry are the prediction and control of events (Flyvbjerg 2001, 26f). Natural science retains its epistemic focus.

A phronetic social science, in contrast, denies any strict parallel between naturalistic and social inquiry. Flyvbjerg accepts Anthony Giddens's formulation of the double hermeneutic of social inquiry (Giddens 1986). Not only is inquiry an interpretive practice carried out by a community of researchers, but the objects of study are themselves subjects who interpret the world. Social inquiry must encounter these subjects as co-interpreters who have the capacity for knowledge and criticism equal to those who study them. Working from this neo-Aristotelian perspective, Flyvbjerg views "theory" as a quest for objective universal knowledge. He contrasts it with phronetic social science as a skilled performance or wise judgment that is internal to a community and always particular. At times, Flyvbjerg seems to reject science, asserting that:

> [T]he study of social phenomena, is not, never has been, and probably never can be, scientific in the conventional sense of the word "science"; that is, in its epistemic meaning. . . . [I]t is therefore not meaningful to speak of "theory" in the study of social phenomena, at least in the sense that "theory" is used in natural science. (Flyvbjerg 2001, 25)

I think, however, that Flyvbjerg does not reject exact knowledge; he simply subordinates *epistemé* to *phronesis*. Since human activities are in Aristotle's sense variable, there can be no fixed laws of action and no paradigms of inquiry. Phronetic social science is primarily concerned with value rational questions such as "Where are we going?," "Is it desirable?," and "What is to be done?" In addition, Flyvbjerg argues, it also has to ask this question: who benefits, and who loses?

> [T]he principle objective for a social science with a phronetic approach is to carry out analyses and interpretations of the status of values and interests in society aimed at social commentary and social action, i.e., praxis. (Flyvbjerg 2001, 60)

For the natural-science approach, inquiry is carried out from the perspective of a third-person observer independent of the value judgments and involvements of the participants. In phronetic social science, assuming the place of an external third-person observer, however, negates the horizon of understanding required by phronetic social science. It reifies practical judgment. Phronetic knowledge, in contrast, can orient us to the social world, but only within the horizon of a culture.

Flyvbjerg seeks an alternate basis for social inquiry. For proponents of interpretive social theory, knowledge of the social world and of the contextual character of social life means that knowledge is never free from presuppositions. It contains unavoidable subjective and intersubjective presuppositions (Bernstein 1978; Fay 1975; also see Bohman 1993). We have access to the social world only though our own belonging together as subjects or participants *in the social world*. In this respect, the participants' perspective is an inescapable presupposition of understanding others as others. While this approach does not rule out viewing social actors from an external perspective, it does imply that social science cannot do without the participants' perspective.

The neo-Aristotelian conception of practical reason, however, is part of a broader family of approaches to mutual understanding. These approaches share the notion that participants in social action are self-interpreting beings who can act to transform the world. Neo-Aristotelians also share the view that practical reason is social; we orient our actions with others through common understanding. They take, however, a narrower view of the scope of the participants' perspective than those who take other approaches. Neo-Aristotelians limit the horizon of the social world to the boundaries of a given culture or ethos shared by members of a community. Mutual understanding approaches encompass a broader range of options. They include not only those who see understanding as culture bound but those who see the horizon of mutual understanding as constituted by the bounds of possible intersubjectivity. In the latter version, mutual understanding is achieved through the medium of a dialogical or discursive form of understanding. The social world is not an ethos but the totality of legitimate interpersonal relations.

The neo-Aristotelian standpoint limits the reflexivity of participants and the scope of self-interpretation to the boundaries a culture. Though participants can grasp other cultures, they cannot employ the full scope of reflection. Mutual-understanding approaches can expand the scope of reflexive understanding. Individuals are born into a particular culture and its horizon of understanding; they have to take up those cultural norms, however, and accept or reject them. In so doing, they have to draw on an independent capacity for mutual understanding that is not culture-bound, yet stays within the horizon of mutual understanding. Seen in this way, interpretive theory is more than the rereading or the translation of a text. It does not simply read a document that has already been produced but is an active element in the ongoing process of linking the actions of participants in social life. The ability to orient and bind action though mutual understanding is *communicative power:* the capacity of mutual understanding to interpret and make sense of the world with others is *communicative freedom* (Habermas 1993; Cornell 1998; Wellmer 2000). While communicative understanding proceeds from the assumption that truth and validity require the free agreement of participants in discussion, mutual-understanding models do not require perfect agreement. Idealizations inherent in discourse refer to what Gadamer and Heidegger called the anticipatory dimension of mutual understanding. Participants have to assume that others can mean what they say and are capable of reasonable evaluation in order to make sense with others. Participants are accountable to others. The consensual character of mutual understanding also includes elements of trust, respect, and care for others. We may carry on in the course of social life with limited degrees of agreement, since we trust others not to manipulate us and respect others' perspectives. In each of these cases, we rely on "expressive" dimensions of language, such as sincerity or authenticity, for binding communicative power.

Although it is not always emphasized, mutual understanding also has a world-disclosing dimension. We can never know a single entity in isolation or as it "really" is but know it only against the backdrop or horizon of mutual understanding. Taken as a whole, this implicit background understanding, elements of which can be made thematic when called into question, disclose a world. While things exist independent of us and exert constraints, rocks exist, gravity exists, other people exist, but they make sense to us only when disclosed within a meaningful world. Still, the world is not given simply as a preexisting structure but is made and renewed in the course of social life. It draws on the communicative power the of participants' perspective. Symbolic universes, though, disclose more that the substance of legitimate relations; they also disclose modalities of world understanding, or what types of relations are legitimate and the ways of assessing legitimacy and truth (Berger and Luckmann 1967).

Flyvbjerg draws on the mutual-understanding perspective in his account of phronetic social science in MSSM, but he sometimes limits its scope. As noted, he employs Anthony Giddens's account of the double hermeneutic but does not accept all its implications. Giddens argues that accountability to others is a basic feature of social life (Giddens 1986). Flyvbjerg, however, operating with a limited notion of reflexivity and self-understanding, reads accountability as a form of making explicit that, when taken to its limits, is inconsistent with strong contextualism. This approach is clear in Flyvbjerg's analysis of the work of Dreyfus and Bourdieu. Each of these theorists argues for the existence of an implicit core of subjective understanding resistant to objectification. This seems to render the status of general or universal concepts problematic. While Flyvbjerg admits the need for universals in some form, he seems to hold that making understanding explicit can become a form of objectifying, context-free social science.

Flyvbjerg also draws on the participants' perspective in his critique of normal social science. No laws of social action or context-free account of rules can provide for the participants' capacity to recognize whether a rule or social practice is being employed correctly or incorrectly, appropriately or inappropriately. Here he uses an example of the interpretive elements in the gift relationship. In the gift relationship, the detached theoretical observer can never determine, simply by analyzing rules, whether the giving of, or reciprocation of, a gift is carried out in the appropriate ways (Flyvbjerg 2001, 42). These judgments require the participants' grasp of the relevance of an action to a situation—that is, the sense of whether the gift is timed correctly, is given in the appropriate proportion, and so on. It implicates the participant in a web of mutual understanding in which participants have a sense of the right thing to do. Mutual understanding is not a preliminary to analysis: it is central to social inquiry. Flyvbjerg's reservations about hermeneutics, however, and his ambiguities regarding mutual understanding are also apparent in this discussion. He holds that this example, which I have held to be consistent with interpretive approaches, cannot be understood with the tools of interpretive social theory. Nevertheless, here Flyvbjerg reads hermeneutic-interpretive approaches in a Weberian manner as the subjective attribution of meaning and not in the broader sense I have outlined.

There are at least two distinctive variants of neo-Aristotelian theory (Benhabib and Dallmayr 1990; Benhabib 1992). In the first version, associated with revival of classical republican theory, moral and political community is secured through an integrated value pattern that is based on an ethos of the community (Macintyre 1997; Beiner 1997). A community has the same identity or an ethos. Usually this ethos is given by lawmakers or anonymously dispensed. The classical republican version of community employs a strong notion of context. The second variant draws on radical democratic or participatory democratic elements. This version advocates a democratic community in which a public sphere of democratic control acts as a barrier against technical and bureaucratic incursions. Here, the participants' perspective draws on the universal context-making and context-breaking power of communicative action. The good is not a preexisting ethos but is created through active participation.

Contemporary critical theories provide a third, broader version of mutual understanding. "Theory" is reformulated in an interpretive social scientific way. Critical theories argue that inquiry can seek universal features of mutual understanding within the boundaries of the participants' perspective. Reconstructive social sciences do not, indeed cannot, take an objectifying standpoint. They have to remain related to the intuitive knowledge of participants. Only in this way can they explicate the generative accomplishments of participants.

Since Flyvbjerg employs a strong version of context, he does not follow the more modernist lines of argument of the participatory view—though at times he alludes to an alternative version of critical theory, which incorporates *phronesis*. For example, Alessandro Ferrara suggests a universality found within *phronesis* (Ferrara 1998). Whether or not Ferrara's proposal is feasible, Flyvbjerg in the end does not take this path. He only criticizes what he thinks is the excessive Kantian formulation of Habermas.

## The Limits of Mutual Understanding

There are two major problems, according to Flyvbjerg, with mutual-understanding approaches as formulated by hermeneutics and critical theory: (1) they are excessively idealistic, and (2) they are excessively rationalistic. In the first case, versions of mutual understanding developed by Gadamer and Habermas are idealistic because they rest on harmonistic notions of a conflict-free consensus (Flyvbjerg 2001, 107). Because these approaches separate validity from power, they prove of limited value in the analysis of social conflict.

The second problem, rationalism, is directed primarily against Habermas. Drawing on an outmoded version of Habermas's theory, the ideal-speech situation, Flyvbjerg argues that this is idealistic since it imposes impossible or at least only perfect possible conditions on agreement and rationalist since it assumes perfect rationality on the part of participants in social life. Flyvbjerg equates this with Kant's transcendental project. For both hermeneutics and critical theory, a transcendental intersubjectivity, like transcendental subjectivity, constitutes a form of objectivism. The ideally rational subject is free from passion and desire, interests and strategy. This subject passes judgment from a standpoint external to society. It is incompatible with Flyvbjerg's conception of *phronesis.*

## The Nietzschean Model: Power-Interpretive Practical Reason

Flyvbjerg views the consequences of Habermas's interpretive idealism as the result of a Kantian emphasis on legality and legitimacy. While Habermas's theory serves as "an abstract ideal for justification and application in relation to legislation, institutional development, and procedural planning," its idealistic orientation "contains little understanding of how power functions" (Flyvbjerg 2001, 107). Typical of the modernist separation of power and knowledge, critical theory studies ideal conditions, not real structures of power and domination. Like Foucault, Flyvbjerg wants to stress the ubiquity and productivity of power. Thus, Flyvbjerg proposes some modifications of *phronesis* to account for the centrality of power in social theory.

These modifications take place in two stages. First, Flyvbjerg employs a phenomenologically tinged conception of subjectivity that views *phronesis* as a virtuoso performance. Virtuosity is a form of know-how. The virtuoso does not employ analytic reasoning but intuitively knows the right thing to do: "a given situation releases a picture of problem, goal, plan, decision, and action in one instant and without division into phases" (Flyvbjerg 2001, 21). These elements of embedded subjectivity can be understood only holistically. This subjectivist turn is linked to a strategic conception of political power.

In his earlier book *Rationality and Power,* Flyvbjerg traces this "strategy and tactics" approach back to the political realism of Machiavelli and Thucydides. The world of republican politics that Machiavelli admires can be created only when power establishes stability and good laws: politics founds the social. With some qualifications, Machiavelli sees the social world primarily as an area of strategic struggles. The conditions of social life are not immediately conducive to cooperation or peaceful coexistence but have to be created. Desired goods and resources to achieve goals are scarce, and individuals will feign cooperation, while acting strategically, to get what they need. Under these conditions, the individual who acts like a saint will, like the unarmed prophet Savonarola, come to ruin. Flyvbjerg reads this idea in terms that are sympathetic to Nietzsche and Foucault.

> The insight that reasoning quickly turned into rationalization and that dia-
> logue becomes persuasive rhetoric under the pressures of reality is already
> present in detail in Thucydides. Machiavelli who like Thucydides, had expe-
> rience with the practical employment of power worked out his insight refl-
> ectively and began developing a concept of power with an emphasis not
> only on power as an entity that is conquered and held based on force and
> law but also on power as strategy and tactics. (Flyvbjerg 1998, 5)

Machiavelli's critique of the impotency of the moral and religious
appeal of the prophet unarmed is seen by Flyvbjerg as a parallel to his critique of hermeneutic idealism and to the idea of domination-free social
order. This reading is premature. Machiavelli represents only the first step
in the power interpretive approach. While politics secures the basis of
social order, human flourishing, including the fine arts, in a republican
society seems to have an independent nonstrategic character. Here Machiavelli is closer to the tradition of Marx, Weber, or Freud in his conception
of politics.

Certainly Machiavelli stresses the importance of success-oriented
action in politics. While purposive rational action can apply to action on
nature, strategic action is a type of *social action* oriented to success. In
social action, individuals are effected by and effect the actions of others. In
contrast, communicative action seeks to create forms of mutual understanding. Unlike pure communicative action, however, strategic action
takes account of others only in order to achieve success in the pursuit of a
goal; in communicative action we have to be accountable to others with
whom we are bound through mutual understanding.

Strategic action, however, represents only one-half of the power-interpretive approach. To complete the picture requires a second element, a
world-generating power whose character has been analyzed in the work of
Foucault and Nietzsche (Foucault 1980, 1984a; Nietzsche 1968b, 1974). In
order to achieve success in social action, control over meaning is essential.
Interpretation, on this reading, is more than a commentary; quoting Nietzsche, it "is itself a means to becoming master of something." Employing
Nietzsche's notion of knowledge, mastery becomes the achievement of a
"fresh interpretation" that gains dominance in an essentially contested
field of interpretations (Flyvbjerg 2001, 123). Power is itself a "productive"
element; strategic power conditions and shapes the character of communicative action. Action is *essentially* power.

Nietzsche linked power, meaning, and interpretation. The will to power is always manifest in interpretation. In fact, interpretation is a primary mode of securing power (Flyvbjerg 2001, 27). As Foucault's conception of power and knowledge illustrates, subjugation and control are dependent upon interpretation. Forms of mutual understanding are here subordinated to a prior world-forming force, which is both strategic and hegemonic.

Power not only secures dominance but does so by defining what is legitimate. A central feature of power, then, is its reality-defining (world-disclosing) character. "Power," Flyvbjerg claims, "is more concerned with defining reality that dealing with what reality "really" is (Flyvbjerg 1998a, 68). Power produces reality. A power-interpretive critique can unmask the strategic rationalizations that hide under the guise of power-free "understanding."

Flyvbjerg employed power-interpretive precepts throughout *Rationality and Power*. He contrasts the seemingly rationalist-modernist approach of the planners with the power politics used by players in the process. Even the technical, value-free rationality of the planners is, in reality, saturated with interest. Such rationality represents rationalizations of preestablished political goals that function to exclude undesired alternatives. Powerful social interests, like the Chamber of Commerce, bypass the notion of discourse altogether. Rejecting the idea that they should proceed rationally through the force of the better argument, the Chamber defined the planning process strategically, as a "war," and worked to defend its position of authority against the incursions of planners and environmentalists. Ideas are employed as tactics. The only players who appeal to reason, pace Nietzsche, are those who are otherwise powerless. Less than a discourse, planning becomes a contest between competing forces to define the situation. Even some opponents of the Chamber came to see the matter as one of tactics, rather than persuasion. The "modernist" project of a rational society must give way to the recognition that the social world requires an infinitely complex practice of strategies and tactics. Rationalist planners, he argues, lack a "realist" sense of the practical (Flyvbjerg 1998, 128).

## From Virtue to Virtú: Reconfiguring Phronesis

Dissatisfied with the tendency to understand virtue as an element in a conflict-free and harmonious mutual understanding, Flyvbjerg draws on the virtú tradition to find an alternative. The latter redefine virtue as a type of heroic performance in an essentially agonistic world (Connolly 1992; Honig 1994). Discourses do not orient action to understanding, but they are tactical elements operating in a field of force relations. This conception is the focus of Foucault's later work. The later Foucault turns away from analysis of objective systems of thought (*epistemé*) and turns to the analysis of practical systems. He rejects the idea that human affairs can be the object of an exact science; *techné* can no longer be applied exact knowledge. The modern notion of technique associated with the application of exact knowledge or epistemé is returned to its premodern sense of practical know-how and making. In Foucault's work, virtú is closely linked to *techné*. Here *techné* is understood as practical rationality governed by a conscious goal—as *phronesis*. Flyvbjerg argues that emphasis on "goals" links Foucault's *techné* to Aristotelian *phronesis* (Flyvbjerg 2001, 111). Foucault's "practical reason," like Aristotle's, avoids universality and focuses on the variable and the particular in human affairs. Certainly power-interpretive analysis still claims to retain a critical dimension. Analysis breaks the aura of naturalness and inevitability of practical systems of thought. In studying how practical systems come to be, we can also imagine them other than they are.

Flyvbjerg employs his strategy-and-tactics approach to link inquiry and action in a practical nexus. Both the actor and the analyst must draw on their practical knowledge of the situation in order to grasp the workings of power. Production extends to questions of (moral) self-formation. "Human life," Foucault wrote, "and the self were objects of certain number of *technai* which with their exacting rationality could well be compared to any technique of production" (Foucault 1988a, 28). Strategies and tactics are a type of know-how, a skilled performance that produces a politics. The analyst gains insight into power though her virtuoso understanding of the workings of power. She illuminates the strategies that achieve dominance and illustrates how groups succeed in making an interpretation dominant. The actor is a virtuoso in the practical use of power. She knows, through experience judgment or intuition, when to apply strategies to achieve a goal and how to take account of others in the situation. In this latter interpretation, moral virtue is a heroic—one might say masculine—quality that requires a wise use of power to achieve the good.

I am not convinced that the power-interpretive reading really explains the virtuoso's performance. Take the example of a musical performance in which someone creates a new interpretation of a Mozart sonata, or, maybe more radically. a composition that puts forward a reinterpretation of musicality itself. We could use the phronetic model to explain these innovations. Not simply judging without rules, the performers enact rules in the performance. The problem with the power-interpretive approach, however, arises with the notion that the audience must also recognize the virtuosity of the performance.

Power-interpretive accounts cannot clarify the link between the audience and the performance. Since they view the novelty as the imposition of a new reality that requires the suppression or exclusion of prior understanding, the independent power of the audience to grasp new meanings or performances is restricted. They must be made to accept the new interpretation though inducement of strategic advantages—not though recognition of its virtuosity. If their prior understanding is suppressed, then it is not clear exactly on what background repertoire the audience can draw on to accept the performance. Understanding power as a ubiquitous reality-forming force is decidedly unrealistic. Strategic power has no world-forming force in this interpretation of power, which in fact conceals the actual dynamics of power. Domination, however understood, needs to draw on conceptions of communicative power rooted in mutual understanding.

### Strategic Action, World-Forming Power, and Domination

While Flyvbjerg employs both the mutual-understanding model and the power-interpretive model of practical reason in his work, his ambivalence about the mutual-understanding model results less in a fusion of the two models than in a subordination of mutual understanding to power-interpretive perspectives. In fusing Aristotle and Foucault, Flyvbjerg favors a teleological reading of Aristotelian practical action. As goal oriented, the control of and the creation of meaning is tied to success in action. This leads to difficulties. Forming power cannot be both communicative and strategic. Contrary to Flyvbjerg's claims, strategic power has no world-forming force; it must draw on the communicative power inherent in mutual understanding.

The power-interpretive analysis represents a step beyond the analyses of domination in earlier critical theories. In the second half of the nineteenth century, analyses of domination employed a purposive rational conception of action, sometimes supplemented with an expressive component.

Here freedom consists of the actor's free pursuit of self-chosen goals. Later it included notions of self-realization in which actors freely use and develop their capacities. In this view, domination consists in the power to get actors to pursue goals that are not self-chosen and that benefit a dominant individual or group while inducing an actor to believing that she is pursuing self-chosen goals or realizing her abilities. In this model, the critique of ideology frees individuals from the grip of domination through reflection and in so doing also frees them to act consciously to achieve their own goals.

The power-interpretive approach marks an advance over its predecessors. It recognizes the limits of the purposive model of social action for analyses of domination. The use of power requires control over meaning. The power-interpretive model however, runs into difficulties when it attempts to fuse strategic action and world formation. Success-oriented action cannot generate worlds; it must rely on forms of mutual understanding (communicative action) to create world-forming power.

The crucial question is, however, not whether interpretation can be employed strategically but whether its basic character is strategic. In opposition to a strategic approach, Wittgenstein identified one element of the intersubjective dimension of interpretation in his notion of following a rule (Wittgenstein 1999). Interpretation of meaning is not simply the subjective attribution of significance to something by a singular actor. It is an intersubjective process in which participants come to use similar meanings. In order to follow a rule, another person (at least one) must be able to understand the speaker, using a proper meaning. For it is always possible the speaker could misinterpret a meaning that she intends, or the hearer could misunderstand the speaker. Each participant must be able to take the perspective of the other in other to establish and fix meaning (which, to be sure, can always be changed).

Certainly Wittgenstein's notion of following a rule was restricted. His examples are primarily semantic, not social. A social conception of understanding entails a world that consists of webs of meaning though which social interaction takes place. In a nascent form, and with many shortcomings, Heidegger's reformulation of hermeneutics as philosophical hermeneutics began this line of thought. In *Being and Time,* Heidegger stresses that neither understanding nor knowing can be seen as a Cartesian quest for certainty by a disembodied mind. Understanding is practical: it is rooted in the structure of action in the world and interaction with others. This practical form of understanding is always interpretive.

Gadamer subsequently clarified this insight and linked philosophical hermeneutics to dialogical processes of mutual understanding. I believe we can further elaborate and clarify this model by incorporating notions of mutual accountability. To use this notion does not imply going back to rationalism or objectivism. It indicates that we interact in practical dealings with one another though structures of giving reasons for action.

Each of these perspectives, then, suggests that interpretation is not primarily a tool or a weapon; it does not create a product but rather is a form of communicative action that is oriented to establishing and renewing understanding. The horizon of a common world that is established through this intersubjective process of interpretation requires the establishment and maintenance of mutual recognition. Language discloses a world only to the extent that we are engaged in understanding each other against the background of embedded understandings and interpretive capacities. Strategic action takes place within a social world but suspends these basic conditions of mutual understanding in defining action as success oriented. Thus, it also suspends the conditions of world disclosure. When interpretation is used strategically to gain success in action, it is parasitic upon the basic sense of interpretation. It draws on the communicative power inherent in our sense of legitimacy but redirects it or constrains it so that ongoing processes of mutual accountability are restricted.

Successful strategic action induces the coordination of actions to achieve desired ends. Actors convince each other not through reasons but through incentives. In pure bargaining, we do not have to change our minds about what we think is correct; we may simply accept an inducement to act. Inducement alone, however, does not in itself imply domination. In cases of successful domination, we have to convince the other person that her action is correct or justified. The power-interpretive view accepts this second account. Achievement of the "goal" of domination entails a control over meaning and over the modes of understanding that participants in a social world use to judge relations as legitimate. These elements, however, cannot be created by strategic action. Strategic action and power-interpretive theories must draw on communicative power and the communicative freedom of subjects in order to achieve domination.

This element of justification comes into play in even in Flyvbjerg's analysis of the Chamber of Commerce. Flyvbjerg lists three principles at the heart of the Chamber's strategy (Flyvbjerg 1998a, 58): "1) What is good for business is good for Aalborg; 2) What is good for motorists is good for Business; 3) Therefore what is good for motorists is good for Aalborg."

However crudely, this informal syllogism forwards a conception of the common good that purports to be accepted or rejected by participants. The Chamber attempts to define the common good for the community. Even in claiming a seat on the planning board, the chamber must make a claim that it deserves the seat, no matter how it acts once it has a position of influence. It asserts that its claims are recognized. Groups like the Chamber appeal not just to the good of the community but to the idea that they are worthy of trust. Power interests may assert that they are trustworthy or caring or otherwise concerned with "our" interests. They try to portray themselves as worthy guardians of a common or public interest. To be sure, those who seek social control act to limit discussion and debate or eliminate it entirely, or to restrict the kinds of claims that can be legitimately held; they may even draw on ways to establish their claim without debate; but in each of these actions they restrict a power that exists independent of strategy. These actions do not create reality, though they may direct or shape it. Powerful interests still have to draw on communicative power in order to achieve legitimacy.

## Social Science and Power

Certainly Flyvbjerg's depiction of the dynamics of the planning processes rings true. Groups like the Chamber or planners act to restrict the alternatives or to structure choices and to exclude participants or ideas from the process of decision making. In spite of its many virtues, Flyvbjerg's power-interpretive reading is inadequate. It cannot accommodate the claims of communicative freedom. One of the basic elements of all freedom is the right to say no. Actors can never be free agents unless they have the ability to assent and dissent. Similarly, communicative freedom entails not just the capacity to create meaning but the ability to accept or reject proposed norms or standards and to judge the authenticity of other participants. While individuals are born into a society and are socialized into the practices of that society, they are not inextricably bound to them. The capacity for communicative freedom is an independent power that draws on our broader capacities for mutual understanding. Participants can judge existing practices because communicative freedom has a context-breaking and context-making capacity. I believe that communicative freedom is an inherent element of mutual recognition. In the latter we must always recognize the power of the other to accept or reject not just shared meanings but the validity of norms and practices.

Power-interpretive approaches also stress the freedom of subjects, but they have difficulty accounting for the type of autonomy that is an element of communicative freedom. While the power-interpretive actor has the freedom to formulate strategies for producing successful results through action, she employs meaning in a one-dimensional way: that is, as strategic action. This limits the communicative freedom of the initiator of meaning and the recipients of strategic-meaning initiatives.

No matter how benignly we view the *agon* as a public space where players struggle to win honor and glory, it cannot adequately capture all elements of communicative freedom. Actors have the freedom to create strategies and tactics to win in the struggle for dominance, and they can initiate forms of meaning. In remaining within the limits of strategic action, however, even initiators employ a severely restricted sense of mutual understanding. The initiator is constrained from reflection upon the legitimacy of norms or practices that will be instituted Losers in the competition and recipients lose the right to say yes or no to practices and norms. They are not recognized as communicative participants. This view cannot account for social order. Even the most sympathetic reading of agonistic struggles would reduce the good to a form of subjective intuition that by passes mutual recognition. Addressors and addresses lack that capacity for full communicative freedom.

Foucault's last work embodies this dilemma. There he invokes the spirit of Kant's essay "What Is Enlightenment?" to forward a notion of critical reflection on the present (Foucault 1988a, 1984b). While this conception is often compatible with critical theory, Foucault cannot marshal the resources of his theory to explain his own critical stance.

A social science that pursues a critical analysis of values and power can best proceed from communication-theoretic rather than a power-interpretive analyses. The power-interpretive approach has difficulty with communicative freedom, but the communicative-theoretic approach can account for the effects of strategic power that concern Flyvbjerg. Strategic power is not a world-constituting force. It is more appropriate to see domination as a process that is constructed of the restriction, redirection, and containment of comunicative power and freedom. It is possible, given the assumptions I have made, to construct a theory that accounts for many of the effects that Foucault and other power-interpretive theorists identify. Strategic power and domination are inherently unstable. When exercised as domination, however, strategic power contains a deeper instability. It must attempt to keep at bay the very powers that it must draw upon for legitimacy. I think it due to this instability that modern forms of power require constant surveillance and vigilance that Foucault correctly identified. He noticed, but did not correctly theorize, the doubly risky character of domination.

One possible objection to my account concerns the nature of struggle. Post-structuralists argue that the social world is essentially a contest for dominance between forms of world formation. In a well-known interview, given a short time before Foucault's death, he argues that discourses were strategic games no different from other "games." This account, however, incorrectly makes discourse into strategies. Discourses are more than strategic games, and they serve nonstrategic goals. They establish relations and bonds among participants.

Critical theory, even that of Habermas, is not a form of idealism based on the goal of a conflict-free world. Mutual-understanding models can accommodate both strategic struggles for power and conflicts over norms. Communicative theories begin not from the position of a transcendental subjectivity but from the standpoint of the practically situated participant who has to make sense of the world with others. Participants do not have a repertoire of perfectly formed understanding but interact though forms of consensual social action that is "good enough" for interactions. In ordinary social life, individuals engage in struggles for recognition. They seek to have individual identities and form their own judgments on the world. This is especially true under conditions of modernity (Giddens 1986). They also may struggle over norms. In each of these cases, however, struggle does not constitute an agon—if by that we mean a struggle for dominance for honor or glory. Rather, it is part of the ongoing attempt to create and renew relations with others.

It is a mistake to interpret the moral capacity of participants along the line of a goal-seeking model. Participants in the social world, as the example of the gift illustrates, have to possess the power to discern the correct from the incorrect employment of practice. This is, however, more than just a sense of the appropriateness of the action. Participants and social-scientific "observers" have to possess the ability to discern the reasons why a practice is appropriate or a norm right or wrong. This aspect of understanding brings us back to the mutual accountability of participants to one another. This capacity is a general competency of the competent speaker/employer of language, but an independent feature of language use that is not reliant on a specific cultural context or frame of reference. It allows us to understand contexts, but also to break them and create new ones. This creative power allows the participants to take a stand on the norms and judgments of a particular society. As long as there is language, hegemony can never be complete.

The structure of ordinary reasoning is more complex than Flyvbjerg allows. Participants invoke communicative reason in two distinct ways. First, as noted, participants orient their action in common through norms that are based in mutual understanding. They constantly renew this understanding in the course of everyday life. In cases where established norms are called into question, participants have the ability to reflect upon the accounts they give for their actions and to engage in discursive process to repair or transform the nature of moral life. Thus, communicative reason possesses the ability to resolve disputes. It has a self-critical capacity.

Elements of self-critical reason can be grasped within an ethos, but in modern societies this self-critical capacity must be extended when a new set of moral questions arises. These questions arise when we consider question of fairness and equal treatment for those who do not share our own ethical religious or national traditions. These moral questions raise issues of justice, which require that we reflect not just within an ethos or traditions but also about the mediation of traditions. Such questions require reflection about the universal capacity of participants to be recognized by others. Though they may transcend the bounds of a particular ethos or tradition, these capacities do not transcend the participants' perspective as such. They are not properties or conditions of an individual subject, as in some versions of rights, but conditions of mutual recognition.

# 8

# Contesting the Terrain
## *Flyvbjerg on Facts, Values, Knowledge, and Power*

## *Mary Hawkesworth*

Bent Flyvbjerg's *Making Social Science Matter* (2001) and some of the reviews and discussion that it has engendered make it clear how difficult it is to envision a new social science. While there is much to admire in this book, it also replays debates and identifies "solutions" that are too familiar and too tainted with failure to offer much hope for a systematic reorientation of the social sciences in general or of political science in particular.

Flyvbjerg's desire to break with the specter of "the unity of science" that has haunted efforts to validate scientific knowledge production for centuries is laudable, but it is remarkably unhelpful to burden that effort with a sterile opposition between the "natural sciences" and the "social sciences," harking back to the *methodenstreiten* that tortured Max Weber (1949) into the flawed artifice of the fact/value dichotomy. Flyvbjerg's narrow conception of natural science reinforces the mistaken idea that there is one "scientific method" shared by all the natural sciences, an idea that has been roundly rejected by philosophers, historians, and sociologists of science, as well as by natural scientists themselves (Latour and Woolgar 1979; Latour 1987; Knorr-Cetina 1981; Lynch 1985; Pickering 1992). And it supports the equally problematic notion that the subject under investigation renders a mode of inquiry "scientific" regardless of the questions asked, the methods of analysis deployed, or the nature of the research findings.

That a faulty opposition, pitting the natural sciences against the social sciences, only serves to shore up methodolatry becomes painfully clear in the exchange between David Laitin (2003) and Bent Flyvbjerg (2004a) in

*Politics and Society.* On the grand assumption that "the scientific method" is at stake and the future of political science is at risk, what might be an engaged scholarly exchange quickly escalates to hurling invectives in a gladiatorial contest. It takes David Laitin (2003, 163) only two sentences to label Flyvbjerg—and all "perestroikans"—"Luddites" in the grips of a potent brew combining "abhorrence of all things mathematical" and "fear of the modern." Not surprisingly, by the end of his essay, Laitin has confidently arrived at the point of "premature burial," self-assuredly forecasting the death of this upstart movement. Invoking the authority of scientific knowledge, he proudly proclaims: "A scientific frame would lead us to expect that certain fields will become defunct, certain debates dead, and certain methods antiquated. A pluralism that shelters defunct practitioners cannot be scientifically justified" (180). Conversely, or perhaps reciprocally, Flyvbjerg (2004a, 395) accuses Laitin of "bombast" and deceit, allowing an "approximation of science" to masquerade as real science. He also berates Laitin for "sloppy science"—misusing statistics and faulty inference, "scientism" (412), and "promoting a dogmatic version of the correct interpretation of what political science is, namely rational choice theory and statistics" (399).

For many who have been in the profession for multiple decades, this anger, animosity, and invective provoke a profound sense of déjà vu. For these debates dominated not only our undergraduate and graduate experiences, but the emergence of social science in Europe and the United States in the early twentieth century.

Appealing to an Aristotelian distinction between *episteme* and *phronesis*, Flyvbjerg (2001, 57) reserves the production of "universal, invariant, context-independent" knowledge to the realm of the natural sciences, while construing social science in terms of pragmatic, variable, value-laden deliberations conducive to the determination of ethical and political action. This dichotomous construction of knowledge, however, caricatures both the natural sciences and the social sciences. Knowledge production, whether in the natural sciences, the social sciences, or the humanities, is far richer, more resourceful, and more complicated than such caricatures suggest. Values structure all modes of knowledge production, more often tacitly than explicitly, and many methods of analysis give rise to generalizations that aspire to the universal. To move beyond facile stereotypes, it is important to recognize that there is no single method that guarantees the validity, much less the relevance, of research findings within or across academic fields.

Rather than restaging a contest between outmoded conceptions of natural science and social science, there are more productive approaches to
questions of disciplinary power and relevance. But these approaches
require that more questions be asked and a more nuanced understanding
of knowledge be achieved. To move toward a more sophisticated grasp of
knowledge production, several questions can be heuristic: to whom do we
want political science to matter? For whom, on whose behalf, should it
matter? What are the consequences, intended and unintended, of political
science mattering? Starting from particular research interests, then, political scientists who want our work to matter might borrow a concern from
the humanities and ask: who is the audience for this research? To whom
do we want it to matter: elected officials, policy analysts, other political
scientists, the public, stakeholders, students, future generations? Any one
of these categories is at once too simple and too grand. For there is no singular characteristic or interest binding all members of any of these groups
together that would generate a uniform reaction to political science
research. Race, ethnicity, gender, nationality, party affiliation, ideology,
religion constitute differences within these categories, structuring recep-
tivity in some instances and evidence blindness in others. Asking questions about "audience" is useful precisely because it begins to chip away at
assumptions of homogeneity. The minute we begin to realize that the
same finding might not matter in the same way within or across these categories, we are positioned to ask some important questions about truth,
power, and the politics of disciplinary knowledge.

Consider for a moment how focus-group methods have proliferated in
political life. Extrapolating from scientific sampling techniques and marketing tactics, focus-group methods have come to matter greatly in U.S.
politics; they are used for everything from devising campaign slogans and
voter mobilization strategies, to vindicating demonstrations of candidate
character and policy proposals, to vetting key political speeches, to managing damage control efforts. Focus groups have become an invaluable tool
for political scientists working in public opinion research and campaigns
and elections. There is no question that the outcomes of focus groups
have come to matter a very great deal to politicians. (Consider, for example, New Jersey governor James McGreevy's resignation speech, in which
the focus-group tested phrase "I am a gay American" was carefully inserted
to divert attention from the issue of corrupt political appointments to a
sympathetic casting of sexual orientation.) Nor is there any question that
focus-group methods generate a form of knowledge that combines

insights of rhetoric into the arts of persuasion, with demographic knowledge, sociological knowledge, and political knowledge. Moreover, this knowledge is profoundly useful to candidates running for election, politicians seeking to maximize their job approval ratings, and marketers trying to sell a product. But the usefulness and reliability of the findings derived from focus groups do not suggest that this method should be made the foundation for scientific research in the social sciences in general or political science in particular.

Two other questions—"for whom?" and "toward what end?"— caution against any such hasty generalization. These questions are raised by critics who have denounced focus-group method as an instrument of strategic manipulation. Their concerns with the well-being of citizens, with the demands of open political debate rooted in reasons rather than causes, and with healthy democratic practices that can enable citizens to hold their elected officials to account raise quite different problems for knowledge production, for they seek to shift the register of political knowledge production from the range of technical interests (i.e., how to produce certain effects) to the sphere of emancipatory interests (i.e., how to enable people to free themselves from ideological distortion and various modes of domination) (Habermas 1971).

Flyvbjerg shares Habermasian concerns about the hegemony of technical interests within social science. His critique of instrumental rationality and his insistence on the centrality of values to social inquiry are designed to rescue social scientists from the grips of scientism. He is quite right to challenge the myth of value neutrality, pointing out that there are always stakes in political knowledge. He is mistaken, however, in assuming that natural sciences escape value ladenness. Whether grounded in fundamental values such as freedom, modernity, or progress, permeated by widely shared cultural beliefs, or informed by idiosyncratic assumptions, disciplinary strategies for knowledge production in the natural sciences, social sciences, and humanities are theoretically constituted, linguistically mediated, and value laden. One methodological question then is whether we openly confront the valuative dimensions of our research or whether we continue to deceive ourselves with outmoded and discredited positivist notions.[1]

To whom and how political science will matter depends heavily on scholars' answers to that question. Consider a second kind of political-science knowledge that has grown increasingly important in the past two decades under the rubric of "democratization studies." Launched during the transitions from authoritarian rule in Latin American and Africa, intensified with the fall of the Soviet system in 1990, democratization studies have become a growth industry, providing consultancies as well as full-time employment in international agencies for political scientists who want to put their knowledge to use in restructuring nations, especially in East and Central Europe, the Baltic, and the Commonwealth of Independent States. While there are, of course, competing views on democratization, certain assumptions of profound importance are shared across these differences. Most notable among these are the assumption that liberal democracy is the *telos* of full democratization and, extrapolating from modernization theory, the bedrock assumption that capitalist modes of economic development are a precondition for the attainment of liberal democracy. Models of "democratic consolidation" posit that marketization, that is, capitalist modes of production and exchange, will generate modernist belief systems, including commitments to and demands for representative democracy. Participation in a competitive market economy will promote norms of instrumental rationality, universalism, and egalitarianism, which will foster mobility and individual achievement, while negating hierarchies rooted in ascriptive status. The rise of individualism will in turn foster demands for increasing political participation, the mobilization of interest groups, the emergence of civil society, and multiparty electoral contests.

The assumptions of modernization and democratization theories (i.e., the process is linear, cumulative, expansive, diffuse, and fundamentally occupied with the tradition/modernity dichotomy) offer little insight into the simultaneous emergence of various forms of ethnic nationalism and fundamentalism during the 1990s. Nor do they square well with the possibility that human freedom is compatible with more than one version of modernity. Nevertheless, they do represent yet another instance of the politics of disciplinary knowledge for they generate a set of prescriptions that can be and have been offered to democratizing states. A cursory list of these prescriptions might include:

- "Democratic elitism" (behind-the-scenes negotiations among elites are posited as critical to successful transition and the only viable form of long-term decision making)
- "Shock therapy" (Unemployment as high as 80 percent is not considered too extreme in the context of transition to a market economy)

- "Regime stabilization" (minimizing "dysfunctional" and "destabilizing" forces such as citizen participation is deemed essential for liberal democratic governance)
- "Structural adjustment" (shifting to export crops, exporting labor, privatization, reduction of health care, education, and social welfare provision, and increasing women's employment in the formal, informal, and subsistence sectors are characterized as "sustainable" development)
- "Private-interest maximization" (substituting self-interested maximizing for community and familial bonds is portrayed as essential to the cultivation of "market mentalities")
- "Competitive elections" (multiparty elections become the primary indicator of "democratic" practice regardless of the principles or policies that the parties espouse)

There is no question that there will be a particular kind of political transformation in states that follow these prescriptions: they will come to look and act a lot more "like us." Whether or not one believes that remaking the world in our own image heightens freedom and democracy, it seems beyond dispute that making political science matter in this way is at great remove from value-neutral inquiry.

## The Quest for Objectivity

The methodological strictures that mainstream political scientists embrace, and that Flyvbjerg calls into question, are part of a strategy to achieve objective knowledge. Objectivity gains its purchase on the basis of specific promises. In the context of scientific investigations, an objective account implies a grasp of the actual qualities and relations of objects as they exist independent of the inquirer's thoughts and desires regarding them (Cunningham 1973). Objectivity, then, promises to free us from distortion, bias, and error in intellectual inquiry, to help the discipline transcend the fallibility of individual knowers. But what if the methods designed to purge distortion and bias actually introduce specific forms of bias? Flyvbjerg's preservation of the demarcation between natural sciences and social sciences does not probe this possibility. Instead, by insisting that the value-neutral, "universal, invariable, context-independent" knowledge possible in the natural sciences is not possible for the particularist, value-laden, praxis-oriented domain of the social sciences, he reinforces the fact/value dichotomy while resurrecting a division of "scientific" labor that assigns objective and theoretical inquiry to the natural sciences and "phronetic" inquiry to the social sciences. Flyvbjerg's consolation prize for social scientists is a renewed understanding that deliberative rationality (*phronesis*) is not only possible in the realm of values but peculiarly attuned to the demands of social science inquiry, for it allows us to answer critical questions: "Where are we going? Is it desirable? What should be done? Who gains and who loses by which mechanisms of power?" (Flyvbjerg 2001, 60).

Laitin's scathing attack on Flyvbverg makes it clear that no political scientist, practiced in the art of formal theory or mathematical modeling, is going to rest content with "social science as public philosophy," when the methods they've been taught offer systematic and predictive theory in the realm of "facts." Had Flyvbjerg been more attentive to recent debates within the philosophy of science, he might have been less sanguine about the fact/value dichotomy as a valid criterion of demarcation between the natural sciences and the social sciences. Debates among "realists" and "antirealists" about the relation between theories and the world, the criteria of truth, and the nature of evidence are intricate and complex,[2] but both realists and antirealists share convictions about the defects of the fact/value dichotomy and accept the broad contours of "presupposition theories of science" (Laudan 1990; van Frassen 1980; Churchland and Hooker 1985; Harre 1986; Putnam 1983, 1988, 1990; Glymour 1980; Newton-Smith 1981; Miller 1987). On this view, science, as a form of human knowledge, is dependent upon theory in multiple and complex ways.[3] The pervasive role of theoretical assumptions upon the practice of science has profound implications for notions such as empirical "reality," and the "autonomy" of facts, which posit that facts are "given" and that experience is ontologically distinct from the theoretical constructs that are advanced to explain it. The post-positivist conception of a "fact" as a theoretically constituted entity calls into question such basic assumptions. It suggests that "the noun, 'experience', the verb, 'to experience' and the adjective 'empirical' are not univocal terms that can be transferred from one system to another without change of meaning. . . . Experience does not come labeled as 'empirical', nor does it come self-certified as such. What we call experience depends upon assumptions hidden beyond scrutiny which define it and which in turn it supports" (Vivas 1960, 76). Recognition that "facts" can be so designated only in terms of prior theoretical presuppositions implies that any quest for an unmediated reality is necessarily futile. Any attempt to identify an "unmediated fact" must mistake the conventional for the "natural," as in cases which define "brute facts" as "social facts which are largely the product of well-understood, reliable tools, facts that are not likely to be vitiated by pitfalls . . . in part [because of] the ease and certainty with which [they] can be determined and in part [because of] the incontestability of [their] conceptual base" (Murray 1983, 321). Alternatively, the attempt to conceive a "fact" that exists prior to any description of it, prior to any theoretical or conceptual mediation, must generate an empty notion of something completely unspecified and unspecifiable, a notion that will be of little use to science (Williams 1985, 138).

Recognition of the manifold ways in which perceptions of reality are theoretically mediated raises a serious challenge not only to notions of "brute data" and the "givenness" of experience but also to the possibility of falsification as a strategy for testing theories against an independent reality. For falsification to provide an adequate test of a scientific theory, it is necessary that there be a clear distinction between the theory being tested and the evidence adduced to support or refute the theory. According to the hypothetico-deductive model, "theory-independent evidence" is essential to the very possibility of refutation, to the possibility that the world could prove a theory to be wrong. If, however, what is taken to be the "world," what is understood to be "brute data," is itself theoretically constituted (indeed, constituted by the same theory that is undergoing the test), then no conclusive disproof of a theory is likely. For the independent evidence upon which falsification depends does not exist; the available evidence is preconstituted by the same theoretical presuppositions as the scientific theory under scrutiny (Moon 1975, 146; Brown 1977, 38–48; Stockman 1983, 73–76).

Presupposition theories of science provide ample justification for rejecting the fact/value dichotomy and for rejecting Flyvbjerg's demarcation of natural science and social science which incorporates that problematic distinction. They also afford more sophisticated criteria for the validity of knowledge claims, offering an alternative to the Nietzschean perspectivism that Flyvbjerg embraces as the epistemic ground for social science. In his effort to explicate an approach to social science that recognizes the plurality of values and the roles that contingency and power play in social and political life, Flyvbjerg draws heavily from Aristotle, Nietzsche, and Foucault.[4] He explicitly rejects foundationalist claims that relativism is the only alternative to universal standards of knowledge and tries to illuminate a variety of strategies for reflexive analysis of values. Yet, in his discussions of narrative inquiry and social science as dialogue, Flyvbjerg's allegiance to the fact/value dichotomy pushes him toward Nietzschean perspectivism.

> Phronetic research is dialogical in the sense that it includes, and, if successful, is included in, a polyphony of voices, with no one voice, including that of the researcher, claiming final authority. Thus, the goal of phronetic research is to produce input to the ongoing social dialogue and praxis of a society, rather than to generate ultimate, unequivocally verified knowledge . . . phronetic research explicitly sees itself as not having a privileged position from which the final truth can be told and further discussion stopped. . . . Hence, objectivity in phronetic research is . . . employment of a variety of perspectives and affective interpretations in the service of knowledge. (Flyvbjerg 2001, 139)

In contrast to objectivist assumptions about "speaking truth to power" (Lasswell 1971; Wildavsky 1979), Flyvbjerg suggests that the validity of any researcher's claims can be determined only by their popular acceptance. "The significance of any particular interpretation in a dialogue will depend on the extent to which the interpretation's validity claims are accepted, and this acceptance typically occurs in the competition with other claims and interpretations" (2001, 139). Adding a democratic twist to the Nietzschean conception, "truth" emerges from a contest of wits and wills, determined by popular assent.

Quantitative political analysts are not alone in having concerns about the conflation of truth and popular acceptance of an idea. Despite the anti-elitist impulse that fuels Flyvbjerg's move to a democratic determination of truth, reducing the grounds for the validity of knowledge claims to popular assent can have far from democratic outcomes.

## Power and Knowledge

Quoting Bertrand Russell, Flyvbjerg advances the fairly uncontroversial claim that power "is the fundamental concept in social science" (2001, 88). In his effort to illuminate the conceptions of power most useful for social science research, however, Flyvbjerg moves from a critique of Habermas to a defense of Foucault that culminates in his conflation of power as an analytic category with power as a criterion of truth. That conflation does not withstand scrutiny. To recognize the politics of knowledge need not commit one to the erroneous view that the validity of knowledge claims can be determined only by a contest of wills.

"The concept of power is at the heart of political enquiry. Indeed, it is probably the central concept of both descriptive and normative analysis" (Isaac 2003, 54). Like many core concepts, however, there is little agreement about how power should be defined, and less about how it should be operationalized for empirical investigations. Jeffrey Isaac (1987, 2003) has provided a helpful taxonomy of power that distinguishes voluntarist, hermeneutic, structural, and postmodern conceptions, a richer array than the Habermasian and Foucaultian options considered by Flyvbjerg. To illuminate the inadequacy of the conflation of power and truth, the final section of this essay uses Isaac's conceptual framework to map a variety of approaches to the study of power in political science. It then surveys feminist critiques of the most popular conceptualizations of power and creative appropriations of less popular conceptions to show how value-laden disciplinary paradigms render certain dimensions of political life invisible, allowing dynamics of gender power to escape serious investigation. Finally, I demonstrate why the validity of these feminist analyses do not and should not turn on their acceptance by popular assent, either of the acceptance of the majority of citizens in a polity, or the acceptance of a majority of political scientists.

Rooted in social contract theory and the methodological individualism that informs behavioralist and rational choice approaches to the study of politics, the "voluntarist" conception of power might be characterized as a staple of modernity. Initially conceived by Hobbes, the voluntarist conception ties power to the voluntary intentions and strategies of individuals, who seek to promote their interests. Within this frame, power is nothing other than "the present means to some future apparent good" (*Leviathan*, Part I, ch. 10, p. 150). Situated in a world of conflicting wills and scarce resources, the Hobbesian individual often uses power to eliminate obstacles to the satisfaction of desire. And since the obstacles to be overcome frequently include the wills of other individuals, the voluntarist conception of power has been construed within political science as the capacity to get others to do what they would not otherwise do (Lasswell 1950; Dahl 1957). Thus, the individual's means to attain desired ends slides easily into coercion: power as the force to accomplish one's objectives, or, perhaps less brutally, power as the capacity to secure compliance by manipulation of rewards and punishments.

Despite its individualist premises, the Hobbesian voluntarist conception of power has also been adapted by "realists"[5] and "neorealists" within international relations to provide an account of the fundamental operations of the international system. Taking Hobbes's depiction of the "war of all against all" as a paradigm for international relations, realists posit "anarchy" as the inevitable condition existing among sovereign states. Arguing that the rational response of states to anarchy is to maximize power, realists conflate "national interest" with the pursuit of power and define international politics as an unceasing struggle for power in a realm devoid of an absolute sovereign capable of enforcing agreements.

Feminist scholars have developed detailed critiques of the voluntarist conception of power, demonstrating that it depends upon a defective and markedly androcentric conception of human nature; it equates individual action and international affairs with a particular model of "abstract masculinity;" it legitimates immoral and amoral action on the part of individuals and states; and it remains oblivious to the social conventions that structure human relationships and the relations among states (Pateman 1988; DiStefano 1991; Tickner 1991; Steans 1998).

Feminist scholars have also pointed out that the voluntarist conception of power arbitrarily restricts the research agenda of political scientists, preventing certain political questions from being perceived and empirically investigated. For example, although, according to the Interparliamentary Union, 85 percent of the seats in national legislatures and more than 99 percent of the offices of president, prime minister, and foreign secretary are currently in the hands of men, the absence of women from national and international decision making is a "nonquestion" according to the voluntarist model of power. For it is assumed that the answer is already known: individual choice mediated by the contest of conflicting wills is the explanation for the distribution of decision-making power. Over the past thirty years, feminist scholars have proven that "individual-choice" explanations for women's underrepresentation in elective and appointive offices are woefully inadequate and serve only to mask the potent operations of gender power and gender structure (Rule and Zimmerman 1994; Flammang 1997; Peterson and Runyan 1999; Chappell 2002; Mazur 2002; McDonagh 2002). These detailed studies illuminate an additional failing of the voluntarist conception of power: it cannot explain how or why agents are able to exercise the power that they do exercise. It is oblivious to forces that shape individual "preferences" or "determine" the will. It is oblivious to institutional contexts that enable and constrain individual action. It is oblivious to structural forces that ensure that individuals are not equally unfettered subjects. It masks recurrent patterns of constraint upon individual choice linked to race, gender, class, nationality, sexuality.

As an alternative to the voluntarist model of power, the "hermeneutic" conception, developed within the tradition of German phenomenology, "conceives power as constituted in the shared meanings of given communities" (Isaac 2003, 58). Attuned to the varying symbolic and normative constructs that shape the practical rationalities of situated social agents, the hermeneutic model of power is keenly aware of the intersubjective conventions that make action, in general, and the use of power, in particular, possible and intelligible.

Some feminist scholars have appropriated the hermeneutic conception of power to investigate the political effects of gender symbolism, that is, the coding of certain forms of human conduct as inherently masculine or feminine. They have suggested that gender symbolism generates a logic of appropriate behavior that shapes individuals' self-understandings and aspirations, thereby structuring social and political opportunities. When rationality, competence, and leadership are coded as inherently masculine characteristics, for example, male power is naturalized and legitimated. When the nation is symbolized as a woman and men are exhorted to risk their lives to defend and protect "her," norms of citizenship and soldiering are masculinized. When nationalist narratives privilege the roles of men as "founding fathers," women's contributions to nation-building are erased. When these invented pasts are institutionalized within founding myths, notions of the "national family" reinscribe fathers' rule and mothers' obedience as natural even as they create and legitimate new race and gender hierarchies. When "national security" is promoted by increasing militarization, the growing physical insecurity of women in areas adjacent to military bases and in areas of conflict is eclipsed, driving a wedge between the interests of states and the physical well-being of women (Enloe 1990, 1993, 2000; McClintock 1995; Peterson and Runyon 1999). Advancing cogent accounts of subtle processes through which male dominance is naturalized, feminist scholars demonstrate how gender power is embedded in intersubjective value systems and structures of belief, which constitute the identities and aspirations of gendered political agents, thereby constraining the possibilities for individual choice and action.

Other feminist scholars have attempted to link gendered asymmetries of power in beliefs and values to structural features of social and political life. They draw insights from a structural model of power, which emphasizes that practices of inequality become embedded in institutions and structures in ways that enable male advantage to operate independently of the will of particular agents. Developing concepts of gender structure and gendered institutions (Duerst-Lahti and Kelly 1995; Kenney 1996), feminist scholars have sought to demonstrate how male dominance in political institutions of the nation-state and in the international arena has been converted into rules, routines, practices, and policies that serve and promote men's interests, normalize a male monopoly of power, and create political opportunity structures that favor men.

Studies of political parties in South Asia, Australia, Canada, Europe, Latin America, and the United States, for example, have demonstrated that male-dominant party elites have been remarkably resourceful in shifting the locus of power from formal to informal mechanisms when women have gained access to formal decision-making sites (Alvarez 1990; Basu 1995; Chappell 2002; Freeman 2000; Jaquette 1989; Jaquette and Wolchik 1998; Kelly et al., 2001). Parties that differ from one another in ideological commitments and policy objectives have been remarkably similar and consistent in allowing male gatekeepers to structure candidate selection processes to prevent women from being chosen for open, safe, or winnable seats in legislative races. Patronage practices within political parties also manifest pervasive gender bias.

Feminist studies of national parliaments and legislatures have revealed the operation of powerful gender norms. The standard operating procedures of parliaments in Britain, Canada, and Australia, for example, feature loud, aggressive, and combative behavior such as screaming, shouting, and sneering that can create "no-win" situations for women members. For women who adopt this combative style are ridiculed and patronized by their male counterparts, while women who opt for a more demure, consultative and collaborative style are labeled "weak" or "unfit" for the job. Indeed, Chappell (2002) has documented patterns of gender harassment in parliamentary systems as women who rise to speak are greeted with increased heckling, coughing, hissing, kiss-blowing, and mimicry in falsetto voices. Within the United States, women legislators who refuse to adopt coercive negotiating strategies are often characterized by their male counterparts as failing to understand the rules of the game (Rosenthal 2000). Women who chair legislative committees confront forms of opposition in hearings—challenges to their authority, refusal to respect their rulings—that men in comparable positions of authority do not confront (Kathlene 1994; Hawkesworth 2003a). Male legislators often perceive women legislators in terms of raced and gendered stereotypes incompatible with the men's conceptions of "power players" (Thomas 1994; Rosenthal 2000; Smooth 2001).

In documenting the operation of gender power within the official institutions of state, feminist scholars have provided powerful evidence that there are political dynamics at work within these institutions that have not been recognized by mainstream approaches. They have also demonstrated that the raced and gendered hierarchies created, maintained, and reproduced within the institutions of state have palpable effects on policymaking and on domestic and foreign policies. The validity of these cogent arguments do not depend on their acceptance by the majority of political scientists, many of whom have never read feminist scholarship. Nor do they rely upon foundationalist claims concerning absolute truth. Keenly aware of the complexity of all knowledge claims, feminist scholars accept antifoundationalist criteria of truth, defending a minimalist standard of rationality that requires belief to be apportioned to evidence and insisting that no assertion be immune from critical assessment. Deploying this minimalist standard, feminist analysis can demonstrate the inadequacies of accounts of human nature and practices derived from an evidentiary base of only half the species; refute unfounded claims about women's "nature" that are premised upon an atheoretical naturalism; identify androcentric bias in theories, methods, and concepts and show how this bias undermines explanatory force; and demonstrate that the numerous obstacles to women's full participation in social, political, and economic life are humanly created and hence susceptible to alteration. In providing sophisticated and detailed analyses of concrete situations, feminist inquiry can dispel distortions and mystifications that abound in dominant disciplinary paradigms. On the basis of a consistent fallibilism consonant with life in a world of contingencies, feminist scholars need not claim universal, ahistorical validity for their analyses. They need not assert that theirs is the only or the final word on complex questions. In the absence of claims of universal validity, feminist accounts derive their justificatory force from their capacity to illuminate existing social relations, demonstrate the deficiencies of alternative interpretations, and debunk opposing views. Thus, feminist researchers provide concrete reasons in specific contexts for the superiority of their accounts. Such claims to superiority are derived not from some privileged "scientific" method, nor from putative popular acceptance, but from the strength of rational argument, from the ability to demonstrate point by point the deficiencies of alternative explanations. At their best, feminist analyses engage both the critical intellect and the world; they surpass androcentric accounts because in their systematicity more is examined and less is assumed.

Perspectivism does not do justice to the need for systematicity in analyses of the structural dimensions of social and political life. Although much can be gained from the recognition that there are many sides to every story and many voices to provide alternative accounts, the escape from the monotony of monologue should not be at the expense of the very notion of truth. The need to debunk scientistic pretensions about the unproblematic nature of the objective world does not require the total repudiation of objective criteria for truth, much less an appeal to popular acceptance. Treating sophisticated feminist critiques as simply one voice among many does not contribute to more democratic political studies or to more democratic polities. On the contrary, it legitimates mainstream political scientists' neglect of the operations of gender power documented by feminist scholars, contributing to the accreditation and perpetuation of distorted accounts of the political world.

The relation of political scientists to the political world they seek to describe and explain has been the subject of recurrent debate (Moon 1975; Gunnell 1998). Post-structuralists inspired by the insights of Michel Foucault have suggested that every scientific discourse is productive, generating power-knowledge constellations that create a world in its own image. Although Flyvbjerg cites Foucault on the productive power of knowledge, he misconstrues the implications of this Foucaultian stance. Feminist scholars working within a poststructuralist frame have suggested that political science itself is a constitutive discourse (Hawkesworth 2003b). The conceptual apparatus of the discipline contributes to the production of the political subject, understood simultaneously as one who is subjected and one who resists subjugation. Disciplinary accounts of politics, law, tradition, and war produce gendered political subjects who both conform and resist gendered divisions of power and opportunity. Failure to recognize the discipline's own relation to the twinned operations of gendered subjugation and resistance can leave political scientists at a loss to explain some of the most profound transformations of political life. For example, mainstream political scientists are ill equipped to explain the sustained mobilizations of

Brazilian women who constituted 80 percent of the activists who ousted military rule in Brazil (Alvarez 1990) or the collective struggles of Korean women against state violence and economic exploitation that helped break down military rule in South Korea in the 1980s. Minimally, the replication of gender bias in political science impedes the discipline's ability to explain the political world. More alarming, the perpetuation of definitions of politics, power, and international relations that privilege the intellectual investigation of masculinist practices in male-dominant sites as the protected preserve of political science reproduces and legitimates male power and gender injustice.

Behavioralism in political science was wedded to the mistaken beliefs that definitions can be value-free, that concepts can be operationalized in a thoroughly nonprescriptive manner, and that research methodologies are neutral techniques for the collection and organization of data. Behavioralism conceived the political scientist as a passive observer who merely describes and explains what exists in the political world. Post-behavioralism challenged the myth of value neutrality, suggesting that all research is theoretically constituted and value permeated. But, in illuminating the means by which the belief in value-free research masked the valuative component of political inquiry, post-behavioralism did not question the fundamental separation between events in the political world and their retrospective analysis by political scientists. In recent years, critical theorists, post-structuralists, and other keen observers of the contemporary world have suggested that this notion of critical distance is yet another myth. Emphasizing that every scientific discourse is productive, generating positive effects within its domain of inquiry, post-structuralists caution that political science must also be understood as a productive force that creates a world in its own image, even as it employs conceptions of passivity, neutrality, detachment and objectivity to disguise and conceal its role (Foucault 1973, 1977a). In a period when "democratization" coincides with a host of gendered economic and political dislocations (Hawkesworth 2001), there are good reasons to treat these cautions seriously, for particular methodologies in political science not only construe the political world differently but also act subtly to promote specific modes of political life.

Contrary to Flyvbjerg's optimistic prescription that social science can "matter," if only it embraces and deploys Aristotelian *phronesis* in the world of social values, any division of scientific labor that reinscribes the fact/value dichotomy will replicate the problems of bias and distortion discussed here. The critical challenge for political science, in my view, is not how to make political science matter—it does, profoundly—but how to assist political scientists to develop sophistication about our knowledge production, heightened awareness of ideological bias, normative presuppositions, and the political consequences of own research.

## NOTES

1. The term "positivism" was first coined by the French sociologist Auguste Comte, who suggested that scientific understanding operates in the realm of the "positive," which denotes "real" or "actual" existence. Advancing a version of empiricism, Comte suggested that scientists must eschew the metaphysical and theological realms and restrict their investigations to observable facts and the relations that hold among observed phenomena. Within this finite sphere of the empirically observable, scientific inquiry could discover the "laws" governing empirical events. In the early twentieth century, a group of philosophers of science, known as the "Vienna Circle," developed "logical positivism," which further restricted the possibilities for valid knowledge by elaborating the "verification criterion of meaning." Focusing on how to establish the truth of specific statements about the empirical world, the verification criterion stipulated that a contingent proposition is meaningful if and only if it can be empirically verified, that is, if there is an empirical method for deciding if the proposition is true or false. Within the natural sciences and the social sciences, positivist commitments generated a number of methodological techniques designed to ensure the truth, not of propositions but of scientific investigations. Chief among these is the dichotomous division of the world into the realms of the "empirical" and the "nonempirical." The empirical realm, comprising all that can be corroborated by the senses, is circumscribed as the legitimate sphere of scientific investigation. As a residual category, the nonempirical encompasses everything else—religion, philosophy, ethics, aesthetics, and evaluative discourse in general, as well as myth, dogma and superstition—and is relegated beyond the sphere of science. Within this frame of reference, science, operating within the realm of the observable, restricting its focus to descriptions, explanations and predictions that are intersubjectively testable, can achieve objective knowledge. The specific techniques requisite to the achievement of objective knowledge have been variously defined by positivism and critical rationalism. For systematic critiques of positivism, see Brown 1977, 1998; Hawkesworth 2003b; Latour 1987; Latour and Woolgar 1979; Longino 1990; Stockman 1983).

2. Within recent work in the philosophy of science, the epistemological and ontological implications of the post-positivist understanding of theory have been

the subject of extensive debate. Arguing that the theoretical constitution of human knowledge has ontological as well as epistemological implications, "antirealists" have suggested that there is no point in asking about the nature of the world independent of our theories about it (Laudan 1990). Consequently the truth status of theories must be bracketed. But antirealists have insisted that theories need not be true to be good, i.e., to solve problems (van Fraasen 1980; Churchland and Hooker 1985). Metaphysical "realists," on the other hand, have emphasized that, even if the only access to the world is through theories about it, a logical distinction can still be upheld between reality and how we conceive it, between truth and what we believe (Harre 1986). Hilary Putnam (1981, 1983, 1988, 1990) has advanced "pragmatic realism" as a more tenable doctrine. Putnam accepts that all concepts are theoretically constituted and culturally mediated and that the "world" does not "determine" what can be said about it. Nonetheless, it makes sense on pragmatic grounds to insist that truth and falsity are not merely a matter of decision and that there is an external reality that constrains our conceptual choices. Following Putnam's lead, "scientific realists" have argued that scientific theories are referential in an important sense and as such can be comparatively assessed in terms of their approximations of truth (Glymour 1980; Newton-Smith 1981; Miller 1987.

3. The term "theory" has multiple meanings, which further complicate understandings of theory's relation to "fact." While positivist conceptions of theories as interrelated systems of "laws" (empirically confirmed hypotheses or inductive generalizations) possessing explanatory power exclude values from the theoretical domain, critical rationalist, contextualist, hermeneutic, philosophical, normative, ideological, and coherentist conceptions construe theory as thoroughly value laden. Post-positivist presupposition theories of science conceive theory as a constellation of culturally freighted presuppositions that structure perception and cognition. For fuller elaboration of competing conceptions of theory and their implications for the fact/value dichotomy and for research in political science, see Hawkesworth 1988 and Gunnell 1998.

4. Political theorists will find Flyvbjerg's extrapolations from Aristotle, Nietzsche, and Foucault troubling. In his effort to demonstrate commonalities in themes and approaches among these philosophers, he ignores Aristotle's teleological ontology that lends objective force to *phronesis* in ethical and political matters; he turns Nietzsche into a pragmatist and Foucault into an Aristotelian proponent of praxis.

5. The term "realist" as deployed in international relations differs markedly from the use of the term in philosophy of science. The realist paradigm, which dominated international relations theory for much of the post–World War II period, assumes that anarchy is the prevailing international condition and that the rational response of states to such anarchy is to maximize their power. Thus,

realist approaches to international relations privilege the state as the key actor in international relations, conflate "national interest" with the pursuit of power, and draw sharp distinctions between domestic politics, which operate in accordance with the rule of law, and international politics, which is understood as a struggle for power in a realm devoid of a sovereign power capable of enforcing agreements.

# 9

# The Bounds of Rationality

## *Stewart Clegg*

Decision making is always bounded in its rationality by the great depths and far reaches of uncertainty and ignorance within which it will always be constituted, which is what makes it an example of phronesis (Flyvbjerg 2001). Phronesis, an Aristotelian term, refers to a discipline that is pragmatic, variable, context dependent, based on practical rationality, and inherently unlaw-like. That is to say, because rationality is bounded, it can never account for itself: hence, reflexivity is inherent to its practice.

Human rationality is always context dependent because, as Ludwig Wittgenstein (1999) demonstrated unequivocally, no rule could ever account for its own interpretation—thus, context cannot be reduced to rules. All science occurs in the context of what realist philosophers of science refer to as "standing conditions." These standing conditions provide for the prevalence of the sense that the science makes of the world of object-relations, against naturally occurring conditions. Standing conditions are definite sets of contextual experimental conditions, such as ensuring a sterile laboratory environment or maintaining a vacuum or a stable temperature. Without these conditions, maintained by the experimentalist, the predicted relations that the research setting seeks to display would not occur. Thus, a context for stable object relations has to be artfully contrived so that the context has no effect other than that sought experimentally. A science of objects needs to appear to be context-free; otherwise, it cannot provide a general theory. By contrast, studies that take interpretations as their frame of reference are only as ontologically secure as these intersubjective interpretations are stable.

We should not be too voluntarist about sense making. One person's sense is rarely as binding as is any other's. All sense is made in a relational world and the relational space is three-dimensional. History, power, and imagination constitute the three dimensions. History represents the dead weight of tradition, like a nightmare on the brain of the living, as Karl Marx once had it. The rules for making this sense, and not some other, have an inertial, historical quality to them. They are such rules because they were established as such interpretive devices in the past. The second dimension concerns power. Without power being exercised in concrete episodic relations and thus disciplining, disposing, and reproducing them, extant traditions could never be preserved or transformed, where an existing circuit of power is broken (Clegg 1989, from which this account is developed). Finally, a capacity to be able to conceive a difference—imagination—has to be allied to the capacity to make a difference—that is, power. Historical traditions change, not inexorably but for reasons of power and imagination. Subjects of rule can cut off their rulers' heads. Monarchies can tumble. What was sovereign becomes debased. What was rhetorically subject—the will of the people—can become rhetorically dominant. Imagination—the capacity to conceive a difference—is at the kernel of planned change.

Not all change is planned. And this is where context comes in. Context is a matter of stable sense-making conditions, for which there are no guarantees. They are ultimately subject to unpredictable, arbitrary, and random variation. (My favorite example of such variation is the combined and interdependent impact of fleas, rats, viruses, technology, geography, and climatic conditions in transforming the balance of power between lords and peasants in fourteenth-century Europe, ushering in the transformation of feudal relations of production—see the account in Clegg 1989).

Natural science is full of cases of random variation: the impact of meteorites or of volcanic-induced climate changes (through the blanket effect of volcanic ash) on the ecosystem are cases in point. Random and arbitrary variation in the contextual standing conditions need not come just from some exogenous source of change, such as a meteorite or geological activity. While these are clearly important, there are other, more mundane sources of variation for social scientists to consider. For instance, in the sphere of organizations, all attempts at organized corporate sense making rely on the organization's power to secure this sense. Potentially, any organization's power to do this may be subject to erosion. Such erosion may be defined as a diminished capacity on the part of the corporate actor to maintain the set of standing conditions that, contextually, enabled this power to structure particular episodes in terms of its preferences. Erosion may derive from the failure of existing imagination on the part of that power, success in implementing its imagination on the part of some other putative power, or random and arbitrary acts that serve to destabilize the existing context. At the margin, they can break existing circuits of power, refixing them on new passage points made obligatory.

History is the representation of what has elapsed, as a sense made from a momentary here-and-now that frames the retrospection that makes its sense possible. An element of contingency resides in those relevancies included and excluded by its retrospection. Power resides in these actions—what I call theorizing power (Clegg 1975). Imagination—by definition—cannot be controlled. And power is always potentially capable of being destabilized if it cannot secure the episodic conditions that contextually enable it to be powerful. History, power, and imagination are both a mighty and an unstable triangulation of forces. Working in harness, they can make particular intersubjective worlds of sensemaking seem stable, almost object-like, in their relations. When such conditions of and for sense making are achieved, they become, simultaneously, both the object and the subject of social science. That is to say, they provide a context that can be assumed in both mundane and scientific sense making.

Intersubjective capabilities may work in ways that are, at any moment in their historical process, potentially ineffable because they are not produced according to rule. Ineffability may arise for many reasons. The imagination of actors may create a rule as yet unknown. Consequently, any extant organizational order will always be rule guided rather than rule governed. There is no external experimentalist holding the conditions of history, power, and imagination stable in order to maintain the existing benefits of doing so, although many of those who do benefit may be expected to try to act as if they were such experimentalists. However, there are no authoritative governors outside everyday life. Only the existing winners and losers and the sense they make, and have made for them, of their human condition can serve to secure the conditions of everyday life.

It is important to realize that these conditions are experienced, simultaneously, as both structure and agency. The rule guidedness that may be observed by social scientists is not the outcome of structures working on agents, as it is often represented as being. Rule guidedness is the outcome of actors and their practices situated in relation to structures, which in turn are instantiated in practices: for example, the Highway Code produces rule-guided outcomes in terms of the semiotic significance of red and green traffic lights for motorists. It is not that red causes an absence of movement and green provokes a presence of movement. In certain contexts, there may be auditory-sense data that contradict those that are visual. For instance, at the sound of an approaching ambulance, police, or fire vehicle siren, the traffic at both the red and the green lights at an intersection may be stationary until the vehicle emitting the auditory-sense datum has visibly passed the intersection. As practical experimentalists, we understand the situational nature of both structures and actions and their mutual implication. Nonetheless, in organization theory we conventionally find research concentrating on one side or the other of the agency/structure divide (usually the structural side), rather than looking at questions about "what structural factors influence individual actions, how those actions are constructed, and their structural consequences" (Flyvbjerg 2001, 138).

Rationality is always situational. And because it is always contextually situational, it is always implicated with power. No context stands outside power. If that were the case, then it would exist nowhere, outside understanding, outside possibility, outside sense. As Michel Foucault (1977a, 27–28) says, in *Discipline and Punish,* "power produces knowledge . . . power and knowledge directly imply one another . . . there is no power relation without the creative constitution of a field of knowledge, nor any knowledge that does not presuppose and constitute at the same time power relations." In such a view, rationalities and powers are fused. Different power actors will operate in and through different rationalities. The different rationalities will have their different rules for producing sense— at the more formal outer limits—for producing truth. In fact, sense and truth cannot be separated from the ensemble of rules that constitute them—and their obverse—as such.

To adopt a discursive analysis of rationality is to see what people say as the means whereby rationality and power become interwoven. People may be in a position to say anything, given the infinity of discourse, but they rarely surprise the well-grounded analyst with their discursive moves. Language games are not predictable, but they are explicable. We can understand and constitute the senses that are being made, as well as the conditions of existence and underlying tacit assumptions that make such sense possible. And in this way we can begin to understand the different forms of agency that find expression in organizational contexts, where the players make sense of rules that they actively construct and deconstruct in the context of their action.

Rather than being law-like phenomena, rules are always constituted locally, in context, by the actors themselves, rather than being the objective instantiation of a general principle or law. Contextualism implies that whatever regularities occur empirically will always be situational. Researchers need to understand that these are not likely to be the result of either remote laws operating behind the backs of the actors concerned or an idiosyncratic researcher's interpretation of the scene in question. To the extent that the researcher has researched the situational ethics of the context at hand, then they will have a sound grasp of the socially and historically conditioned context within which sense is made. With these understandings, researchers can avoid the relativism that they are sometimes charged with: their understandings will be framed within deeply embedded foundations that the actors find normal and acceptable to use. In matters of interpretation there is always room for disagreement, and it is no different for the organization researcher. One interpretation is rarely as good as another. Some will always be more plausible in terms of the contexts within which they are produced and received.

Unlike phenomena in an object realm, where the matter at hand has no understanding of itself, actors who possess understanding always populate organizations. Their understanding extends both to an appreciation of each other and to those artifacts that they constitute (which sometimes constitute them—for instance, a machine operator) and with which they interact. Thus, organizations are always more subject-realms than merely object-realms, although, as objects of reflection, they can be subjected to object-like treatment and routines. But this does not inescapably secure their nature as something ontologically just so. Of course, there is no shortage of theories in organization studies that presume to offer abstract, context-independent concepts, but on close examination these theories always betray the origins of their context-dependent assumptions. It could not be otherwise. These assumptions may be more or less tacit or more or less reflexive, but their context cannot be excluded, because such context always defines the relevancy of the phenomena that any theory addresses. Like its precepts for practice, organization theorists always study what is bounded rationality. And they do so with bounded rationality.

## Organizing Power

Many accounts of power that were available in the social sciences have been limited in their imagination: almost entirely framed by the assumption that if power was not a causal phenomenon, it was nothing. The lack of imagination was, in fact, the result of an excess of (Anglo-Saxon) history. Since at least the time of Thomas Hobbes, power had been considered as a causal concept. For power to be able to be identified, someone had to do something, directly, observably, unmediatedly, to another. In this model—epitomized by Robert Dahl (1957)—one could focus only on directly observable causal relations between definitely mediated actors. Causal relations required such connectivity to be clear. However, in the broader literature on power in social theory, a central debate had been sparked around concepts of "nondecision making" and "nonissues," after the impact of Morton Bachrach and Peter Baratz's (1962) work. Basically, they were interested in trying to surmount the behaviorist frame of dominant models in which something had to be seen to have happened in order for it to be considered a phenomenon. In the terms of Sherlock Holmes, they were more interested not in the things that did happen, but the things that did not—like the famous dog that did not bark in the night in one of Holmes's mysteries. Why were certain issues kept off the agenda? Why were some things not an occasion for power contestation, their very legitimacy seen as a part of their power?

The broad social-theory agenda within which power has been constituted in the wider social sciences was shaped in its outer coordinates by a continuing debate with Marx and Friedrich Nietzsche. The debate with Marx was conducted most notably by Steven Lukes (1974), the English political philosopher, especially in his use of the concept of "hegemony," a concept that had become inexorably associated with the work of the Italian Marxist and theorist of civil society Antonio Gramsci (1971). Nietszche's influence could be seen most clearly in the French historian Foucault's (1977a) *Discipline and Punish,* although it was also evident in Max Weber's (1978) work. Each of these theorists had a significant impact on the scholarship on power. Foucault introduced a new mode of analysis of power and was opposed to any such opposition as "science" and "ideology" or "true" and "false" consciousness. He opposed the assumptions of imperial and imperious correctness contained in either side of the oppositions: the security of the ground from which ex cathedra judgements about the "truth" could be dispensed could invariably, he would argue, be shown to be historically changeable, rather than constant. For Foucault, one should not think of power without also thinking of knowledge. Power operated not only in a prohibitive way, telling one what one could not so, but also operated through knowledge, through everyday ways of sense making that were more or less institutionalized in disciplinary knowledge, in a permissive, positive manner—constructing the normalcy of the normal.

For those scholars for whom Weber and Foucault are a source of vital questions about the nature of research, foundational assumptions, methodologies, evidence, and ethics, a quite different pragmatics of research flourishes to the dominant model in the U.S. discourse on power, which has clearly been one of "positivism" (ten Bos 2000; Clegg 2002). At issue are the unequivocal establishment of a casual relation and the direction of that causality in determining matters of power between phenomena treated as if they were a part of the object world. Positivism is doubly functional: it enables one to create an illusion of consensus in both theory and reality. So, those voices that might disturb the consensus by raising issues that cannot be answered within the causal, objectivist apparatus must be ignored. Instead, research should search for the nature of reality as that which is open to inspection rather than that which is beneath the surface, beyond the gaze, of an objective observer recording what is. In Andrew Wicks and R. Edward Freeman's (1998, 125) terms, positivists seek to be finders, not makers, of reality (even as they artfully construct their domain assumptions and standing conditions to do so). Essentially, they are naive descriptivists, neutral observers of what just happens to be. They take no stance toward the nature of being; in other words, they simply register that which is without reflection—which could only be speculative and prescriptive—or why it might be that way. Their ethic of value freedom places them beyond ethics—it is a kind of ethics that you have when you don't presume any other ethics. Of course, these articles of faith are designed to protect science from contamination by other, lesser forms of knowledge.

Against this view of the world, one may argue that, phronetically and pragmatically, while the nature of reality is unequivocally real—it is "out there"—our ways of knowing it as such are somewhat more contestable. While we have highly elaborated codes for making sense of phenomena— such as the methods of empirical science—we should recognize these for the codes they are. They are sophisticated ways of narrating the stories

that matter to us as scientists and people, of giving them credence, of pass-
ing them on in the world. Reality cannot be represented in some propositionally pure form that is untouched by the context of meaning in which it
is embedded. Hobbes's contemporaries were mightily impressed with
springs, flywheels, and forces, seeking out signs that would enable them to
unravel the mechanical nature of the universe and of being in it, as Isaac
Newton did soon thereafter. In speaking in the scholarly language of his
day, Hobbes bequeathed a view of power that could not encapsulate action
at a distance, that could not conceptualize how the standing conditions for
any action might constitute the mechanics of its outcome, and could not
cope with the power of abstracted representations—its own included.

One conclusion that we can draw from all this is that all inquiry is fundamentally narrative—it tells a story about states of affairs that is more or
less plausible within the conventions of particular narrative communities.
Or, as Wittgenstein (1999) puts it, science is a language game—like any
other. Or, in Richard Rorty's (1991) similar terms, experience ordered
though our sense data may cause us to hold certain views of the matter in
question, but it cannot tell us which views we should be considering in the
first place. The insight is old, however. Weber quoted Leo Tolstoy in a
speech to students at Munich University in 1918:

> Science is meaningless because it gives no answer to our question, the only
> question important for us: "What shall we do and how shall we live?" That
> science does not give an answer to this is indisputable. The only question
> that remains is the sense in which science gives "no" answer, and whether or
> not science might yet be of some use to the one who puts the question cor-
> rectly. (Weber 1948: 143)

One consequence of positivism has been to obscure this most basic question. It has created an epistemic context in which such a question cannot
even be considered. Instead, ethics are something else outside the questions one asks of reality as a scholar: that certain causal regularities may be
empirically observed of a phenomenon does not enable one to ask, Why
these regularities and not some others? How, for instance, is authority
achieved as a set of patterned preferences whose prevalence demonstrates
its facticity? Moral rearmament around functionalism may suppress internal conflict concerning methods and epistemologies, which may be seen as
dangerous, corrosive of moral authority, and destructive of professional
reputation and discipline. I would argue that intellectual communities—

just as political communities—that suppress conflict do so at considerable risk to their vitality. As Flyvbjerg (2001, 108) suggests, "suppressing conflict is suppressing freedom, because the privilege to engage in conflict and power struggle is part of freedom." He goes on to suggest that "perhaps social and political theories that ignore or marginalize conflicts are potentially oppressive, too."

Any theory that allows for debate only on its own terms would be repressive, oppressive, and antithetical to the spirit of an intellectually open society. It is conflict that sustains openness, and without such conflict the genuine democracy that is essential to the articulation of reason is lacking. Reason resides not so much in what is said, as Jurgen Habermas (1971) argues, as in the formal conditions that constitute the conditions within which what is said can be expressed. The more democratic a discourse, the more legitimate will be the inevitable conflicts of interest that arise and the less there will be barriers to their expression. And there is every reason for democratic discourse as the basis of science: if there are barriers to expression, if certain styles of work are demonized, are disdained, then there is no open society, just a certain exclusively cultivated clubbishness, cultish commitments to things being seen the way that people like us (and not people who are not people like us) see them. Sterility, banality, orthodoxy—this is what ensues when debate is stifled in the name of order. In political science, it is called totalitarianism. It is what happens when power overwhelms imagination—especially the imagination of those out of power, whose imagination could rewrite history.

One of the advantages of Foucault's approach to power is that it "integrates rationality and power, knowledge and power, reason and power, truth and power" (Flyvbjerg 2001, 124). Power is the axis. Power frees imagination, and power writes history. Without power, poverty, disease, and despair are what face the human condition. Only power—the capacity to make a difference to existing conditions of existence in ways that are significant for the actors concerned—can free imagination. Otherwise, it rots in the gutters of history. Power writes history. That the histories we inherit have overwhelmingly been those of the dominant actors strutting their stuff in the various stages of the human comedy—the men, the whites, the colonialists, the rich, the powerful, the educated—is hardly surprising. Life on the margins, in service, bondage, or slavery of one kind or another, rarely affords room, time, or tools for intense reflection. As Foucault (1977a, 27) suggests, in *Discipline and Punish,* "we should abandon a whole tradition that allows us to imagine that knowledge can exist only where the power relations are suspended and that knowledge can develop only outside its injunctions, its demands and its interests." On the contrary, as he goes on to suggest, power produces knowledge; they are directly implicated in each other. Reflexivity is essential to understanding this relation, suggests Foucault. We need to be able to see how power actually functions in context. Elsewhere, in the context of a discussion of the significance of reflexivity, I have elaborated a general and guiding theoretical point:

> Those theoretical positions able to account, reflexively, for their own theorizing, as well as whatever it is that they are theorizing about, will be clearest about their own identity, and the extent to which it is partial or formed in dialogue with other positions. The recognition of the 'other' is crucial: self-regarding behaviour in the absence of the recognition of the and by others is of no value in itself. On these criteria it is not the alleged 'disinterestedness' of a position that makes it worthwhile, but the degree of reflexivity that it exhibits in relation to the conditions of its own existence. Severing the conversational elements that nurtured the theory in the first place and which link it t practice makes it harder to attain this reflexivity. Thus we argue for the grounding of theoretical claims in local and specific circumstances rather than their radical and rapid translation out of them. In an organizational world that is part of the social, which is inscribed with the materiality of words, and the indeterminacy of meaning, such conversational stretch is essential. Otherwise the paradigm closes, conversational practice becomes monologue, and reflexivity declines accordingly. (Clegg and Hardy 1996, 701)

Reflexive analysis is never innocent of context—that is its beauty and its strength. It situates itself on the boundaries between the seemingly possible and the impossible, with the desire to shift these boundaries. Such a position is the ideal place from which to think differently in order to act differently, as Flyvbjerg (2001, 127) puts it. It is from such a position that one is best able to use power in the service of imagination and the making of history.

## Conclusion

Theory and analysis are best cultivated not in an ideal world of paradigm consensus or domination but in a world of discursive plurality, where obstinate differences in domain assumptions are explicit and explicitly tolerated. A good conversation assumes engagement with alternate points of view, argued against vigorously but ultimately, where these positions pass the criteria of reason rather than prejudice, tolerated as legitimate points of view.

What constitutes reason? Well, we can start by observing what does not. It seems barely reasonable to hold to a standard for analysis that Flyvbjerg (2001, 1) and Richard Sennett (1995, 43) refer to as "physics envy." Conventionally, it is proposed that organization studies should "model reality and search for essentialist underlying structures via scientific study" (Wicks and Freeman 1998, 130). Essentially, in philosophical terms, this is the propositional strategy that was outlined by Wittgenstein (1922) in the *Tracatus Logico-Philosophicus*. And in the *Philosophical Investigations* (1972), the same author decisively repudiated such a position. The earlier philosophy suggests that one should seek to make ideal representations, in an eternal, unchanging way, through absolutely lucid and unequivocal propositional statements, concerning the essential qualities of the social world of organizations—as if they were as simple to read as iron filings around magnetic poles. The later Wittgenstein (1999) suggested that one should explore a phenomenon firsthand, instead; he used a very clear representational, cartographic metaphor to make his point.

> Imagine this case: I tell someone that I walked a certain route, going by a map which I had prepared beforehand. Thereupon I show him the map, and it consist of lines on a piece of paper; but I cannot explain how these lines are the map of my movements, I cannot tell him any rule for interpreting the map. Yet I did follow the drawing with all the characteristic tokens of reading a map. (Wittgenstein 1972, 653)

Wittgenstein wrote about maps on several occasions (Gasking and Jackson 1967). His use of maps, rather than establishing the unequivocal mapping of a reality in a precise representation, was more a means of knowing a phenomenon, such as the City of London, to be used to enable one to walk highways and byways, side streets and main streets. In parlance more contemporary than that which Wittgenstein had available to him, perhaps of one who aspires to explore the underbelly and side streets of a city, such a mapping would probably be considered a "rough guide." Rather than construct some Whiggish history of the discourse that peaks in the latest paper in the most prestigious journal, one should seek to show some of the byways and side streets, not just the main highways through which traffic passes today (see Andrew Chan's 2001 discussion of "Whiggish history").

Wittgenstein's metaphor of the city can be extended further. Organizations are somewhat like the city: organic, constantly recreating themselves, tearing out the present heart and soul, routing new freeways through the existing geography, creating new aesthetics that overwhelm but never entirely eradicate the old, leaving traces of lost realities, past triumphs, and buried beliefs. Having no static essence, the city can never truly be represented cartographically, any more than organizations can ever be truly represented propositionally. The city is its conflicts, its power struggles over real estate, its aesthetic imagining of its possibilities, as well as its history. It is alive, organic, contested, and peopled, a space for human possibilities, impossible dramas, overweening ambitions, and great tragedy. Lacking faith in the existence of an underlying, all-knowing but ultimately unknowable order, one should instead gradually allow the case narrative to unfold from the diverse, complex, and sometimes conflicting stories that people, documents, and other evidence tell them. This approach leaves ample scope for readers to make different interpretations and to draw diverse conclusions (Flyvbjerg 2001, 86).

Hence, the possibility of multiple interpretations is admitted and structured into the accounting that one does. "There are multiple interpretations of events and different concepts and classificatory schemes could be used to describe phenomena" (Wicks and Freeman 1998, 134).

Having multiple interpretations does not mean an embrace of nihilism, an abrogation of perspective to the relativism that all views are equal. One does not simply celebrate difference for the sake of difference. Not all accounts are as good as others. Some are more useful for the purpose at hand than are others. Which of various accounts will be most useful will depend, precisely, on the purpose at hand. The criteria of reasonableness must include some notion of fitness for purpose: some accounts will better serve the task at hand and thus better enable people to accomplish relevant goals than will others. And that is a compelling reason why organization studies should not be rigidly scientistic in its forms of method and writing: these may not be the most appropriate forms of communication for the particular audience one is seeking to address. And, as Ralph Stablein (1996) has taught us, in writing organization studies (or anything else), the intended audience should not be ignored. Not being positivistic does not mean that one abandons scientific rigor. A persuasive narrative must provide reasons—it must be reasonable—and must recognize that reasons, reason, and positivistic science are not the same thing. A compelling narrative is one that persuades rigorously, aesthetically, and through the conventions of its chosen mode of discourse. It can never be paradigm-independent, in the jargon. Hence, it does not mean that "social scientists should stop using control groups, double-blind studies, regression analyses, and other techniques that are associated with social scientific research" (Wicks and Freeman 1998, 137). However, it is how and for what purposes one uses these that matters. As Flyvbjerg (2001, 166) stresses, "we must drop the fruitless efforts to emulate natural science's success in producing cumulative and predictive theory; this approach simply does not work in social science." The use of such methods should be oriented toward understanding and explaining contextual particulars, rather than be seen as elements for a law-like grand theory of predictive power. Such a colossal immodesty in the face of the many standing conditions that cannot be controlled is at worst sheer stupidity or at best the worst kind of cultural cringe. Case studies, documentary analysis, or other forms of narrative are not, a priori, second-rate science.

An outstanding example of a case-based approach to science that is based on a materialistic and ontologically realist approach to knowledge is available in the work of Jared Diamond (1998). He takes as his model of science not an ahistorical causal science, such as physics, but historical science, such as astronomy, palaeontology, climatology, ecology, evolutionary biology, and geology. To these, Diamond adds the interpretive opportunities offered by the fact that, of all the subjects of science, only humankind is a speaking and writing subject. What differentiate these sciences—as knowledge—are four methodological features that set them apart from nonhistorical sciences such as physics.

First, the methodology of physics places great store on the experimental method. With this, one creates a set of standing conditions in the laboratory that are such that one may create the effects that one is interested, theoretically, in investigating. Methodologically, one uses what, early in the methodology of modern science, the philosopher John Stuart Mill referred to as the method of systematic co-variation. Using this method, one manipulates the parameters of the experiment in such a way that one systematically varies theoretical controls in the experiment until causal efficacy is established. Different parameters are held constant—such as temperature or length of time that there is exposure to some variable—while others are systematically varied. Once the desired causality is achieved, one seeks to replicate that experiment systematically, in order to ensure the constancy of results, given the standing conditions. It is this strategy of systematic co-variation that is the fundamental axiom of laboratory-based sciences, such as physics, chemistry, and molecular biology.

Second, there are no laboratories in nature. By definition, the laboratory is an artfully contrived environment. When we look at naturalistic phenomena that vary in nature through time and space, the research questions that we seek to address are such that one cannot control their parameters. For instance, with the global warming hypothesis, one cannot isolate a low-lying Pacific atoll, such as Kiribati, and systematically increase the ecological heat surrounding it, perhaps by systematically thinning its immediate ozone layer. And, even if one could, there is the not so small ethical question of what happens to the nature so fried and drowned through increased sea levels—including the Kiribatians and other organisms that inhabit the atoll. The ecology, like the subject of other historical sciences such as evolution of species, linguistics, or the galaxy, is not something that can be artfully constructed into a temporally and spatially bounded sphere of co-variation.

> Historical sciences are concerned with narrative chains of proximate and ultimate causes. In most of physics and chemistry the concepts of "ultimate cause," "purpose" and "function" are meaningless, yet they are essential to understanding living systems in general, and human activities in particular. . . . In chemistry and physics the acid test of one's understanding of a system is whether one can successfully predict its future behavior. . . . In historical sciences, one can provide a posteriori explanations (e.g., why the an asteroid impact on Earth 66 million years ago may have driven dinosaurs but not many other species to extinction), but a priori predictions are more difficult (we would be uncertain which species would be driven to extinction if we did not have the actual past events to guide us). (Diamond 1998, 422)

Third, in historical science, there are an enormous number of variables, great complexity, unique actors, and no possibility of artful laboratory closure. One response to this is to restrict explanation to probabilistic statements that prevail at the level of ontological adequacy (McKelvey 2002). We can compare the behavior of a statistical model, based on trend data, as an idealized pattern against which parallel properties of real-world phenomena that are defined as falling within the scope of a theory may be contrasted in a model-phenomena link. So, for instance, Diamond (1998, 423) can predict the model parameters of statistical probability for an event occurrence, such as the number of births of boys and girls in any population, without being able to predict the outcome for any specific case before its conception. There are other approaches available in the historical sciences as well, such as the use of naturally occurring experiments (Garfinkel 1967), an approach used not only by ethnomethodological investigators but also by cultural anthropologists and evolutionary biologists.

Fourth, there is one great advantage when researching socially constructed phenomena: provided we are able to translate the language in use, we are able to interpret the understandings that its subjects have of themselves and the phenomena that they found salient. Ultimately, we can seek to understand interpretively the stories that people construct to explain reality for them. (While this is easier if we are able to be co-present and ask directly, historical traces can also yield great returns.) Essentially, the human condition is a narrative condition—it is a story of unfolding origins, sometimes charted but more often unknown destinations, and ways of telling the stories that matter. These ways of telling are what we can refer to as narrative techniques.

While all narratives that establish prime movers display a degree of fetishism—sometimes extreme—what characterizes more ontologically adequate accounts of phenomena is the relation of narrative prime movers and proximate causes. In natural history, evolution is one such metaphysic; in organization studies, it can also serve that function for some cases of large-scale populations over relatively long periods of time, such as Diamond (1998) studies, in the cases of the social organization of peoples, their foodstuffs, ecologies, crafts, and germs. Narratives make sense not simply by fetishizing certain techniques but because they also address existential dilemmas in meaningful ways. That is how Rainbow Serpents, Sons of God, and Laws of Science are named into Being. They speak to our human and organizational conditions of existence in ways that we find useful and desirable. They may propose ways of extending our powers and freeing our imagination, while sometimes they represent ways of enslaving the imagination of others or limiting their powers.

There is an ethical dimension to the contextual, pragmatic conception of a field such as organization studies as a human science with a natural history. Being a part of the social scenes that she investigates, the organization analyst has a responsibility toward the subjects of that science. When we investigate organizations, we are messing with people. We are not just observing rats in a laboratory or iron filings around a magnet. We address the impact of major structures of society on the lives of ordinary people. We have a responsibility to these people—as human communities—just as much as to the professional communities of methods and theories that sustain us. Indeed, if we cannot effect a conversation, a dialogue, between the two, then it is not clear what we are doing that is useful—although it may be very clear what privileges we are abusing by doing so. Hence, it matters not only how we study what we study but also how we choose to study such phenomena in the first place. We can address ourselves to issues that are arcane and inconsequential for all but an elite community of scholars—perhaps no more than two or three people. Or we can engage in the human comedy and address things that matter to people in their everyday lives.

It is because I hold these views that I have placed power, history, and imagination at the center of the analytic scheme that I recommend. Nothing matters more than these three abstractions, for they are the most likely proximate cause of the natural history of organizations. It is through these abstractions that I suggest we make sense. First, we make sense of who we are, what and where we have come from, and why—the dimension of history. Second, we make sense of where we want to be, what we want to do, and why—the dimension of imagination. Third, the capabilities we have and the capabilities that we need to achieve redress of some of those histories that we have had chosen for us—often, as Marx (1964) remarked, not under circumstances of our own choosing, which I would term the dimension of power. The history of the past, the imagination of the future, and powers in the present to affect these—with these we can know what is to be done—and undone. So, as Flyvbjerg (2001, 166) suggests, "we must take up problems that matter to the local, national and global communities in which we live, and we must do it in ways that matter." And, finally, as he goes on to suggest, "We must effectively communicate the results of our research to fellow citizens."

Signs of past traces of power, imagination, and history prefigure present organization studies. Such pasts are not privileged as something already elapsed and fixed but remain relevant to contemporary understanding only in as much as that understanding makes its sense of them (Burrell 1997, 5). Such past practices, sedimented structures, and materialized meanings, in the memorable rallying cry, "weigh like a nightmare on the brain of the living" (Marx 1964, 30). Yet, the living cannot easily shrug them off, for they frame our condition even as we cease to believe in the ways in which they have been represented in the past. The past of analysis is not so much another continent but a landscape that can be constantly redrawn in terms of contemporary aesthetics, techniques, and concerns. It is the landscape on which we project our dreams and our nightmares, our imagined futures and our fabled pasts; it is the context that frames our powers as it defines our limits.

Today, no one can pretend to understand the human condition who does not understand the organizations in which it is constituted, constrained, and transformed. Organization studies should be at the core of the study of the human condition, because without such subject matter—how, why, and in what ways we collectively organize, dispute, do, and change the things we do—we would have nothing of any consequence to discuss. Organizations frame the outer limits of our humanity and how we choose to express it—whether through the systems of slavery that brought the world such wonders of the world as the pyramids or through the learning bureaucracies that first propelled humankind into space.

In conclusion, organization analysis implies a substantial moral responsibility, if only because the history of human achievement is a history of organization. The responsibility should not be shrugged off lightly or reduced to a mere technical discourse, to a physics of necessity made out of social contingency. It should be acknowledged for what it is: a conversation with the living and the dead about those conditions of social existence that we imagine for the future, as well as a struggle to establish powers that can transcend those histories we inherit, in the service of those futures we can imagine.

*10*

---

# Making Intuition Matter

## *Leslie Paul Thiele*

Rather than indulging their "physics envy" for another fruitless century, Bent Flyvbjerg entreats social scientists to develop practical reason grounded in contextual judgment. By integrating an updated Aristotelian notion of phronesis into social-science inquiry, Flyvbjerg argues, practitioners can gain the knowledge and skills appropriate for their enterprise and ensure its practical relevance. Phronesis is an intellectual and moral virtue that develops out of experience. As a reflexive form of knowledge and inquiry, it allows one to interpret the meaning of social practices and negotiate the networks of power that generate and sustain them.

Flyvbjerg argues that the highest level of social science practice cannot be achieved without extensive worldly experience. In this respect, the social sciences parallel many other fields of skilled performance, where novices may demonstrate book knowledge but fail to exhibit flexible talent. As novices gain worldly experience, however, adaptive practices play a larger role. By the time the status of expert is reached, the context-sensitive practice of phronesis is all important.

Virtuosos do not apply rules. Rather, they act on the basis of a holistic, intuitive understanding. Following rules and abiding by logic allows competency. Proficiency is achieved only through intuitive knowledge and skills acquired over years of effort. If one remains caught in rule-following procedures and limited to strictly analytic rationality, progress towards virtuosity will be stymied. To become an expert social scientist, Flyvbjerg insists, one must move beyond the antiseptic massaging of data and get one's hands dirty grappling with the real world.

*Making Social Science Matter* provides a compelling argument for the development of phronesis, understood as a form of contextually grounded, practical judgment. Unfortunately, Flyvbjerg does not bring the full weight of science to bear in his effort. Consequently, he does not adequately penetrate the nature of practical judgment. Perhaps Flyvbjerg is reluctant to rely on standard scientific inquiry to legitimate the role of an alternative, experiential style of inquiry. Perhaps the normative nature of phronesis, understood as moral and political judgment, suggests that value-free science cannot make a contribution. Or, perhaps, Flyvbjerg is aware that most scientific investigations of judgment—studies in the field of decision theory—aim to counteract the biases of intuitive thinking that intrude on rational decision making. In any case, his argument for phronetic inquiry is weakened by a lack of reference to recent empirical research, particularly that in cognitive psychology and neuroscience.

The literature in decision theory has much to offer. By exploring cognitive heuristics and probability theory, it aims to improve judgment by strengthening reason. There is much to be gained from this endeavor, for intuitive biases are many and their influence in decision making is often pernicious. An education in reason is all for the good. The problem is that this education is generally portrayed as a means of *replacing* intuition with rational thought. Any such effort will prove counterproductive. The alternative, however, is not simply to give freer range to intuitions. The task is to educate them.

If we are to become more proficient moral and political judges, we must acknowledge and cultivate, rather than deny or deprecate, the role of the intuitive unconscious. The idea of explicitly cultivating a part of ourselves that we do not cognitively control, or even well comprehend, may seem strange and perhaps dangerous. But it is a common feature of our efforts to achieve excellence in many other endeavors, and there is much evidence to suggest its relevance to social and political affairs. Decision theory rightly gives us pause when we rely on intuition. At the same time, recent research in cognitive psychology and neuroscience demonstrates the crucial contribution of unconscious, intuitive capacities to practical judgment. Social science has much to gain from greater familiarity with this research.

## Perceptual Skills and Implicit Memory

Unless one is able accurately and richly to perceive one's world, good judgments cannot arise. No doubt, one can make a deliberate effort to cultivate fine perception, trying to be more attentive to the intricate features of human character and the complex interdependence of opportunities, obligations, and constraints that structures moral and political life. But the lion's share of our perceptions are not intentionally sought or gained. They arrive unannounced. We can deliberately choose to close our eyes and ears. But once these conduits to the world are opened, what they take in, and what they fail to take in, is not primarily under conscious control.

Neuroscientists assert that our eyes absorb and pass on to the brain more than 10 million signals each second. The other four senses also contribute extensively. But our conscious mind can process only about forty pieces of information each second. That is a small share of what becomes available to us. Indeed, it is estimated that our sense organs collect up to one million bits of information for every one bit of information that enters our conscious awareness (Zimmerman 1989; Wilson 2002, 24). Conscious perception represents only the smallest fraction of what we absorb from our worldly encounters. It is the tip of an iceberg.

Perceptions are next to useless unless they can be stored and retrieved. Memory, like perception, is a crucial skill without which good judgment cannot arise. And memory, like perception, is not fully, or even primarily, within our conscious control (Toth 2000; Koh and Meyer 1991; Lewicki et al. 1987). We remember much more than we can ever recall.

Consider experiments that inform a field of cognitive psychology known as implicit learning or implicit cognition. Faced with a computer screen divided in four quadrants, participants of one study were asked to press one of four buttons corresponding to the quadrant upon which a target character, hidden among other characters, appeared in an apparently random fashion. The target character actually appeared, unbeknownst to participants, in specific sequences that followed a very complex algorithm. Participants became increasingly adept, that is to say, faster and more accurate, at pressing the correct buttons as time progressed. Yet they remained wholly unaware of the rules that determined where the target character would appear. When the rules were changed (without notice), the participants' performance deteriorated.

What was happening? Without knowing it, the participants were acting in anticipation of the target character's movement on the computer screen. They had unconsciously perceived, stored, and retrieved for use—that is to say, learned—the complex algorithm that was determining the placement sequence of the target character. Yet they had no conscious awareness of this knowledge. When offered a cash reward ($100) to identify any systematic feature of the sequencing none of the participants, all college students, could identify a pattern despite hours of effort. (Lewicki et al. 1992; Wilson 2002). Their learning was implicit.

Implicit learning is demonstrated when traces of past experience affect behavior, yet the influential experience remains largely unavailable to self-report or introspection. In other words, proficiency grounded in unintentionally acquired knowledge develops without (or well in advance of) the ability to articulate or even detect useful patterns of information. Distinct neural structures (particular areas of the brain) are devoted to or feature prominently in implicit learning (Willingham and Preuss 1995). For example, conscious, short-term memory, also known as explicit or declarative memory, while stored in related cortical regions, is wholly mediated by the hippocampus (a curved ridge located on the floor of each lateral ventricle). Implicit memory, also known as procedural memory, is mediated by other regions, including the amygdala (an almond-shaped mass of gray matter located near the hippocampus).

The study of implicit learning originated with an experiment conducted by the Swiss psychologist Edouard Claparede (1951). In 1911, Claparede worked with a forty-seven-year-old woman who had been in an asylum for five years suffering from Korsakoff's syndrome. The patient, owing to her brain malady, had no short-term memory. Every morning the woman would have to be reintroduced to her caretakers and co-patients, as she bore no recollection that the same event had taken place each of the previous days.

One morning, Claparede concealed a pin in his palm when he shook hands with the amnesiac woman. She reacted as one might expect, by wincing and retracting her hand. Shortly thereafter, the woman completely forgot about the episode, as she forgot about all recent events. Yet when Claparede introduced himself the following day, the woman withheld her hand (Glynn 1999, 318). The patient did not recognize Claparede and could not recall the pinprick. The damaged hippocampus that would normally allow such short-term, declarative memory remained nonfunctional. The undamaged part of her brain that was involved in the formation of procedural (implicit) memory, however, worked fine. Like the subjects who unconsciously learned the complex rules that dictated the sequencing of target characters on a computer screen, the amnesiac woman was able to learn without consciousness, acting on the basis of memories she could not recollect.

The preponderance of the millions of bits of information that comes our way every second of our waking hours is processed through implicit means. Our conscious minds do not get much involved. But it is not simply a matter of the quantity of information that makes implicit cognition important. In many circumstances, it also has the edge over conscious learning in terms of quality. Our capacity for implicit learning is often more robust and resilient in the face of a complex, demanding world (Reber 1993, 18–21, 88–94; Claxton 1997). Resorting to conscious rationality in stressful situations, for instance, often produces a decline in skillful performance. People under pressure who rely on implicit learning tend to perform better (Masters 1992). Studies also demonstrate that declarative (i.e., conscious) memory is significantly impaired when attention is demanded simultaneously from multiple sectors. Subjects perform quite poorly, for instance, when attempting to recall a list of words if, while reading the list, they are asked to take on a secondary task, such as monitoring a sequence of digits. In contrast, implicit memories are not severely impaired by multiple demands on a subject's attention (Toth 2000).

The conscious mind is like a serial processor, addressing tasks sequentially. It is inhibited from taking on more than one job at a time. The unconscious mind, in contrast, works more like a parallel distributed processor. It addresses numerous complex tasks simultaneously by funneling multiple independent sources of information through multiple information-processing units (Bargh 1997, 53; Rumelhart et al. 1986). To the extent that we engage in "multitasking," the unconscious mind takes over. As much of our lives are characterized by multiple demands on our attention, it is not surprising that implicit cognition plays a very large role in our ability to function effectively (Marcus, Neuman, and MacKuen 2000, 30).

## The Modularity of the Brain

Alfred North Whitehead said that "Civilization advances by extending the number of important operations which we can perform without thinking about them" (1911, 61). Whitehead's formula may be too tidy, but empirical evidence demonstrates that implicit cognition plays a significant role in our lives and often produces qualitatively superior results. All of us possess skills that we are not consciously aware of or, in any case, do not consciously control; riding a bicycle, playing a musical instrument, and typing are good examples. To comprehend the nature of such skills, we must understand how the brain divides its workload. The hind brain, or cerebellum, controls fine motor movement and complex movement patterns. The pianist who completes a fast and intricate passage without a thought to the fingering, like the touch typist, has stored the necessary instructions in his cerebellum (Glynn 1999, 167). The prefrontal cortex, where most conscious thought occurs, remains largely uninvolved. Likewise, when grandmasters and good amateurs play chess, brain scans indicate that the amateurs are using primarily the medial temporal lobes of their brains, whereas the grandmasters employ their frontal and parietal cortices. At a certain level of skillful performance, when people operate most proficiently, distinct brain regions take over the show.

Such findings have led neuroscientists, psychologists, and philosophers to propose the brain to be *modular* in structure and function. Rather than viewing the mind as a general purpose computer, modularists understand it to operate more like a Swiss army knife, with distinct neural networks, which may or may not occupy a single area of the brain, demonstrating distinct capacities. Modules are hard-wired, specialized brain systems whose operations remain unavailable to conscious awareness. These modules carry out specific, independent tasks while remaining "cognitively impenetrable" (Hoffman 1986, 8). Many, if not most, of our mental capacities appear to be modular to some degree, though the precise extent to which modularity operates and the level of interactivity between modules remains unknown.

Modularity is most evident in the (evolutionary) older regions of the brain, such as the thalamus. But even in the neocortex, which demonstrates much more fluidity, parallel processing, and interconnection, a form of modularity is evident. The frontal lobes, for instance, are mostly involved in "adaptive" or practical judgments—those that entail a choice among alternatives whose relative merits are ambiguous. They do not much participate in computational tasks involved in producing "veridical" judgments. In turn, the right hemisphere primarily assumes the charge of grappling with novelty, while the left hemisphere is concerned with more routine tasks (Goldberg 2001, 79–80).

Modularity is well demonstrated in the act of smiling. When asked to smile on command for a camera, or trying to smile in front of a mirror, many of us produce strange grimaces. Yet we may have beautiful smiles that appear on our faces without effort when encountering a good friend. These two kinds of smiles differ so markedly because distinct brain regions handle them. The consciously orchestrated smile is produced by the motor cortex. The spontaneous smile is executed by the basal ganglia, clusters of cells found between the brain's higher cortex and the thalamus.

A person who has suffered a stroke in the right motor cortex (which controls movement on the left side of the body) is able to produce a half smile (on the right side of the face) with conscious effort. But this same stroke victim can exhibit a full spontaneous smile on both sides of his face. Likewise, voluntary arm movements are impossible for such a stroke victim on both sides of his body. Try as he might, the person who recently suffered from a stroke in his right hemisphere will not be able to lift his left arm. But an involuntary yawn will raise both arms. The reason, again, is that the voluntary and involuntary movements are controlled by different brain regions, only one of which was damaged by the stroke (Ramachandran and Blakeslee 1998, 14).

Such neuroscientific findings prompt the following questions: is there a significant sense in which practical judgment, like smiling, is best accomplished by nonexplicit, involuntary, unconscious means that are grounded in distinct brain regions? Is social science, therefore, impoverished if it cuts itself off from the many forms of perceiving, remembering, learning, and acting that remain cognitively impenetrable? Would a social scientist exercising practical judgment solely through conscious effort be in the position of the pianist who refused to employ her cerebellum and consequently produced choppy, ear-bending executions rather than mellifluous music? The phenomenon of tacit knowledge offers a means for launching inquiry into such concerns.

## Tacit Knowledge and Intuition

The notion of tacit knowledge was given a wide audience beginning in the late 1960s by Michael Polanyi. Polanyi described in phenomenological (rather than neuroscientific) terms how we can have "subsidiary" knowledge of things without that knowledge ever rising to the level of consciousness. He posited as the paradigm case for tacit knowledge the way we "know" our own bodies (1969, 183). The sense of balance exhibited in walking, running, or jumping demonstrates that we can do many things with our bodies without knowing *how* we do them. We subsidiarily know how to ride a bicycle, for instance, yet we remain largely if not wholly unable to identify the precise movements that allow this complex activity of balance and propulsion to take place.

Tacit knowledge is generally understood to be a type of "know-how." It is exemplified in fine and gross motor skills (e.g., playing a piano, riding a bicycle); in skills involving one or more of the five senses (e.g., that exhibited by wine tasters or music conductors, or the more general ability to discern and discriminate among smells, tastes, colors, shapes, sounds, and touch); in skills that employ various senses in combination (e.g., the ability to predict weather patterns through sight, sound, smell, and bodily reactions to changes in barometric pressure); and in largely cognitive but no less unconsciously directed skills (e.g., many aspects of language use).

Some forms of tacit knowledge appear innate. Certain people, for instance, are "born" with perfect pitch. Most of our tacit knowledge, however, is acquired. We do not arrive in the world with knowledge of how to walk, ride a bike, or speak a language. Rather, we are born with the potential, if we are typical, of developing the muscular coordination, sense of balance, and the linguistic skills that make walking, riding a bike, and speaking nearly effortless activities. We are not "hard wired" to do these things in the same sense that we are hard wired to breathe. But, one might say, we are hard wired to learn to do these things, given a sufficiently supportive environment (see Reber 1993). We can and generally do achieve such feats without ever consciously gaining knowledge of their basic structures (e.g., the physics and physiology of walking or riding a bike or the grammatical rules of language use). Explicit learning in these arenas, if it ever occurs, happens long after we have acquired the respective tacit skills. Thus, when my four-year-old son remarked, after sampling both his and my treats, that "The chocolate ice cream is the goodest," he was neither imitating something he had heard nor consciously applying memorized rules of grammar. Rather, he was (mis)applying tacitly learned linguistic knowledge. When appropriating such knowledge, we are engaged in what Polanyi called "learning without awareness" (1969, 141–42).

Building on Polanyi's work, the political theorist Sheldon Wolin sketches the importance of tacit knowledge for politics. Tacit political knowledge, or practical political wisdom, he observes, is "mindful of logic, but more so of the incoherence and contradictoriness of experience. And for the same reason, it is distrustful of rigor. Political life does not yield its significance to terse hypotheses, but is elusive and hence meaningful statements about it often have to be allusive and intimative. Context becomes supremely important, for actions and events occur in no other setting" (Wolin 1969, 1070). In contrast to methodologically rigorous, highly directed inquiry, tacit political knowledge derives from "an indwelling or rumination in which the mind draws on the complex framework of sensibilities built up unpremeditatedly and calls upon the diverse resources of civilized knowledge" (Wolin 1969, 1071). Understanding political theory to constitute a "sum of judgments," Wolin observes the merits—and indispensability—of tacit knowledge for those who adopt the "vocation" of theorizing (Wolin 1969, 1076).

Like Wolin, Michael Oakeshott worries about the modern effort to rationalize politics. And, like his fellow political theorist, Oakeshott decries the discounting of implicit forms of learning. "By 'judgment,'" Oakeshott writes, "I mean the tacit or implicit component of knowledge, the ingredient which is not merely unspecified in propositions but is unspecifiable in propositions. It is the component of knowledge which does not appear in the form of rules and which, therefore, cannot be resolved into information or itemized in the manner characteristic of information" (2001, 49). Oakeshott, like Polanyi, differentiates between the "knowing-how" of tacit knowledge and the "knowing-what" of explicit knowledge (information). He admits that most if not all "knowing-how" has within it certain elements of "knowing-what." But he argues that knowing how is primary and foundational. In turn, he insists that tacit knowledge is exhibited not only in physical skills but in "all abilities whatever, and, more particularly, in those abilities which are almost exclusively concerned with mental operations" (2001, 51).

Oakeshott's claim regarding the importance of tacit knowledge for intellectual effort has been vindicated by empirical research. Though it proves difficult to measure, tacit knowledge does indeed augment our more deliberative, explicit bases of knowledge. Students who demonstrate high levels of tacit knowledge, for example, achieve better academic grades than students who are low in tacit knowledge but equal or higher in explicit knowledge (Somech 1999).

When tacit knowledge is involved in mental efforts, such as decision making, these efforts are often said to be *intuitive* in nature. Intuition may be defined as a form of awareness that occurs without the involvement of conscious reasoning or attention. As such, it reflects our access to and use of tacit knowledge. Intuition tends to be automatic (experienced passively), rapid, effortless, holistic (pattern oriented), and associational. It is idiographic, grasping reality in concrete images and metaphors, is self-evidently valid, and is prone to stereotyping. Intuition is immediately compelling and is resistant to change; its alteration generally requires repetitive or intense experience. In contrast, rational thought is intentional, relatively slow, structured, analytic, and deductive or inductive. It grasps reality in abstract symbols, words, or numbers, requires logical justification and evidence, and is generally responsive to new evidence and arguments (Epstein et al. 1996). Both intuitive awareness and rational thought have their respective, context-dependent strengths and weaknesses. They often work separately but can also fruitfully be utilized in tandem.

When the grandmaster plays chess intuitively, he is operating in a fashion analogous to that of the expert pianist playing a concerto or the tennis pro playing a match. In each case, tacit knowledge and implicit learning are at the forefront, leaving a much diminished but by no means absent role for deliberation. When conscious thought does come into play for the chess expert, it occurs, most times, not as a completely separate, purely analytic activity. Rather, it involves his critical reflection upon existing intuitions (Dreyfus et al. 1988, 32).

Empirical studies suggest that moral and political judgment operates similarly, with the lion's share of the work accomplished by intuitive processes. For most people most of the time, practical judgment is a product of intuitions that have been shaped though active participation in sociocultural environments, occasionally refined by propositional deliberation. When conscious refinement takes place, it typically occurs not as the imperial pronouncement of reason but as the use of reason to break a deadlock between conflicting intuitions (Haidt 2001; Greene et al. 2001; Greene and Haidt 2002). As James Schlesinger, one-time director of strategic studies for RAND and subsequently U.S. secretary of defense, observed, "Analysis is not a scientific procedure for reaching decisions which avoid intuitive elements, but rather a mechanism for sharpening the intuitions of the decision-maker" (1968, 335).

We frequently learn and act wholly on the basis of tacit knowledge and skills, with rational thought playing no role whatsoever. The obverse never occurs. As Michael Polanyi writes, "While tacit knowledge can be possessed by itself, explicit knowledge must rely on being tacitly understood and applied. Hence all knowledge is *either tacit* or *rooted in tacit knowledge*. A *wholly* explicit knowledge is unthinkable" (1969, 144). It follows, for Polanyi, that "any attempt to gain complete control of thought by explicit rules is self-contradictory, systematically misleading and culturally destructive" (1969, 156; and see Oakeshott 2001, 50).

Even if one acknowledges the impossibility of reason operating in the complete absence of tacit knowledge, one might still seek to limit the role of nondeliberative, intuitive knowledge to a minimum and expand rational analysis to a maximum. While our perceptual skill, implicit memory, tacit knowledge, and intuitions may constitute a necessary starting point for any critical reflection, might it be the case that the less we engage the unconscious capacities of the mind, the better our practical judgments will be?

The answer is no. When the conscious mind crowds out the unconscious mind, a tremendous resource is being wasted. Cognitive psychologists have demonstrated that the performance of subjects working on a given problem may be significantly undermined if they are asked to "think aloud" through their problem solving. Thinking aloud effectively restricts the subjects to conscious mental processes, eliminating the often more fecund capacities of the unconscious mind, namely implicit memories and intuitions (Simonton 1999, 47–49). Likewise, many forms of tacit knowledge, such as that which operates in face recognition, become impaired if people are initially required to describe verbally the world they observe (Schooler and Engstler-Schooler 1990). Words and the conscious thoughts behind them get in the way of perception and recall. People also may demonstrate increased problem-solving skills and improved recall of the perceptual cues or other memory traces that guide judgment when they relax their conscious efforts. A willful attempt to focus the mind actually interferes with access to the knowledge that figures in the making of judgments or the solving of difficult problems (Greenwald and Banaji 1995; Ellis and Hunt 1993, 93–94; Simonton 1999, 44–45). With this in mind, we can understand why the vast majority of Nobel laureates (seventy-two out of eighty-three in science and medicine) indicate that intuition played a significant role in their success (Marton et al. 1994).

Consider the following study. Participants were asked to give their preferences for strawberry jams (based on tasting them) and college courses (based on a review of syllabi). Left to their own devices, control subjects produced preferences that corresponded very well to the ratings of trained sensory experts and faculty members, respectively. Subjects who were asked to think about why they liked or disliked the jams and why they would choose or not choose a particular course, however, performed quite poorly. Why did this occur? The more deliberative decision makers brought to mind, as requested, attributes and reasons to ground their judgments. But these did not well correspond to the attributes and reasons deemed important by experts. When the subjects proceeded to base their judgments on these suboptimal attributes and reasons, they produced suboptimal judgments (Wilson and Schooler 1991). Looking for and employing reasons when making a judgment does not guarantee that one will find and choose the right reasons. Intuitive judgments—based on unconscious sorting mechanisms—often prove superior to the results of deliberative efforts (Woolhouse and Bayne 2000). This is particularly true if the task at hand is oriented less to the determination of facts or figures than to the determination of values (McMackin and Slovic 2000).

The point is not that practical judgment should restrict itself to the unconscious powers of the mind. Research demonstrates that judgment is often improved when complex, ambiguous situations force us to reason more carefully (Pizarro and Bloom 2001; Lieberman 2000). The question is: how large of a role should unconscious capacities play? Our brains, over eons of evolution, have figured out which modules to employ to achieve the best results when attempting many physical feats. As often as not, the less conscious the activity the better. We have a lot further to go in discovering when and how practical judgment is enhanced by tacit capacities.

Intuition has been identified as a "new cottage industry" (Myers 2002, 3). It is valorized in popular culture and even in business affairs, with magazines, Web sites, pay-per-call "hot lines," and best-selling books devoted to it. While abilities do vary from person to person (Woolhouse and Bayne 2000), in general people tend to overrate their intuitive powers. Empirical research demonstrates that individuals making "seat-of-the-pants" decisions based on their "gut feelings"—including reputed experts in their own fields of expertise—often perform quite poorly (Elster 1999, 295; Dawes et al. 1989; Hogarth 2001, 144–45; Camerer and Johnson 1991; Janis 1989; Kahneman et al. 1982). Let there be no mistake: intuition is very fallible. Nonetheless, one cannot accurately account for good judgment without reference to the prominent, often positive, and generally indispensable role it plays.

Scooping Freud by more than a decade, Nietzsche argued that the conscious mind is mostly a façade and that the vast majority of what goes on in the brain remains unavailable to us. In turn, and unlike Freud, he argued that prodding the unconscious into speech would result not in enlightenment and liberation but in further corruption. I will briefly present Nietzsche's case for the irreducibility and incommunicability of the unconscious features of judgment and subsequently back away from the extremity of his position.

"For the longest time, conscious thought was considered thought itself," Nietzsche writes in *The Gay Science*. "Only now does the truth dawn on us that by far the greatest part of our spirit's activity remains unconscious and unfelt" (1974, 261–62). The conscious, deliberative mind is but a pale reflection of more important "hidden roots" (Nietzsche 1920–29, 60). What eventually comes to consciousness is simply "the last link of a chain" (Nietzsche 1974, 203).

The foundations for our judgments remain ineffable and inherently unavailable to consciousness. Once judgments find their way into speech, Nietzsche insists, they have already become misrepresentations (1968a, 82; 1968b, 243). If and when our instincts and intuitions become available to reflection, we can be sure that we are gaining consciousness only of a veneer. Explanation of them, it follows, is always a sham. Nietzsche writes: "The world of which we can become conscious is only a surface-and-sign-world, a world that is made common and meaner; whatever becomes conscious *becomes* by the same token shallower, low, thin, relatively stupid, general, sign, herd signal; all becoming conscious involves a great and thorough corruption, falsification, reduction to superficialities, and generalization" (1974, 299–300).

In what might be taken as an update of Nietzsche's position, Tor Norretranders speaks of the "user illusion." The user illusion occurs whenever we believe that the conscious self is driving the car of life when, in fact, the unconscious self is mostly at the wheel. The cogitating mind that thinks and explains (Norretranders calls it the "*I*") plays a very useful but quite limited role. Norretranders writes that "The role of the *I* in learning is precisely to force the nonconscious, the *Me*, to practice, rehearse, or just attend. The *I* is a kind of boss who tells the *Me* what it must practice. The *I* is the *Me*'s secretary" (1998, 303). Norretranders both buttresses and challenges Nietzsche's position. He puts the conscious mind in its place but does not unduly diminish its contribution. Being a good secretary is no small task.

Athletes understand that cognitive thought can interfere with peak performance. When at their best, the *Me* is in control. At the same time, the best athletes also work with trainers or are adept at training themselves. Through drills and instruction, athletes improve their performance. Second nature, in this case, often bests first nature. And this second nature is gained, in large part, by way of explicit learning and training. Conscious thought can never replace unconscious processes on the playing field. But unconscious capacities are often improved through practice and pedagogy.

There is no need to gainsay the importance of rationality to practical judgment, whether supplied in the form of conceptual analysis, strategic planning, probabilistic thought, general instruction, or retrospective reconstruction. At the same time, we must acknowledge that the perceptual skill, implicit memory, tacit knowledge, and intuitions that ground our judgments often remain unavailable to the conscious mind and that this implicitly acquired knowledge, as cognitive psychologists attest, is "always richer and more sophisticated than that which can be explicated" (Reber 1993, 64, and see Horgan 1999, 220; Greene and Haidt 2002; Nisbet and Wilson 1977). Expunging the unconscious features of the mind that resist assessment and explanation undermines rather than improves practical judgment.

## Cultivating Good Judgment

In many respects, good judgment is best identified by the diversity and quality of its input rather than by the rationality of its output. The pertinent question to ask is whether a judgment relies on a singular faculty or whether it makes use of a wide array of deliberative and intuitive capacities. The mysterious aspect of practical judgment concerns our ability to integrate these diverse elements. I employ the word "mysterious" because the mind remains a largely undiscovered continent, notwithstanding tremendous advances in neuroscience. Commenting on the dearth of knowledge of how the brain integrates myriad perceptions and memories to arrive at a coherent picture of the world, John Horgan aptly writes: "Like a precocious eight-year-old tinkering with a radio, mind-scientists excel at taking the brain apart, but they have no idea how to put it back together again" (1999, 23). Fortunately, the judging mind functions quite well despite our patent ignorance of its workings.

If good judgment is grounded in a well-integrated mix of diverse capacities, it follows that relying on a single mode of perception or assessment will generally result in bad judgment. As Isaiah Berlin observes, bad judgment consists "not in failing to apply the methods of natural science, but, on the contrary, in over-applying them. Here failure comes from resisting that which works best in each field, from ignoring or opposing it either in favor of some systematic method or principle claiming universal validity . . . or else from a wish to defy all principles, all methods as such, from simply advocating trust in a lucky star or personal inspiration; that is, mere irrationalism" (1996, 30). Bad judgment is bad because it is monolithic and lacks integration. Good judgment, in contrast, puts a panoply of (conscious and unconscious) capacities to work in tackling multifaceted problems.

What makes for good judgment, effectively, are the countless microjudgments that go into it. These microjudgments determine when perceptual skill, implicit memory, tacit knowledge, and intuition should play their respective roles and when these intrinsic elements of judgment ought to be subjected to the watchful eye of reason. In turn, other microjudgments determine how much and what kind of information to gather, how many and what sort of alternative perspectives to entertain, which principles and rules to apply, how much analysis to undertake, and when and where to direct its force. The question being begged in each case, of course, is, What makes for good microjudgments?

Rational analysis may certainly play a part in our microjudgments. But you cannot have rational analysis all the way down. Calls for analytic reason to fully ground decision making harbor a *reductio ad absurdum.* Good judgment can proceed only on the basis of sound knowledge of alternative choices and their relative worth. The decision to seek (particular kinds of) information or to examine (particular) alternatives before making a judgment, however, must be based on a set of reasons. These reasons must be well chosen, which is to say that their selection must be based on sound judgment. But the merit of such judgment depends on the reasons that support it. An infinite regress threatens. Ultimately, an authoritative decision is required. Typically, it comes from the gut, from intuition. And the buck stops there.

Thomas Edison famously observed that "genius is 1 percent inspiration and 99 percent perspiration." Good judgment is also a combination of what we might broadly label intuitive capacities and the hard work of gathering information, considering alternate viewpoints, and rationally analyzing options. But the optimum ratio may be quite different for practical judgment than that suggested by Edison for genius—and it assuredly varies from context to context. The good judge, somehow, finds the right mix given the situation at hand.

If the thesis that practical judgment significantly and unavoidably involves tacit skills and knowledge is correct, then understanding how to make the best use of these skills and knowledge is of great importance. Neuroscientific research offers useful insights. Consider the discovery that the brain's right hemisphere generates and grapples with innovation and is considered "highly sensitive to perturbation," whereas the left hemisphere is more oriented to routine tasks and fitting new phenomena into preexisting models. At times, the "conformist" left hemisphere goes so far as to push individuals into extreme acts of denial (Ramachandran and Blakeslee 1998, 141). Stroke victims whose right hemispheres have been damaged and, consequently, whose left arms are left paralyzed, for example, have on occasion exhibited an uncanny tendency to deny their paralysis. They even invent—and fully believe—elaborate stories to explain why they cannot perform tasks that require the use of both arms.

One woman who suffered from this affliction was asked to lift a tray holding drinks. Rather than placing her functional hand in the middle of the tray, as stroke victims who are conscious of their paralysis would do, she grabbed the tray from one end with her right hand. The left arm remained lifeless at her side. Not surprisingly, the tray tipped over, and the drinks spilled onto her lap. When asked what had happened, the woman stated matter-of-factly that she had successfully lifted the tray. Incredibly, she remained oblivious to the mishap and her soaked legs.

The right side of the brain that normally would have allowed the woman to grapple with a changed body image (left-side paralysis) had been too badly damaged by the stroke. Her conformist left hemisphere therefore went about the Procrustean task of fitting a different world (where partial paralysis disallowed certain actions) to a preexisting body image. Consequently, she acted as if both her arms were fully functional and subsequently rewrote her personal history to mesh with this framework.

Scholars of decision making suggest that one of the best things one can do to offset common (intuitive) biases that impede rational judgment is to regularize the use of a devil's advocate. This tactic facilitates a surveying of alternative perspectives and options while mitigating excessive optimism, inaccurate self-images, stereotyping, and other common biases. From a neurological perspective, it is a good suggestion. Effectively, we must find ways to stimulate the right hemisphere of the brain, lest the left side carry through its conformist mandate of rationalizing and legitimizing expectations, habits, and prejudices.

With the aforementioned stroke victim, the physical stimulation of the damaged part of the brain did indeed produce welcome results. By irrigating the left ear of the afflicted woman with ice-cold water, researchers were able to stimulate her right hemisphere. Directly after the ear irrigation, the patient acknowledged the paralysis of her left arm and acted accordingly. However, in as little as half an hour, her former state of denial returned. The physical stimulation of the brain's right hemisphere provided only temporary relief from the left hemipshere's conformist tendencies.

Good judgment may be cultivated by the equivalent of recurrent ear washing. At times, the primary need might be arousal of the right hemisphere, perhaps by using a devil's advocate or some other means of engendering the appreciation of novelty. At times, the arousal of the neural networks that bear implicit memories or tacit knowledge might be most useful. This might be achieved by stimulating the motor cortex or the visual occipital lobe near which a particular form of learning finds its cerebral home. And, at times, the stimulation of the seat of reason in the frontal cortex proves most useful. The point is that good judgment is a *whole-brain* activity that involves not only our cognitive, rational capacities but also our implicit capacities and their accompanying visual, auditory, tactile, and proprioceptive skills. We are operating at a severe deficit if we limit ourselves to the conscious, rational effort that is the specialty of a relatively small section of the forebrain.

Whole-brain judgment is based on whole-brain learning. Such an education was traditionally offered in apprenticeships, but it may occur in any broadly experiential encounter with the world. Antonio Gramsci wrote that knowing yourself is a matter of insight into the "historical process" that has "deposited in you an infinity of traces, without leaving an inventory" (1971, 324). Practical judgment makes use of the uninventoried resources deposited over a lifetime of experience. Utilizing these deposited traces may on occasion lead one astray. Too often, we intuit badly and glean the wrong lessons from our worldly experiences. So we are well advised to study reason and mitigate common biases. Learning, in most cases, is enhanced when it makes good use of explicit knowledge and rationality (Reber 1993, 159). At the same time, relying solely on the small portion of neurological capacities that we have managed to inventory— the conscious mind—can produce only impoverished judgments.

Good judgment, most everyone since Aristotle agrees, cannot well be taught. It has to be gained through experience. That is why Aristotle deemed politics a field of study and practice unfit for the young. But Aristotle never tells us what it is about experience, as opposed to formal pedagogy, that lends itself to the cultivation of judgment. In this regard, Flyvbjerg follows in the Peripatetic's footsteps. Cognitive psychology and neuroscience help remedy this shortcoming. Formal pedagogy well conveys explicit information, but most of the knowledge that goes into our practical judgments is implicitly acquired. The cultivation of practical judgment demands the whole-brain learning that is primarily offered in the school of life. To properly educate intuition, we must concern ourselves with the awesome task of understanding—and improving—the lessons learned in this academy.

Flyvbjerg is right to challenge the hegemony of rational analysis and scientific methodology in social-science research and to highlight the benefits offered by practical engagement. But we should not neglect what standard science has to teach us about the intuitive, experiential nature of practical judgment and how we might improve it. There is no substitute for experience in the development of expertise. But it would be mistaken to believe that we best foster experiential learning in the social sciences by turning our backs on science. Athletes improve with practice. But they also benefit greatly from the scientific investigation of optimal training methods. Likewise, the best social scientists integrate experientially grounded knowledge and skills into their work. But their efforts can be improved only by the rigorous investigation of the psychology and neuroscience of learning. We need not shun science to embrace Aristotle. The best way to make intuition matter to social scientists is to bring the full weight of science to bear on its investigation.

# Part III

# Making Political Science Matter

# 11

# Conundrums in the Practice of Pluralism

## *Peregrine Schwartz-Shea*

> Rather than "either-or," we should develop a nondualis-
> tic and pluralistic "both-and." Hence, we should not crit-
> icize rules, logic, signs, and rationality *in themselves.* We
> should criticize *only the dominance* of these phenomena
> to the exclusion of others in modern society and social
> science.
> —Bent Flyvbjerg (2001, 49, emphases added)

> [I]f the knowledge-seeking project is always . . . a politi-
> cal project, then it is in some important sense irreducibly
> oppositional. . . . To assume that the one or the other
> [approach] can or should simply accept the other is per-
> haps to not take seriously enough what they both take
> the political (=world-affecting) stakes to be.
> —Elizabeth Wingrove (personal communication, 2001)

There has been much attention in recent years to increasing the plurality
of knowledge approaches in political science. In contrast to the arguments of Kuhn (1970) and Lakatos (1970) that in a competition of
approaches the "best" approach will and *should* win—producing a dominant paradigm and a "mature" discipline that practices normal science—
Flyvbjerg (2001) and others (Dryzek 1986, 1990; Rule 1997) have argued
that a plurality of approaches in the social sciences is desirable because
such diversity provides societies with a full repertoire of possible

approaches to societal problems, some yet unknown. In this view, it is not particular approaches that are problematic but the *dominance* of particular approaches and, presumably, the dominance of *any* approach. Flyvbjerg's "both-and" perspective on pluralism implies a practice for scholars, that, at a minimum, we should accept other approaches' existence on principle and, perhaps, should even be on the lookout for complementarities among approaches.

Flybvjerg's "both-and" perspective has been embraced by perestroikan proponents of pluralism, perhaps, in part, because it deftly handles the hypocrisy charge—that perestroikans don't "really" want pluralism but, instead, want *their* methodological and theoretical approaches to become dominant in the discipline. The reply to such charges is: "No, we don't want dominance. We simply want space in the disciplinary journals, curricula, conferences, granting agencies, and other venues. We are committed to pluralism because we believe pluralism will be good for the discipline as a whole and for the pursuit of knowledge in general." And, indeed, when it comes, for example, to methodological pluralism, perestroikans have argued not for eliminating graduate offerings in statistics or formal theory but for "balance" in the curriculum, that is, for increased offerings in case study and other qualitative methods as well as in interpretive methodologies (e.g., Schwartz-Shea 2003, 2005).

The "balance" perspective on methodological pluralism has been further strengthened by the call to conduct problem-driven research (Shapiro 2002; Flyvbjerg 2001), which requires, at a minimum, that a variety of methodologies be taught so that researchers may select among them as a function of the specific research question. While some envision researchers capable of moving almost seamlessly from variables-based survey research to in-depth, meaning-centered interpretive research as a function of specific research questions (Soss 2006),[1] others envision specialization by individuals with pluralism at the collective, disciplinary level such that societal problems (say, democratic vitality) may be attacked from a variety of directions by distinctive communities of researchers (APSA Task Force on Graduate Education 2004).[2]

The feasibility of the first vision is questionable. The graduate program that could produce researchers capable of competently applying modeling, ethnographic, semiotic, statistical, and narrative methodologies as the research question dictates would seem to require incredibly talented, flexible students (not to mention faculty), with access to that broad array of course offerings, as well as the time to absorb, if not master, these wide-ranging methodologies. The attraction of the vision, however, is its emphasis on scholarly curiosity and a commitment to substance that promises a vibrant pluralistic practice, with researchers swapping techniques and ideas in the pursuit of solutions to problems about which they care deeply. In contrast, the vision of the APSA Task Force—specialization by program with an ensuing pluralism at the collective level—appears more feasible (because it does not imply that departments need offer such broad-based methodological training), but it may run afoul of what is known about the sociology of professions. Ingroup-outgroup social psychological processes, shown by Tajfel and Turner (1979) to be exceedingly robust, arise such that scholarly *identities* become entangled with theoretical and methodological approaches—producing the sort of "tribal warfare" remarked on by Anderson (2000, 8): "Judging from the way most American doctoral students are trained today, disciplines are as much gangs, with handshakes and colors, initiation ceremonies and secret passwords, as they are research traditions. Their members are jealous of their territory and quick to resort to 'trash talk' when confronted with the work of their rivals." Notably, these group processes are legitimized wherever a Lakatoisan, let-the-best-paradigm-win perspective on scientific knowledge persists. Accordingly, the Task Force vision may produce a structural pluralism at the collective level, but the scholarly attitudes and practices likely engendered by it do not seem consistent with the ideal of "both-and" pluralism nor likely to produce the cooperative, exploratory spirit of the first vision of problem-driven research.

This sketch and very brief analysis of these two visions of the practice of pluralism imply, although not necessarily so, quite different portraits of scholarly motivations. On the one hand, in the first vision, the scholar is driven by a passionate interest in a substantive topic such that her identity is not bound up with methodological approaches; she uses whatever approach suits the question, producing an ethnographic study for some problems and a survey-based quantitative study for others. She simply ignores—or imagines she can ignore—the politics surrounding the competition among knowledge approaches. On the other hand, in the second vision (structural pluralism *lacking* the "both-and" spirit), the scholar is deeply identified with her methodological approach—"her" paradigm for research—and convinced of its superiority (at least for "the important" questions); her "politics" could be characterized as the politics of scholarly self-interest in the sense that advancement of her paradigm furthers her career regardless of the paradigm's validity or appropriateness to the question at hand. And whether she can really be trusted, as a self-interested actor, to support structural pluralism seems questionable, particularly if she endorses a Lakatosian epistemological perspective that the "best" paradigm will and should win.

What both of these caricatures have in common is a very "thin" understanding of "the political." It may seem plausible that one can be above the politics of knowledge approaches when the choice is represented as one of "methods," as if "methods" were neutral tools to be chosen from the fully stocked tool box provided by doctoral education. Not only is it questionable whether the tool box will be fully stocked, but, more important, choice of method is entangled with "methodology," which, in turn, is connected with particular theoretical and epistemological commitments. For example, it is difficult to imagine a researcher choosing between feminist and evolutionary psychological (e.g., Ridley 1994) approaches to gender *as if* the research question itself would indicate which of these two should be chosen to address it. *Both* of these approaches are deeply political in their distinctive assessments of the possibility of personal and social change for addressing gender issues. More broadly, research questions are not simply "given" by nature or society but flow out of a complex combination of theoretical, methodological, ethical, and political commitments. As Atkinson, Coffey, and Delamont put it, "in the world of real research, social scientists do not dream up 'problems' to investigate out of thin air, divorced from concerns of theory and methodology, and only then search for precisely the right method" (2003, 99).

Similarly, the reduction of "the political" to self-interest, as in the second caricature, ignores the ethical element that is part and parcel of politics as a commitment to "the good." Continuing with the same comparison of contending approaches used earlier, individual scholars choose feminism over evolutionary psychology not only because they consider it a better approach to understanding gender but also for "political" reasons beyond scholarly self-interest, that is, because (in their view) evolutionary psychology contributes directly to contemporary constructions of gender that decrease human freedom, particularly for women. Likewise, individual scholars who choose evolutionary psychology over feminism consider it the better approach; but, whereas they would likely admit (or, if a Lakatoisan, even claim) the scholarly politics of self-interest (because, in this view, self-interested competition is consistent with the disciplinary, collective interest in a dominant paradigm), they eschew other, broader sorts of political concerns as "unscientific" (see, e.g., Alford and Hibbing 2004, 707), claiming scientific "objectivity" for their results and denigrating feminists as the ones who are inappropriately "political." These contrasting understandings of "the political" highlight a conundrum for the practice of pluralism—that one critical commitment that divides many of the social sciences in patently incommensurable ways concerns conceptualizations of research processes and communities as "objective and apolitical" *or* as "fundamentally and ineluctably political." Therein lies a direct challenge to the "both-and" conceptualization of pluralism. Whereas Flyvbjerg would have me criticize only the dominance of evolutionary psychology, I feel an ethical duty to criticize its very existence because such explanations often imply an immutability to gender that itself creates gender inequality in the here and now.

This conflict over the political nature of research is broader than just this example of feminism versus evolutionary psychology; it has its roots in epistemological debates about the fact/value dichotomy that are many decades old. Scholars who claim "objectivity" for their research (implicitly) endorse a positivist conception of knowledge that post-positivist scholars contest as epistemologically impossible, that is, "the view from nowhere." It is notable that, despite the compelling nature of the epistemological claims of post-positivist philosophers of science (Hawkesworth 2006), these *same* researchers who claim objectivity have relinquished positivism (because it has been so thoroughly discredited); still, they continue with their research approaches *as if* their theoretical concepts could be treated as transparently reflecting "reality" in an apolitical manner. Yet, at the bottom of every "count" of a phenomenon (from gross domestic product to the incidence of rape) are researchers' acts of categorization, decisions about inclusion and exclusion that are ineluctably political. (In my observations of conference presentations and discussions, the politics of categorization are often brushed aside with a disinterested shrug and the excuse that "these are the data that we have.") Such an inconsistent practice has led Bevir (2003) to observe that many who claim a technical rigor (in their use of quantitative-statistical methodologies) lack "philosophical rigor" in that their research practices rest on untenable philosophical premises. In contrast, feminists (e.g., Harding 1993) and others working in the qualitative-interpretive tradition[3] have worked hard to theorize the place of political commitments in research, developing an extensive literature on "reflexivity"—the ways in which individual scholars and scholarly communities can assess how values intertwine with and impact research processes and findings.

This situation, then, sets up the following scenario: (implicitly positivist) scholars claim an "objectivity" for their research, denying that their approach is political; post-positivist scholars claim that all research, their own included, *is* political and that the political consequences—of not only research findings but also research approaches—must be owned by all scholars. Ironically, those with the epistemologically untenable position (i.e., denying the political nature of their work) have the political upper hand *because of that very denial;* contemporary power holders from Congress to NSF to the society at large still hold philosophically unsustainable, if unstated, epistemological positions, so that scholars who admit "values" to their social scientific research are labeled as "biased" and may be denied resources. Thus, feminists and interpretive researchers are continually on the defensive (e.g., Marshall and Rossman 1999) even as they do the substantive work to develop reflexivity so that the entanglements of values and research are better understood.

These complexities, then, require a more nuanced analysis of recommendations for the *practice* of pluralism. If, as one commentator put it, "positivism is reflexivity denied,"[4] then how should researchers with these incommensurable commitments interact? One clear principle should be a commitment to pluralism at a structural level supporting *the right* to exist of what might be called one's "research others"—those who use methodological and theoretical approaches incommensurable with their own favored approaches. This commitment is rooted in what Yanow (1997) has called "a passionate humility"—belief in the validity of one's own research approaches, coupled with the classically scientific attitude that anyone, oneself included, could be wrong. On such grounds, then, it would be wrong of me as a feminist researcher to deny training and funding and journal space to evolutionary psychologists. My aim, as a feminist, should not be to eliminate this research by such power moves but to contest its findings on theoretical, empirical, *and* political-ethical grounds. It does not follow, as Flyvbjerg's epigraph seems to imply, that a commitment to structural pluralism (out of a passionate humility) should mean silence on my part. Rather, it is my ethical duty to criticize those who falsely claim an impossible "objectivity" and to point out the political implications of chosen research approaches. In sum, for me, the practice of pluralism entails a commitment to structural pluralism coupled with an ethical duty to analyze, assess, and criticize the political stakes inherent in knowledge approaches.

The example used earlier—feminist versus evolutionary psychological approaches to gender—clarifies the political stakes involved in competing research approaches, but it may strike some readers as somewhat marginal to the concerns of many political scientists. It is not as if evolutionary psychology is in the mainstream of the discipline (although recent high-profile publications may indicate a change in that regard; see, e.g., Alford and Hibbing 2004; Alford, Funk, and Hibbing 2005). Another, seemingly less contentious comparison may better illustrate the argument that epistemological positions on objectivity/reflexivity constitute a division with which visions of pluralism must cope. This example involves the political positioning of research "subjects" ("participants" is the preferred nomenclature in ethnographic and interpretive research traditions) *and* researchers in two literatures that address decision making—the heuristics literature and the tacit or local knowledge literature. My familiarity with the former literature stems from my graduate training in the early 1980s in experimental methods and rational-choice theory, whereas I encountered the latter literature only as I began learning about interpretive methodologies in the 1990s—even though the classics in that literature predated and were contemporaneous with my graduate training.

The experimental dissertation that I completed (Schwartz-Shea 1983) examined the "framing" of public goods problems, where "framing" was understood in terms of the ideas of the psychologists Kahneman and Tversky (1979) and others working on "decision-making heuristics." So, for example, Tversky and Kahneman performed experiments that showed that "choices involving gains are often risk averse and choices involving losses are often risk taking" (1981, 453). In other words, the subjective disutility of a unit loss is greater than the subjective utility of a unit gain, reflecting the "commonplace that the pleasure of winning a sum of money is much less intense than the pain of losing the same sum" (Kahneman and Tversky 1981, 164). In the context of the decision-making literature of that time (which had co-evolved with game theory), this lack of equivalence is "wrong" and leads people to make "poor" decisions. Tversky and Kahneman (1981, 457) compare the effects of frames on preferences to the effects of perspectives on perceptual appearances:

> If while traveling in a mountain range you notice that the apparent relative height of the mountain peaks varies with your vantage point, you will conclude that some impressions of relative height must be erroneous, even if you have no access to the correct answer. Similarly, one may discover that

the relative attractiveness of options varies when the same decision problem is framed in different ways.

Numerous subsequent decision-making experiments supported this particular finding and demonstrated other decision-making problems as well (Kahneman, Slovic, and Tversky 1982). This literature was extensive in the 1980s and has continued to this day (Gilovich, Griffin, and Kahneman 2002). Psychologists, economists, and others have produced research that shows the ways in which everyday decision making by ordinary people is predictably "biased" because of the use of heuristics that distort their judgment. People commonly use decision-making short cuts (or heuristics) that do not conform to the dictates of pure logic.

What strikes me about this literature, thinking about it so many years later, is how different it is from what I know of the research on what has been termed "tacit knowledge" by some (Polanyi 1966; Polanyi and Prosch 1975; Ingersoll and Adams 1992) and local knowledge by others (Geertz 1983; Yanow 2004). In the heuristics literature, researchers want to know how "real people" make decisions, but they investigate this topic using quite artificial paper and pencil exercises, often in laboratory settings. The result of this voluminous research is a consistent set of findings, the implication of which is that ordinary people need to be taught to think like the experts (meaning the researchers themselves). In contrast, in the literature on tacit and local knowledges, researchers begin with the assumption that ordinary people have reasons for what they do; that is, they know something about their own situations that the researchers do not. For example, Schmidt (1993) analyzes the collapse of a dam to show that the knowledge of low-level workers was superior to that of engineers but their knowledge was dismissed, not only because of their lower hierarchical status but also because of assumptions about what constitutes "real" knowledge.

As summarized in Table 11.1, these two literatures paint very different portraits of ordinary people and, as important for my purposes here, very different portraits of researchers. In the heuristics literature, ordinary people are portrayed as flawed and befuddled, whereas researchers are, implicitly, experts who can teach them how to be better, more effective decision makers. In the tacit-knowledge literature, ordinary people are portrayed as informed and reasonable, as having reasons for their actions that derive from their intimate knowledge of their own lived experience, even if they cannot articulate these reasons as fully or as carefully as would befit experts' standards. (See Soss 2006 and Maynard-Moody and

TABLE 11.1 *Portraits of subjects/participants and researchers in two literatures*

| Literature | Subjects/Participants | Researcher |
|---|---|---|
| Heuristics | Flawed, befuddled | Expert, teacher |
| Tacit knowledge | Reasonable, have knowledge | Investigator |

Musheno 2006 on methods for accessing tacit and local knowledge; and Yanow 2000). Instead, in this second situation it is the researcher who is lacking expertise in that lived experience, and she goes to ordinary people precisely because they are experts on their own lives and the contexts of those lives.[5]

What do these contrasting literatures imply about the *practice* of pluralism, that is, about the sorts of scholarly interactions we might expect? Additionally, how might we make sense of their quite different perspectives on ordinary people's capacities and their contrasting, if implicit, portraits of researchers? At least three possibilities present themselves.

One construal of a "both-and" understanding of pluralism is that both approaches to knowledge about decision making are "correct" and that the findings—the respective "truth claims"—simply imply different "knowledge domains" to which the literatures apply. There is a certain plausibility to this interpretation. Ordinary people fail to live up to the standards of pure logic in paper-and-pencil tests that ask them to use probability reasoning, but they have in-depth, worthwhile knowledge about their own daily activities. On this reading of the two approaches, one can imagine a pluralism that "carves up" research space and assigns the best theories to parts of that space, what sociologists call specifying the scope of a theory. Notice how this interpretation gives credence to both research approaches so that one can imagine fruitful, cross-boundary scholarly exchanges on, say, doctoral committees or in the peer-review process consistent with the "both-and" vision of pluralism. Additionally, it is an interpretation that does not inquire into the political positioning of researchers vis-à-vis their subjects/participants, leaving to the side the potential conflicts over researchers' societal roles.

A second possibility is to argue that the heuristics literature tackles a problem that can be documented in the laboratory but that doesn't matter in other contexts because "the problem" is a creation of the research experts. Or, from the other side, it might be argued that the tacit knowledges found in specific locales are marginal phenomena with little potential to contribute to social scientific understanding of the human world.

Here, individuals committed to pluralism make their own judgments about the usefulness of research agendas but are still willing to adopt an attitude of "live and let live": "I don't do research on that sort of intellectual puzzle, but it's no skin off my nose if someone else does." This attitude reflects a commitment to structural pluralism, but it is the sort of acceptance that is likely to produce few, if any, cross-boundary exchanges because both sets of scholars simply do not judge the others' problems as worthy of their own time and energy. And, again, the politics inherent in research approaches do not loom large when there is little interaction between research communities.

Finally, a commitment to reflexivity produces a third possibility, that the heuristics researchers are part of a professional-technical class that creates and solves problems given to it by elites, and then regular people are in some senses "disciplined" and "taught" ways of being that will help them to better "get along" or "adapt to" the contemporary economic-consumer world. The very same critique might be made of local knowledge researchers because they are part of the same professional-technical class. Yet, their research approach, unlike the heuristics approach, is explicitly reflexive, and many local knowledge researchers explicitly seek knowledge to empower research participants. This third interpretation, then, asks about researchers' roles in social-political-economic power structures and eschews the possibility of innocent research approaches and findings. (For analyses of social science in these terms, see Mitchell 2002 and Hawkesworth 2006) Those who take this perspective, then, have an ethical duty to point out these political consequences to all involved—an exchange that is likely to raise the ire of, in this example, heuristics scholars so targeted who, predictably in the contemporary period, will claim that *they* are the "objective" ones, whereas those criticizing them are illegitimately "political."

The first scenario is consistent with Flyvbjerg's "both/and" admonition in the first epigraph to not criticize "rules, logic, signs, and rationality in themselves." It implies a "happy" pluralism in which researchers can imagine themselves contributing to the proverbial house of knowledge, though perhaps to different wings of that structure. In the second scenario, judgments are made about the significance of the problems defined and researched by different research approaches. This snapshot results in a less sanguine perspective on the practice of pluralism; some researchers believe that they add whole floors to that house and that others add barely a brick. Finally, in the third scenario, researchers think more critically about the value of their research and how it will be used—not only in a pragmatic way but also in a political way that goes beyond "both-and." Here, the "oppositional" stakes pointed out by Wingrove in the second epigraph become most apparent. What kind of a house do we want to build, and for whom? Once this question of reflexivity is asked, and taken seriously, it seems impossible to go back to the previous "innocence," now understood as dangerously naïve, in which researchers may unknowingly (or knowingly) serve power rather than promote freedom and justice.

Perhaps there will continue to be pockets of happy pluralism in the social science disciplines in which scholars encounter other approaches and appreciate the relevance of each other's contributions. This is indeed a plausible outcome when distinct research approaches share fundamental epistemological and ontological assumptions (and, so, many will continue to believe, on the basis of such a comparatively narrow set of experiences, that politics needn't affect research). A recent example is the NSF-funded summer institutes in Empirical Implications of Theoretical Models (EITM) that bring together formal modelers and statistical researchers (e.g., http://eitm/berkeley.edu/ last accessed June 2, 2005). The more likely outcome may be the second scenario described earlier, in which judgments are made by diverse scholarly communities about what topics matter most to them (with little interest in the absorptions of others). Cross-community scholarly exchanges about what constitutes significant research—to the extent they occur—are an indicator of a more vibrant pluralism than that advocated by Flyvbjerg because they force scholars to think more deeply about what research is worth doing. But the greater the epistemological distance between such communities, likely the more acerbic the exchanges, particularly to the extent that scholarly identities are bound up with theoretical and methodological approaches.

I argue that we should strive for the third possibility, despite the fact that it is likely, in the short run in particular, to be rather acrimonious—at least while many persist in their faith in positivist versions of objectivity. It is this third sort of pluralism that can, in the long run, produce a more honest and relevant social science—a social science that matters because it asks questions of justice about every facet of the research process. To be clear, I am not arguing that the answers to such questions are straightforward. And facile judgments—that one set of research questions, methods, theories or approaches are automatically on side of justice, whereas others serve only the powerful—must be vigorously resisted. Rather, individual scholars and scholarly communities need to more consistently and persistently ask questions about who benefits from research and to theorize researchers' complex positioning in the political world. It is reflexivity on, rather than denial of, our politics that will make structural pluralism more productive of social science research that matters.

A very brief version of these remarks was prepared for the roundtable "Making Political Science Matter" and presented at the American Political Science Association Annual Meeting, Chicago, IL, September 2–5, 2004. Thanks to Dvora Yanow for organizing the roundtable and inviting me to participate and to the other fellow panel members, Timothy Luke and Mary Hawkesworth, for their stimulating contributions. Joe Soss and Mark Button provided valuable critical perspectives in the development of these ideas. Finally, thanks especially to Mary Hawkesworth for her encouragement and to Elizabeth Wingrove for her thoughtful criticism on a related project.

## NOTES

1. An important part of Soss's argument is that reification of scholarly identities decreases individual scholars' freedom and flexibility to pursue diverse projects over the course of their careers (2006, note 2). I do not disagree with this point but, instead, seek to show the ways in which the politics inherent in research approaches complicate the relationship of scholars to their chosen research projects.

2. The APSA Task Force position on graduate education is more nuanced than this representation of it might suggest. Its authors emphasize the importance of breadth of training and exposure to a variety of research approaches for first- and second-year graduate students as a "fundamental duty" of departments (5). But they also acknowledge the need for in-depth training in at least one research area, and they note that "some departments may well choose to specialize in particular approaches to political science" (4). The report goes on to explore a variety of ways to mitigate the problems produced by mismatches between students' interests and skills and departmental specialization.

3. The literature developing the concept of "reflexivity" in relation to interpretive research is extensive (Schwandt 2001), such that "reflexivity" has become a general criterion for assessing the quality of research. Texts have been written on its philosophical status (Bartlett 1992), the role of emotion therein (Carter and Delamont 1996), and practical techniques for accomplishing it (Finlay and Gough 2003).

4. This was a comment by an audience member in the discussion at the 2004 Chicago APSA Roundtable entitled "Making Political Science Matter."

5. This assumption does not mean that interpretive researchers cannot be critical of the people they study (as in much feminist analysis), but *that* critical move must, in an age of reflexivity, be explicitly theorized and defended. And, usually, the relative power positions of researchers and study participants are brought specifically into the analysis.

# 12

# Unearthing the Roots Of Hard Science
## *A Program For Graduate Students*

## *Gregory J. Kasza*

Quantitative analysis, formal modeling, and other forms of hard science dominate the leading journals and research institutions of American political science. These approaches to the study of politics raise fundamental philosophical issues, but one by-product of the hegemony of hard science has been the banishment of political philosophy to the margins of the discipline. Indeed, political philosophy is the most distinguished victim of today's "normal science." This essay offers graduate students a program by which to test the claims of hard science, demonstrating how you might use personal experience, the study of history, and the study of philosophy to scrutinize today's dominant scholarly ideology.

Today's Perestroika movement presents a radical critique of hard science as a means to study politics. This critique revolves around the definition of "science" as it is applied to the study of human beings. Today's protest movement is not antiscientific, as some adherents of the hard-scientific establishment have tried to stigmatize it. Contrary to David Laitin's claim that the rebels have "abandoned the project of a scientific discipline" (Laitin 2003, 163), most protesters associated with Perestroika think of themselves as scientists. But what sort of science is possible when the object of study is a human society? Science has always been a contested concept, even in the realm of the physical sciences, and it remains so today. The Perestroika critique raises three core questions related to the reach of "science" in the study of politics:

First, what is the character of political life? This is the ontological question. In particular, does politics exhibit the high degree of consistency and regularity demanded by hard science, or do choice, complexity, and accident limit its regularities? Formal theorists and quantitative researchers seek a political science comparable in precision and breadth to the natural sciences, but does the character of politics resemble or differ from the character of physical nature?

Second, how and what can we know about politics? This is the epistemological question. Given the character of political life, what sort of knowledge about it is possible? Does the character of politics lend itself to the equilibria of formal theory? Are most significant aspects of politics meaningfully convertible into numbers? Moreover, to what extent can scholars transcend their personal interests and their position in society and history to offer an objective, comprehensive, and thus scientific account of the social world?

Finally, what purpose should political knowledge serve? This is the normative question. What good follows from the study of politics? What ends should guide our work? How might we integrate research on the mechanical features of politics with reasoning about its proper ends?

In short, what is out there, what can we know about it, and why should we want to? Perestroika questions hard science on these radical grounds. The answers to the ontological, epistemological, and normative questions are complex, and no one should enter this profession without addressing them, yet graduate education today largely ignores these core questions. Instead, it offers students a sterile training in hard scientific methodology that embodies what C. Wright Mills long ago disparaged as "the ethos of the technicians." Once upon a time, philosophers of social science thought they possessed a set of persuasive answers to the fundamental questions, but these have now proved unsustainable. In response, most practitioners of social science, rather than altering the way they conduct research, have simply dropped these questions from the curriculum.

How should you who are entering the profession of political science investigate the ontological, epistemological, and normative questions related to politics? This essay directs graduate students to three sources for help, and it explains briefly why my answers to these questions have led me to adopt a more humble conception of social science than that which dominates the discipline today.

The first place to seek answers to the basic questions is in your personal experience. Examine your life. Evaluate your character. How would you explain where you are today? Has your life conformed to rational-choice equilibria? Could the significant elements in your life be meaningfully reduced to numbers? What does your self-reflection tell you about the nature of human beings and their politics?

Although this is the easiest place to turn for insight into the core questions, most scholars decline to use their personal experience as a standard for evaluating their research. They behave as if social science constituted an abstract world of truths that existed independent of the experiences of the social scientist. Consequently, young people considering political science as a profession typically make no effort to increase their range of life experiences in preparation, and scholarly books tell us little about their authors.

I will now share some reflections on my experience to illustrate what a person's self-analysis might look like, and to explain how mine has led me to reject the claims of hard science. My fascination with politics began at age 11, when I decided that I would become a diplomat. Being born into the American middle-class, I had a better chance to control my life's course than most people. But today I am a scholar of Japanese politics, and both my becoming a scholar and my focus on Japan occurred more by accident than on purpose.

When I graduated from college, in 1971, I thought I might have to serve in the military, but, thanks to chance, that did not happen. I had made no other plans beyond graduation, so I did menial jobs for a while. I then met a Japanese teacher who was visiting my home town of Los Angeles, another chance event. He taught English to children at a private academy in Japan, and he was looking for an American to teach there. I took him to my grandmother's house for Thanksgiving dinner and to the USC-UCLA football game (I have not been entirely a pawn of fate!), and he offered me the job. When I got the offer, I looked to locate Japan on a map. I had never taken a course on Japan as a college student. Had I been hired to teach in Nigeria, Bolivia, or Malaysia, I would have been just as happy. Teaching English in Japan, I met my wife and began to study Japanese, and my life moved in a new direction.

A few years later, while doing an internship at the Carnegie Endowment for International Peace, I took the U.S. Foreign Service exam to enter the diplomatic corps, but I failed the oral part of the test. Afterwards, I mentioned this to one of the VIPs in the Department of State whom I had been interviewing as part of my work at Carnegie, and he said, "Greg, if only you had told me!" He didn't put it in so many words, but he was the Inspector General of the Foreign Service at the time, and it was clear that he could have put in the fix for me. Not making a phone call to him before that test cost me a career in diplomacy, something I had aspired to for fifteen years. A phone call—and I would have dealt with Gorbachev's Perestroika rather than our modest academic version.

When I examine my character, I find inconsistencies. I find acts of courage alongside acts of cowardice, periods of commitment alongside periods of procrastination. In short, my life has not conformed to anything like a hard-scientific theory of human behavior. There are certain regularities, to be sure, but they coexist with elements of chance and unpredictability. In this, I suspect, I am not alone. Howard Becker (1998, 30) cites one study of social scientists that found that, despite their commitment to "highly deterministic models of social causation" in their research, all resisted the application of these same models when discussing their own lives.

Examine your life not only to grasp the nature of society but also to ponder the epistemological and normative questions. How clearly are you able to see into the souls of the people you know? Looking at the people you interact with every day, do you know how they got where they are? Could you describe the crucial junctures in their lives? What does that tell you about your ability to explain the decisions of millions of voters, or the life of a great leader whom you have never met?

In what respects does your experience suggest the good ends that political knowledge might serve? What injustices have you experienced that this knowledge might set aright? My research interest in war springs partly from the immense consequences of the Vietnam War for my life and the lives of my friends, even though I never fought in it.

At this point, you may be thinking, "Greg, why should anyone care about your little life? Why should one person's experience be the measure of anything? Isn't the whole idea of 'science' to look beyond one's experience to discover the general experience?"

This challenge sounds reasonable, but when I read theories of politics that obviously do not apply to the life of the scholar who concocted them, I become suspicious. As a graduate student, I spent a one-semester reading course on Hobbes's *Leviathan*. The introduction bothered me because it appeared utterly unscientific and out of character with the rest of the book. There Hobbes wrote that readers would ultimately have to consult their experience to determine if what he had written was the truth.

[R]ead thyself . . . for the similitude of the thoughts and passions of one man, to the thoughts and passions of another, whosoever looketh into himself, and considereth what he doth, when he does think, opine, reason, hope, fear, &c. and upon what grounds; he shall thereby read and know, what are the thoughts and passions of all other men on like occasions.... [T]he characters of man's heart, blotted and confounded as they are with dissembling, lying, counterfeiting, and erroneous doctrines, are legible only to him that searcheth hearts. And though by men's actions we do discover their design sometimes; yet to do it without comparing them with our own ... is to decipher without a key, and be for the most part deceived.... [W]hen I shall have set down my own reading orderly, and perspicuously, the pains left another, will be only to consider, if he also find not the same in himself. For this kind of doctrine admitteth no other demonstration. (Hobbes 1962, 20)

At the time, this struck me as a half-baked way to introduce a book of rigidly formal modeling. I have since come to think that Hobbes's preface was profound.

Scholars who offer theories of politics that do not apply to them are deceiving themselves and deceiving others. If your political views and actions are not guided mainly by material interests, why should you imagine that the views of others will be? If your life has not followed rational choices or mathematical equations, why should that be true of others'. Let your experience and self-reflection as a human being be your first guide as you seek to answer the basic questions about politics.

The moment you begin to take your experience seriously as a source of knowledge, you will start to think differently about the character of your education. Scholars who spend countless hours in the library or in front of a computer in the land of nerd-dom are infamous for their lack of experience of the world outside. If experience matters to our work, it follows that we should seek to expand our range of experiences and also to embrace those research methods that combine direct experience with other ways to acquire knowledge. Ethnographic methods and field work are designed to incorporate experience into research. In his ingenious exposition of the Aristotelian concept of *phronesis*, Bent Flyvbjerg has reformulated our notion of political wisdom to include the lessons of experience.

To learn from your experience, you must trust yourself. Do not accept the assertions of your mentors if these clash with the lessons of your life. Instead, question such assertions by asking your professors if what they are preaching accords with their life experience. My experience and self-reflection lead me to conclude that formal theories and quantitative research would be poor tools for explaining most of my life, so I will not use them to explain most of yours. How can an explanation be true of everyone that is not true of anyone?

A second way to grapple with the big questions about politics is to reflect upon the lives of others, that is, to study history. People in history departments do many types of scholarship. What I mean by history is old-fashioned, narrative-descriptive-chronological history. This is the type of history found in books with titles like *George Washington: The Early Years,* or *The Peasants of Alsace, 1665–1885.* Such work enables a person to experience vicariously the lives of others. It allows you to see if other people have lived life the way you have, giving you a broader basis upon which to judge the claims of hard science.

The reading of history is a humbling experience for most social scientists. In graduate school, I spent a summer reading about the French Revolution. Regional nobles started the revolution to regain privileges they had lost to the crown, but the revolution ended with the urban rabble putting those nobles to death and elevating a populist demagogue in their place. None of those who started the revolution could have foreseen or desired its end.

Another piece of history I know well is that of the Peruvian military regime that took power in 1968. The initial junta had revolutionary aims, but more conservative generals took control in a countercoup in 1975. Political scientists alleged many systemic reasons for the countercoup: economic conditions, the prior junta's failure at popular mobilization, and other causes open to theoretical argument. But years later, after the military had returned power to civilians, a Peruvian journalist named María del Pilar Tello interviewed the officers who had led the regime. They had arranged a peaceful transition from the first president to the second. Some uncertainty always attends such arrangements, but there was never a plan to launch a countercoup. One night a few months before the scheduled transition, several generals got drunk at a party, and in that state they telephoned local military garrisons and ordered them to march on the presidential palace. At the time, they believed that the chosen successor would continue the regime's revolutionary program. He surprised them all a few months later by changing course (Tello 1983, 1:275). Just as the failure to make a phone call cost me a career in the diplomatic corps, so a drunken phone call toppled a government in Peru. Its consequences were no clearer to most of the perpetrators than were those of the French Revolution to its aristocratic sponsors.

History is not completely haphazard, but it resembles my life in that chance and inconsistency are sometimes decisive. There is room for theoretical explanation, but only of a limited, qualified sort, not for the grand, elegant explanations required by hard science.

There are other lessons to be learned from history in regard to the big questions. When you study a topic like the French Revolution, about which historians and social scientists have written for two centuries, you will find differences in their accounts. They rely on different sources; they highlight different aspects of the same events; they use different concepts to explain what happened. This will sensitize you to the problems we confront when we attempt to transcend our place in society and history to analyze events from a neutral, objective perspective. In struggling to explain why scholars have written and interpreted history so differently, you will become more aware of your own limitations as an objective observer of politics. Too often, what practitioners try to market as an objective, universal theoretical outlook turns out to be a culture-bound and time-bound perspective, like rational-choice theory. But you may not become aware of it unless you study the development of ideas in their historical context. The results of historical processes also enable you to reflect on the normative outcomes of political action and some of the ways that the political knowledge you seek might make good outcomes more likely.

A third way to educate yourself about the basic ontological, epistemological, and normative questions is to read political philosophy. Indeed, one might define political philosophy as the effort to grapple with these core questions. The great philosophers are those who have produced important, original insights into these matters. My graduate education included six courses in political philosophy. If you want to enter the Perestroika debate at a high level, start by reading Machiavelli and Hobbes. Machiavelli, who attributed much of politics to *fortuna,* would be a perestroikan today, whereas Hobbes originated many of the hard-scientific notions that I now rail against. My education also required extensive reading in the philosophy of science, covering writers like Karl Popper, Abraham Kaplan, Peter Winch, and Alan Ryan. These scholars knew the major philosophical traditions and discussed the scientific project in that larger context. The study of political philosophy is the most sophisticated way to explore the basic questions of what is out there, what we can know about it, and why we should want to.

Alas, the graduate education we offer today, crafted in the interests of hard science, does not encourage you to ponder these big questions. Nor does it offer you many courses in political history or philosophy that you would have to take in order to grapple with them. The opportunity to examine political history used to come in courses with titles like "The Politics of the Soviet Union" or "The Politics of Mexico." Such courses were once the backbone of the curriculum in comparative politics, but they are few these days. Most courses focus instead on ahistorical, theoretical topics that many students lack the background to evaluate with reference to real-world political systems.

Hard science has practically driven political philosophy from the curriculum. A two-semester sequence in political philosophy used to be a common requirement, but philosophy is rarely required at all now. Except for students who intend to write dissertations in the field, most of you will probably not take a single philosophy class. I once required Marx's *The Eighteenth Brumaire of Louis Bonaparte* when I taught the graduate survey in comparative politics. This important work is the source of many current arguments about state autonomy, but I dropped it because students did not have the historical or philosophical background to understand it. Many departments now handle the big questions perfunctorily in one-semester classes billed as "introductions to political science." The purpose of excluding philosophy from the curriculum is to crush dissent, for it offers the most profound critique of the dominant trends in the discipline. Most students today do not even read extensively in the philosophy of science. If they did, they would find that there is little philosophical foundation for the assumptions that guide today's hard-scientific research (Diesing 1991).

Why are you saddled with such an impoverished education? Hard scientists seek to forge what Thomas Kuhn called a "normal science" of politics. Kuhn argued that progress occurred in the natural sciences when the scientific community agreed on the basic questions and devoted itself to applied research. Only in rare moments of scientific revolution would the big questions return to the table. In an effort to turn the study of politics into such a normal science, today's hard scientists ignore the basic questions about the nature of our enterprise.

They assume away the "what is out there?" question by simply equating politics with general patterns of social action. This removes from the table all those troubling questions about the nature of the social world, such as, how much of it actually conforms to patterns? By definition, a "scientist" is one who unearths patterns. Do not worry about the rest; the history department will handle it.

Hard scientists assume away the "how do you know?" question by focusing all of your attention on methods. This is the fatal perversion of today's political science: the methodology fetish. The idea is that if you follow your methods textbooks to the letter, the result will be a perfectly objective contribution to scientific knowledge. This illusion of perfect-objectivity-through-method means that there is no need to consult your experience. Master the latest form of regression analysis, and you need not worry about how your values or your social position might color your work (as if the bureaucratic mindset inherent in the methods fetish were not a "value" in itself). Reducing politics to the language of mathematics, you will not have to supply a single adjective. *You* are out of the picture.

And as for the normative goals of political knowledge, why, they are assumed away, too. Democracy and human rights pretty much cover the field. If you entertain any doubts about this, there is no need for concern, because values do not really matter anyway. The goal of our discipline is not to make politics better; it is to produce grand, elegant theories that explain why politics is as it is, to find those patterns that we assume are ubiquitous out there. The fact that political leaders make stupid decisions is not a problem we need to solve. Our business is only to develop a theory that explains why they do so on such a consistent basis.

There is an intricate set of professional norms that locks the prevailing outlook into place. These norms are now so institutionalized that most scholars accept them without thinking. Academic journals, for instance, impose a conventional format on the articles they carry. The article must start with a review of the literature on a given topic, indicating a gap or a problem in previous research. The article then fills that gap or solves that problem with new data, preferably expressed in unnecessarily complicated mathematical equations with an addendum on some arcane question of methodology. The article then concludes by noting some new gaps or problems that it has brought to light, so that the next seminarian can get his research published. Dissertations take the same format. Depart from it, and the gatekeepers of the establishment will slam the door in your face. The journal's referees will reject your work for not citing the relevant literature, and the faculty considering your job application will reject it with the comment that "this research does not speak to the theoretical literature I know on this subject." The format in which you are forced to write is designed to keep your work within the bounds of "normal science." This format rewards derivative research, while the dismissal of truly original ideas calls to mind the Japanese saying that "the nail that sticks out will be hammered down."

Another institutional trait that protects the existing dogma of hard science is the lack of outlets for expressing dissent in the profession. Alone among the major academic associations, the American Political Science Association does not hold regular, competitive elections for its officers, so there is normally no electoral campaign in which one might raise issues about the profession. Nothing illustrates better the complete disconnect between what political scientists teach and write, and their personal experience. Transitions to democracy have been the foremost research topic in the discipline for the past fifteen years, yet we cannot seem to manage a transition to democracy in our own professional association. After all, what has all that research to do with us?

Except for *PS: Political Science and Politics,* there is no journal in political science that regularly welcomes articles on controversies within the discipline. Given the severe page limits on articles in *PS,* this means that most pieces on the topics addressed in this book go begging for a publisher. Even our newest journal, *Perspectives on Politics,* whose mission is to restore the relevance of political science to the real world, systematically excludes essays that might explain how political science became divorced from the real world in the first place. There has never been a conference of the American Political Science Association or an issue of the *American Political Science Review* (APSR) devoted to the subject of what should be the proper role of mathematics in the study of politics. Consequently, the shift to hard science has occurred without an open discussion of the relevant issues. If you are unaware of the alternatives to today's hard science, it is not because hard science has proven its superiority in an open contest of ideas but because professional norms and institutions lock the prevailing outlook into place.

What sort of soul emerges from today's graduate education in hard science? Its star product is the research technician, whose scholarly life revolves around quantitative methodology. C. W. Mills (1959, 105–6) wrote of this type:

> I have seldom seen one of these young men . . . in a condition of genuine intellectual puzzlement. And I have never seen any passionate curiosity about a great problem, the sort of curiosity that compels the mind to travel anywhere and by any means, to re-make itself if necessary, in order *to find out.* These young men are less restless than methodical; less imaginative

than patient; above all, they are dogmatic. . . . They have taken up social research as a career; they have come early to an extreme specialization, and they have acquired an indifference or a contempt for "social philosophy." . . . Listening to their conversations, trying to gauge the quality of their curiosity, one finds a deadly limitation of mind. The social worlds about which so many scholars feel ignorant do not puzzle them. . . . [E]xplicitly coded methods, readily available to the technicians, are the major keys to success . . . once a young man has spent three or four years at this sort of thing, you cannot really talk to him about the problems of studying modern society. His position and career, his ambition and his very self-esteem, are based in large part upon this one perspective, this one vocabulary, this one set of techniques. In truth, he does not know anything else.

Perestroika's challenge to hard science concerns the basic ontological, epistemological, and normative questions that lie at the heart of the scholarly enterprise. Thus far, hard scientists have offered no response to this challenge. We are met with the silence of the wolves. The reason, I suspect, is that most hard scientists, like most of you, entered their graduate education as though jumping on a moving train. They had no idea of the train's origins or ultimate destination, and their abiding concern was only to reach the next station. They did this by immediately going to work on some theory in some subfield of political science, blindly following their methodology textbooks, and striving to publish an article or two that might get them a job. Nowhere along the line—not in class, not in the methods texts, not in the editorial screening of the journals—did anyone bother them with the big questions. Their eyes have been focused on the next station . . . and the next, ever since. Never having asked themselves the big questions about political life and political knowledge, hard scientists have no idea how to respond to the radical challenge that Perestroika poses. So they ignore it and hope that by throwing some resources our way, a few articles in the *APSR* perhaps, they will satisfy us.

I do not imply that those who investigate the big questions will all reach the same conclusions I have. Some, like John Dewey and Richard Rorty, have come to question the project of positivistic science altogether, while others, from Auguste Comte to Ludwig Wittgenstein, have investigated those questions and produced answers more supportive of hard science. A pluralistic discipline must accommodate a variety of philosophical perspectives.

The problem that confronts us today is that most hard scientists would not know Comte from their aerobics instructor. Today's hard-scientific orthodoxy is a prejudice, not the reasoned product of self-reflection, historical study, and the reading of philosophy. To sustain that prejudice, the big questions about politics have been expunged from your education. Welcome to "normal science."

The reform of graduate education is a primary goal of the Perestroika movement. Until we achieve it, students will continue to find themselves in a difficult situation. It is a discouraging admission for me to make, but to become a scholar worthy of respect these days, to a great degree you will have to educate yourselves.

# 13

# Political Science and Political Theory
## *The Heart of the Matter*

## *David Kettler*

When Bent Flyvbjerg raises a call to "re-enchant and empower social science" (2001, 166), he may be understood, at least in part, to be renewing the demand for a "new political science" that had already mobilized an earlier generation (Kettler 1974; Wolfe 1970). Like the members of that cohort, he rightly despairs of the disciplinary preference for studies that are designed more to display and refine techniques of analysis than to seek answers to the questions that attend efforts to respond to the political urgencies of the times. Social scientists in general and political scientists in particular, intoxicated with methodology, are forever looking where the light of science is deemed to shine brightest, and not where the key objects of value have been lost. The question was then and the question is now, however, whether the best antidote is, so to speak, a hair of the dog. Flyvbjerg asks us to set about reversing the situation where social science is the "loser in the Science Wars." I am not persuaded that this is a valuable or achievable objective, and I will argue that those of us who share his larger concerns would do better to "declare victory" and to withdraw from that theater of operations, which is not of our choosing.

Philosophy is a demanding autonomous discipline with its own claims to respect; the self-reflection of critical intellectuals in the social sciences is best served by steady attention to what other working social scientists say and do in close conjunction with their actual studies. Mediations between the two domains take varied forms. Obviously, there will be learning from and bargaining with philosophical writers, but judgments will be more commonly made good by social science results than by improvised "refutations" of philosophical writers or definitive programmatic claims. The task is to redefine the interconnection without negating the tension. Surprisingly little thought has been given to such vital operations as "learning from" and "negotiating with," when it comes to encounters on the way to and from our own studies. What does seem clear is that these are properly constructive and even opportunistic relationships, too selective and decontextualized to bestow leverage for legitimate critique and evaluation.

To illustrate an alternative strategy for rendering social science politically instructive, I shall recall the work of Franz L. Neumann (1900–1954). To declare a rather massive interest, I must say, first, that Neumann was my teacher at Columbia and that I have been intermittently puzzling over his political theory/political science project since my very first published paper to the present (Kettler 1957, 2001). A Social Democratic labor lawyer in Weimar Germany and a graduate of the London School of Economics under Harold Laski and Karl Mannheim in the first years of his exile, Neumann was author not only of the seminal *Behemoth,* which offered a model for understanding Nazi Germany no less influential and generative, in its earnest way, than Hannah Arendt's spectacular *Origins of Totalitarianism* (Neumann 1944; Sollner 2004), but also, somewhat later, of an instructive project for interrelating the work conventionally divided between political theory and empirical political science. The latter undertaking can be best understood if his writings of the postwar years are read in the context of his exchanges with colleagues, not least in conjunction with his extensive dealings with foundations. Some reflection on his design may effectively complement, especially for political studies, the attempts in this volume to extract and extrapolate the insights that are doubtless present in Flyvbjerg's bold work.

A reflection on Neumann seems an appropriate bit of history, above all, because he strongly opposed his own time's versions of the present-day divorce between "political theory" and "empirical political science," which I consider to be the heart of the matter. Political theorists today are largely satisfied to be intellectual historians, epistemological explorers, or moral philosophers, often displaying extraordinary talent and virtuosity in these activities. Political science, for its part, puts the subject matter that the discipline used to class as political theory under the heading of ideology, and it admits theory, in the analytical sense of the term, only in one or another of the modes legitimated by the science that is characterized as empirical, although it actually leaves room for a good deal of rationalist constructivism. Neumann's program was not a "refutation" of such "political theory" or "political science," insofar as he could anticipate them fifty years ago, but a rejection of the categorical separation between the domains and the claims of either to exclusivity. "Empirical" work represented a continuum from narrative history to statistical analysis: it was all of intellectual importance, but also in need of contextualizing by a "theoretical" statement of questions and problems. The political theorists of the "canon" and others provide vital intellectual resources, but only insofar as engagement with their work helps contemporary thinkers to enrich their understanding of political relations and possibilities, past and present.

This requires a construction of the theories in conjunction with an account of the factual evidence to which it is meant to apply, with the value assessed by reference to the theories' worth as practical guide to judgment and conduct, given human aspirations to freedom. For Neumann, this implied indifference to precisely the structural features of theories that philosophers quite properly care about, which he dismissed as metaphysics in the pejorative sense. The models for his concept of theory appear to be the justificatory and organizing theories of law in the approach that Neumann learned from Hugo Sinzheimer and practiced as a labor lawyer in the Weimar years, where theory must conjoin but cannot fully synthesize the formal qualities of legality (which comprehend its core normative worth as well) with a sociological apprehension of the changing realities to which the law applies. Such complementarities between jointly relevant but incompatible models of understanding human conduct have been praised as asserting "the value of human action in time—which is to say, of history, of drama" (Burckhardt 1969: 183–84). Political action is the common ground—the shared reference point—between the two modes of thinking, but it cannot be exhaustively comprehended by either.

In a memorial delivered, as dictated by convention, by the head of his Columbia department to the assembled council of the Faculty of Political Science soon after Neumann's death but written in quite an unconventional, almost challenging manner by Neumann's closest friend, Herbert Marcuse, it is said of him that he "was a scholar for whom political science was closely linked to political action" and that "theory was for him not abstract speculation, not a digest of various opinions on state, government, etc., but a necessary guide and precondition for political action." His lifelong cause, according to the friend who knew best how he would want to be remembered, even in this academic setting, was to reverse the Weimar failure of social democracy, and his most pressing concern was the condition of his time. Referring to the situation in both Germany and the United States in 1954, Marcuse claims: "He became ever more appre-hensive of the intensified anti-democratic and neo-fascist trends the world over. He did not compromise; he did not recant." The motif of the talk was set at the outset, when it was stated as a puzzle that Neumann's last work should have addressed "Anxiety in Politics," since "he had always rejected the interpretation of politics in psychological terms." The conclusion returns to the puzzle, striking a political tone that lent urgency to what might otherwise have appeared as a commonplace:

> The "Anxiety in Politics" came to be his last word; it was not an escape into psychology. The title calls reality by its name; it epitomizes the political situ-ation of man in contemporary society. The traditional notions of political science are here absorbed into the overriding category—anxiety. The cate-gory does not seem to be alien and extraneous to political science today. (Political Science Faculty 1955)

Neumann's legacy, in my view, consists not of his particular political convictions or his distinctive diagnosis of his time but of his placing the starting point and endpoint of the two distinct aspects of political study in the practical domain of political action, understood not as a locus for self-enclosed projects, however worthy, but as the arena where system-related, long-term conflicts are adjusted or fought out. Specific aims, bargained settlements, and wins or losses in that political domain are understood in strategic perspective, as moments in unending campaigns by collective and socially embedded actors; both political theory and empirical political science have to be good enough, critical and remote from ideological tru-isms, to provide clarification and orientation. There is always something to be done: "No freedom without political activity" is the formula Marcuse ascribed to him in the memorial. But there is no assurance that situations rightly understood and aims rightly reflected will endorse dramatic mea-sures likely to bear large consequences in the short run.

In the address "Politics and Anxiety," cited by Marcuse, for example, Neumann starts with a concept of alienation derived from Schiller, Hegel, and Marx, links alienation to anxiety with the help of Freud's suggestions about mass psychology and the identification with leaders, and empha-sizes the heightening of these effects through an institutionalization of anxiety by means of the pervasive spread of conspiracy theories and mea-sures of terror. These continuing trends, he contends in 1954, make "the world more susceptible to the growth of regressive mass movements," if also in modes different from the 1930s. He asks whether the state or education can be relied upon to counteract these dangers and answers both questions with quotations from Schiller, discrediting both formulas, to all appearances, since both agencies are implicated in the "barbarous civil polity"; Neumann concludes, nevertheless, that "for us as citizens of the university and of the state," there nevertheless remains only "the dual offensive on anxiety and for liberty: that of education and that of politics" (Neumann 1957, 294).

"Anxiety and Politics" was presented at a ceremonial occasion at the Free University of Berlin, of which Marcuse credited him with being "the chief architect." What is important in the present context about Neumann's efforts on behalf of the Free University is, first, that they were a prime locus of political activity for him, involving not only the municipal government and American military authorities but also the principal foundations whose conduct of American cultural policies was closely coordinated with public agencies. (Neumann's activities on behalf of the Free University in 1951 can be followed in Ford Foundation 1951.) Second, and most important in the present context, one of his principal aims was to integrate political studies at the Free University with the work of the *Hochschule für Politik,* a site of important involvement for him already during the Weimar years and the center for a conception of "political education" (*politische Bildung*) that both embodied and embedded a way of doing social science. For Neumann, the institutionalization of political education, the shape of political inquiry, and the logic of political action are linked, although each of the three constituents has its own integral norms and none is merely instrumental to the others. To turn from the logical categories of two-term dialectics and complementarity to a more strictly political simile, Neumann's conception of political studies resembles a constitution, understood as a dynamic conjunction of formal and political elements. Such a reconstitution of political studies is a largely lost but retrievable legacy from Neumann and, as Ira Katznelson has recently argued, from the generation of American academics most directly responsive to the impetus of the émigré intellectuals of the 1930s (Katznelson 2001). The constitutional simile is especially applicable because Neumann, like Flyvbjerg, pushed for the reconceptualization of two categories that a political inquiry he considered as either too idealistic in its rendering of normative dimensions or too reductionist in its realism compartmentalized in air-tight boxes, and it is precisely the unresolved conjunction of political ideals and power that Max Weber puts at the center of constitutional law.

Neumann announced these dual themes in one of his first sustained encounters with American political scientists, the Columbia University Seminar on "The State," during the academic year 1946–1947, when Neumann was an adjunct professor in the School of International Relations (University Seminars 1946–47) The subject under discussion was bureaucracy, taken up by the group as a theoretical problem, after two years of descriptive historical treatments involving specialists in Egyptology, Greek and Roman classics, and medieval history. At the beginning of the new academic year, in October 1946, however, Robert K. Merton is applauded by Karl Wittfogel and Arthur MacMahon when he opens the proceedings with the remark that "we have had no clear statement of problems in two years; we didn't formulate the question *why* we are concerned with aspects of bureaucracy" (University Seminars 1946–47, October 4, 1946, 1). Neumann is asked for his views, as a new member with "individual experience in this field." Wittfogel and Merton had spoken to the issue first. Wittfogel wanted a focus on the social structural conditions under which bureaucracies are strong or weak, as well as their inner power relations, while Merton proposed a focus on the "factors which tend to limit bureaucratic power," in the wider context of a typology of bureaucracies. Neumann's remarks, his first recorded intervention in the seminar, are completely in character, responding openly to the ideological motifs implicitly present in the remarks of the others, not to denounce them but to bring them expressly into discussion:

> That bureaucracy and democracy are incompatible is untrue. Democracy would then be procedural. Might not our approach be to inquire where the locus of power is in the modern state? Is it in the bureaucracy? Is it outside the government? . . . We should analyze bureaucracy, and the external conditions making bureaucracy rule in our social process. Militarization has taken place in the human relations of society; external conditions have become so powerful that they may make democracy a sham and bureaucracy the power. (University Seminars 1946–47, October 4, 1946, 2)

Having injected this political urgency into the discussion, Neumann makes it clear that he does not mean by this to replace analysis with prophecies of doom. In fact, he adds immediately that such a development is not a realistic threat in the United States, since there is not really a bureaucracy in that country, in the sense of a cohesive social formation capable of exercising power, but only a "civil service."

In the course of the eight meetings of the semester, Neumann built an argument against a conflation of the functional and sociohistorical (or "institutional") aspects of bureaucracy, which he claimed to find in Max Weber, and against the erroneous assumption that a growth of bureaucracy in either of those senses necessarily implied an increase in bureaucratic power. Rather than assuming that the growth of officialdom and the increased need for the functional qualities associated with bureaucracy opened the door to rule by administrative agents of the ever more complex state, Neumann saw the accession of bureaucrats to a share of that decision making on discretionary, contested, and weighty matters he identified with "power" as a puzzling anomaly, given the impossibility of governing a dynamic society by the established rules inherent in bureaucracy, and thus as a symptom either of temporary conditions or of pathological malformations of state. When actors within the institutions of bureaucracy have power, they are not in any case acting bureaucratically. The question is how the locus of power came to such an unexpected place. His first assumption was always that power in the modern state, strictly speaking, would be exercised by other actors, whether public or private, and that bureaucracy would be instrumental, restricted to the functions that Weber identified as peculiarly bureaucratic. The problem of adapting democracy to modern conditions is not addressed by an attack on bureaucracy or on the expansion of governmental functions that brings with it a growth of administration (University Seminars 1946–47, November 29, 1946). The correct question is about the special circumstances that lead to an exercise of power by the bureaucracy as institution.

This analysis set him against the other two émigré intellectuals who played a prominent part in the proceedings, Karl Wittfogel and Gottfried Salomon-Delatour. Wittfogel charges: "Your definition is your personal definition and competes with others. . . . You have simplified the scope of analysis by referring to modern society, which is something different from Max Weber's teachings." Salomon, in turn, challenges Neumann: "Do you accept Weber's modern theory of rationalization in defining bureaucracy?" Neumann's reply to Wittfogel denies that his distinctions between bureaucratic and nonbureaucratic conduct fail to fit Weber's expositions of the phenomenon, but his reply to Salomon is "I do not accept [Weber's theory] because our society is not foreseeable as Weber says it is; it is even less so today. [ . . . In any case,] we must distinguish between discretionary and non-discretionary decisions, as was developed in Locke's theory" (University Seminars 1946–47, November 29, 1946, 4–5). For Neumann, theories are provisional guides to the reading of dynamic situations, and the primary objective is always to orient the discussants to a scene for action: the perspective is that of the actor, not the spectator. The records of the seminar are instructive not because Neumann is invariably right or clear but precisely because Neumann is always endeavoring to make social science matter.

Except for the introductory meeting and one meeting devoted to a frequently interrupted report on bureaucracy in the Soviet Union by an economist who apologized that he had not studied the phenomenon at all, the sessions were led by the three German exiles. Wittfogel, who had been a Communist in Weimar and member of the Institute for Social Research in New York but had broken with both, had three sessions to comment on the historical presentations of the preceding two years; Neumann spoke on bureaucracy in wartime for another three sessions; and Salomon-Delatour, the intellectual successor of Franz Oppenheimer, whose Frankfurt chair went to Karl Mannheim instead, was asked to lead the last two meetings by offering his views on the semester's work. The Americans taking part were themselves quite influential academic figures, notably Robert K. Merton, on his way to being one of the foremost sociological theorists of his generation; Walter Gellhorn, a leading writer on administrative law; and Arthur Macmahon, a very respected figure in American political science, noted for his work in public administration and American institutions and president of the American Political Science Association at the time. The 1946–1947 Columbia University Seminar on the State, in brief, was an important site for Franz Neumann and his two compatriots in acculturation to bring their competing macrotheoretical approaches, each possessing political overtones familiar to the competitors from Weimar debates—notably in conflicting judgments of socialism—before several prominent representatives of the older, more narrowly problem-centered, as well as the newer, science-building, American intellectual strategies. Neumann made a special impact because he showed that a broader historical and comparative framework need not detract from the circumstantial citation of urgency, relevance, and experience (notably his experiences as Weimar lawyer and as bureaucrat in wartime Washington), qualities of special value to most of his American partners in the seminar.

From a different point of view, Neumann's strategy in the Columbia seminar can be understood as an implementation of the overall design developed by the members of Max Horkheimer's Institute of Social Research, of which Neumann was an associate during his first years in

America and with which he remained allied, in their attempt to work with and transmit the adaptations of Marxism they called "critical theory," without appearing alien or esoteric to American social scientists. In the *"Debate about the methods of the social sciences, and especially about the conception of social scientific method represented by the Institute [of Social Research],"* held among the associates in January 1941, in which Neumann played an active part, pressing the case for meeting American expectations about empirical verification of claims, Horkheimer closes the discussion, as follows:

> The decisive element we will be unable to reveal—that we actually take science so seriously, in the end, that the decision of our lives and the turn of our lives as a whole depend on it—that theory is linked to practice, and that our attitude to practice changes when our knowledge changes. For us, science retains its practical and political seriousness. The contrast between the American and the European is that science is philosophy for us. One can act either on the basis of religious belief or out of theory and knowledge. That's also what it is that unsettles those people so much. (Horkheimer, 1941 Archiv IX, 214)

While there is no doubt that Neumann continued to speak in the accents of the Institute when he came to Columbia, and equally little doubt that Wittfogel and Salomon-Delatour opposed him as a representative of that school, it may be said that Neumann's measured distance from Horkheimer on the "subjectivity" of bureaucrats and his more vehement disagreements with his fellow-exiles in the State Seminar had a common ground in Neumann's conception of political power and of political studies as focused—in theoretical reflection, empirical inquiry, and strategic orientation—on the historically variable relationships between political power and political freedom, none of which figure importantly in the "political culturism" that emerges as the distinguishing theoretical practice of the "Frankfurt School" (Sollner 2005).

"Approaches to the Study of Political Power" (1950) and "The Concept of Political Freedom" (1953) are consequently the titles of the only two articles that Neumann published in periodicals with wide circulation among American political scientists (Neumann 1957, 3). In the opening paragraph of the essay on power, Neumann says disarmingly that he does not pretend to say "add any new idea to a discussion of political power" but rather hopes to aid "younger students" by laying "bare the approaches to its study" (Neumann 1957, 3). Neumann opens with a rejection of approaches that identify politics completely with power politics and that treat the psychology of power as the core problem, a position he imputes to a line of thinkers from Machiavelli to Harold Lasswell. This, he claims, "appears to have become the predominant trait of American and, perhaps, of modern political science in general" (4). The key to his rejection of this "technical" view is that political control is "always a two-sided relation-ship"(3), entailing at least the question whether and to what extent the acceptance of commands in a given context is a function of the rational, as well as emotional, capacities of human beings. The mode of analysis must be capable of recognizing when power claimants do not address rational capacities (or subjects of power do not expect or demand it) or when power is wholly reduced to the threat and infliction of violence, ending in liquidation. He concludes his preliminary argument thus:

> The rejection of the psychological approach involves in its positive aspect the view that politics (and thus history) is not simply a struggle of power groups for power, but an attempt to mold the world according to one's image, to impress one's view upon it. The historical process has a meaning. (5)

Having asserted that reasoned rationales for power are relevant to both the exercises and the study of political power, Neumann proceeds to a typology of value-laden attitudes toward power, which must be uncovered by the "soul searching of the political scientist" (5), because one or the other will invariably shape their approaches. "The valuative premises must be made clear," he adds, "so that objective analysis may be possible" (5).

His nine types, which cannot be developed here, are introduced by a sharp contrast between the community-centered affirmative concept of Plato and Aristotle and "the Augustinian position" for which all political power is evil and then extended to the "common-sense" Thomistic view, whose ambivalence toward political power "prepared the way for the lib-eral attitude." This is, of course, a crucial type for Neumann:

> Its sole concern is the erection of fences around political power which is, allegedly, distrusted. Its aim is the dissolution of power into legal relation-ships, the elimination of the element of personal rule, and the substitution of the rule of law in which all relationships are to become purposive-ratio-nal, that is predictable and calculable. (6)

Having characterized the first three approaches without evaluation, he asserts that this is "of course, in large measure an ideology" to obscure the locus of power, since "power cannot be dissolved in law" (7). His typically provocative citation in support of the last conclusion is a passage from the most unliberal Joseph De Maistre, pointing out the presence of hidden forces behind the law as written, which are indispensable to the state (20). Such unexpected evocations add a recurrent element of surprise to Neumann's works, even when he seems to be doing routine cataloguing. Accordingly, he next offers an "Epicurean attitude" as an approach, which makes the barest demands on political power and treats the rest with indifference, and he sees similarities to the "psychological consequences" of the former in his next type of approach, anarchism, inasmuch as its denunciation of all political power may lead to aloof indifference or putschist moves to establish an associative society at will (7). This brings him to Marxism, which he credits with a "positive attitude towards political power" but only until political power has smashed the conditions for its historical—not "natural"—existence (7). Rousseau's "positive attitude" in turn moves back in the direction of Plato and Aristotle, inasmuch as power is everywhere present but nowhere separate from other communal relations in view of "the alleged identity of rulers and ruled." Neumann ends with "the liberal democrat," who differs from the "total democrat" of Rousseau primarily because he does not accept "the total politicizing of life" and thus insists on the "separate character of political power." On balance, however, "he is increasingly concerned with the potentialities of a rational use of power" (8).

After this introductory section, which illustrates very well Neumann's uses of the political theory literature as an analytical resource, there follow sections on the significance of political power, the roots of political power, the identification of political power, and political power and freedom. The argument is an elaboration of Neumann's principal points in the 1946–1947 seminars. He points, first, to the growing complexity of the mix of persuasion, benefits and violence in the constitution of political power, and its expansion overall, to cope with the growing complexity of society. Second, then, the relationship between economic and political power becomes more difficult to delineate, and political power becomes ever more independent in its dynamics (up to the limiting case of the Soviet Union, where economic power seems to arise out of the political). This is the context in which the question of bureaucracy belongs, since the rise of politics and of bureaucracy go together. The extent to which bureaucrats exercise power is an empirical question, although it is clear that they exercise some. The blanket hostility to the "ascendant role of political power" is antidemocratic in inspiration and implication, as is the ideological misuse of distrust of bureaucracy. The typology of attitudes to power makes it clear that there is no univocal opposition to political power in "the tradition of Western civilization," which is frequently arrayed against these changes. "Certainly one can say," Neumann maintains, "that Rousseauism is a more important element in the political tradition of democracy than the essentially self-contradictory and arbitrary doctrines of Locke and the natural law" (16). He concludes this part of the argument thus: "The problem of modern democracy is much less the fencing of political power than its rational utilization and provision for effective mass participation in its exercise" (16). After a short interlude, in which he recurs surprisingly to Carl Schmitt's thesis that the locus of power is most clearly revealed in an emergency situation, Neumann picks up the liberal democratic thesis, which forms the transition to his "political freedom" article, but he does so in a markedly pessimistic vein.

To say, as he provisionally did at the outset, that ideas are as relevant to political study as power is "too ideological," Neumann now argues: "If history were a conflict between power groups and ideas, ideas would invariably be defeated" (18). The problem is to identify the power group among those in conflict that may more nearly, in that context, represent the "idea of freedom." Sweepingly, he asserts that "the task of political theory is thus the determination of the degree to which a power group transcends its particular interests and advocates (in Hegelian terms) universal interests." Having made this seemingly guileless statement, he turns immediately to the difficulty of distinguishing truth from ideology when attempting to make such judgments, especially because of the weight of a public opinion that submits so easily to authority, so that the persuasiveness of an idea says nothing about its rationality. The liar may become the hero, because he evades the weight of this force. Neumann ends with another of his unexpected citations, a long quotation from Charles S. Peirce, who speaks of the role played by "moral terrorism to which the respectability of society will give its full approval" (19) in maintaining uniformity. Beyond that, Neumann quotes Peirce as saying, the "peaceful and sympathetic man" will persecute himself until he finds himself forced "to submit his opinions to authority" (19, quoted from Peirce 1940, 20). Neumann's habit of partially subverting his own argument by the insertion of points taken from political opponents and unbelievers (De Maistre, Schmitt, Peirce) enacts his self-monitoring against ideological conformity: there is always that edge that sustains the provisional, exploratory character of the inquiry, even when it is punctuated as well by flat assertions on the borderline of dogmatism. In his writings, as in his studies, there is always a speaker present, and a voice.

Neumann's essay on political freedom opens with a reassertion of his thesis on "the task of political theory," now restated as the seemingly hopeless but indispensable "attempt to pierce the layers of symbols, statements, ideologies and thus come to the core of truth" (Neumann 1957, 162). Political freedom, he asserts, is the truth of political theory, but no political system can ever fully realize freedom. In consequence, he maintains, echoing the position of Horkheimer, "all political theory must by necessity be critical" (162). As the article goes on to make clear, however, the criticism must always be validated by a measure of realism; it presupposes as accurate understanding as possible of the situation and its possibilities. This is what Neumann calls the "cognitive" element of freedom, which he traces to the apothegm "freedom is the recognition of necessity." Neumann's other two aspects of freedom are the "juridical," which comprehends the ethical element in the doctrine of rule of law (which also possesses instrumental and ideological elements) (Neumann 1986, 1957, 22–68) and the "volitional," which concerns participation and takes up the problems of alienation and fear, which we have encountered so often in his work:

> If the concept of "enemy" and "fear" do constitute the "energetic principles" of politics, a democratic political system is impossible, whether the fear is produced from within or from without. Montesquieu correctly observed that fear is what makes and sustains dictatorships. If freedom is [among other things] absence of restraints, the restraints to be removed today are many; the psychological restraint of fear ranks first. (194)

Neumann underlines this emphasis by closing with another mainstay of American pragmatist philosophy, John Dewey, in a passage where he speaks warningly of "the stage of development in which a vague and mysterious feeling of uncertain terror seizes the populace" (194, quotation from Dewey 1929, 819).

Neither the dark overtones of these writings nor their emphasis on models, problems, and theses derived from the political thinkers of the past means that Neumann despaired of empirical study to give a realistic handhold for political practice. These articles, in fact, were proposed as the opening chapters of Neumann's unfinished major project "Political Systems and Political Theory," for which he received funding from the Rockefeller Foundation, at a unique moment at the end of 1952, when the Social Science Division under John Willits suddenly decided that its policy of fostering behavioral and quantitative methodologies required a balancing emphasis on "law, morals, and ethics." Neumann's role at that moment in the Foundation's history was not limited to his precisely timed application, since he also played a vocal part in the "First Conference on Legal and Political Philosophy" convened by the Rockefeller Foundation from October 31 to November 2, 1952, at its conference center at Arden House, in Harriman, New York (Rockefeller Foundation Archives 1951–52).[1] His initial intervention at that Conference, spoken with the confidence of his professorial status and wide student following, lays down a challenge:

> The question is, shouldn't political theory be dangerous? Isn't that the very function of political theory—to be dangerous? Don't we face a situation that, in many cases, political theory and propaganda becomes indistinguishable? Isn't it the function of political theory to be, so to speak, the critical conscience of political science? That is the primary role of political theory, as I see it. This, however, requires that political theory, apart from the study of its history, should not be taught *in vacuo,* but it should be taught in very close contact with the other segments of political science and other social sciences. To me it is not understandable that a course in political institutions should be taught regardless of political theory; and that theory, political theory is, so to speak, a segment where you learn certain things which have no bearing whatsoever on public administration, on comparative government, on American government, and so on. There is already a setting in of a fragmentation in which political theory appears merely as a segment in addition to other segments. This is, in my view, due to the fact that the critical role of political theory in the analysis of political phenomena and political structures is not properly recognized, and that the injection of political theory considerations into the teaching or the writing of political institutions leaves very much to be desired. Therefore this twofold orientation, to be critical but to cooperate very closely with the other segments of political science is, in my view, one of the principal and main problems that ought to be discussed. (Rockefeller Archives 1951–1952, 54–55)[2]

Neumann underlined this dualistic position in two follow-up letters to J. W. Willits at the Rockefeller Foundation and to his Columbia junior colleague, Herbert A. Deane, who had been selected by Robert I. MacIver to manage the new Rockefeller departure. Having written briefly immediately after the conference to underline his strong dissent from "political theory-empirical studies" dichotomy, which he calls a "very dangerous confrontation," he lay out his position at greater length ten days later. In this letter, he offers a list of neglected historical figures, whose thought has a special bearing on the present; he urges studies using methods of sociology of knowledge and history of ideas; but then he returns to his prime theme:

> Yet our primary task to determine the truth of a political theory is to develop a true political theory for today. . . . My own view . . . is that the truth of political theory is determined by its ability to maximize the freedom of man in a specific historical situation. I reject both [skeptical and dogmatic] extremes and I base the determination of the truth on the empirical analysis of a concrete historical stage as well as on philosophical thought. The reason is this: political theory is not and cannot be pure philosophy. It does not deal with eternal categories (like time, space, being, essence, accidents). It deals with politics and thus with power, which is an historical category. The great attraction—and the great difficulty—of political theory is precisely the need for this dual approach: theory and its empirical validation. (Neumann to Willtis, Rockefeller Archives 1951–1952)[3]

Neumann's use of commonplace scientific language is misleading, since his concept of "validation" is quite different from any notion of empirical verification. A clearer idea of his meaning is provided by the research proposal that he presented to the Rockefeller Foundation as a specification of his general themes. (All of the following quotations are from Rockefeller Archives 1951–1952).

To "validate" a political theory is to show that its normative and interpretative elements apply to the realities of the day, as we have seen, that it can make sense of them and orient conduct appropriate to them. Present-day democratic theory, Neumann asserts, is merely a "myth" because it is unrelated to the present-day state of knowledge, material advance, and power. The changes include dramatic shifts in economic power, the rise of new social groups, the displacement of individualistic by pluralistic competition (and other changes in mechanisms of society), changes in governmental structure, especially the rise of the executive and bureaucracy, the increased weight of political power in socioeconomic processes, and "the shift from enlightenment to propaganda and the resulting increased role of the communications media." He asks whether a system geared to an agrarian society can suffice, and he contends:

> This question can . . . be answered only through a genuinely comparative study of political systems. The comparative study must also be theoretical and historical, that is, they must be seen in the process of social and political change. Only then can we hazard a forecast whether our institutions will be capable of peaceful adjustment to a fundamentally changed environment.

Because in present-day political science American institutions are treated apart, political theory is separated from the study of institutions, an almost exclusive emphasis is given to behavioristic aspects, interconnections among economy, social systems, and political systems are neglected, "very little historical awareness illuminates current political thinking,"—for all of these reasons, "there is no longer a theory of political institutions." In order to gain for the present day what Aristotle, Bodin, and Montesquieu achieved for theirs, Neumann proposes to follow the procedures anticipated in his articles on political power and political freedom (which he anticipates as forthcoming). Through a typology of various political power-political freedom interrelations, he hopes to generate a reclassification and re-evaluation of the Aristotelian scheme of constitutions. The principal focus and objective will be the problem of change from democracy to dictatorship and from dictatorship to democracy, with major changes in predominant political ideas studied as symptoms and precursors of such changes. Revealing the implicit diagnosis out of which the project arises, Neumann turns at the end to the observation, which he claims was anticipated by Aristotle and Montesquieu, that changes from democracy to dictatorship depends upon the ability of antidemocratic groups to mobilize and manipulate anxiety and fear. He concludes: "The analysis of the socio-economic changes, the techniques for coming to power, and the changes in the thought structures will thus be focused on the psychological processes which make man a fearful animal."

It was noted much earlier that "learning from" is a poorly understood process. I think of it as a negotiation, where the parties bring their resources and needs to the table and seek to strike the best possible bargain, an especially difficult matter when only one of the parties is actively present, and he can pay off only in respect. Although I offer this account of Neumann as an instructive bit of history for the present stage of the recurrent effort to make social science work an activity whose ethical content goes to social and political responsibility, beyond the immanent ethics needed to shape any credible claim to knowledge, I cannot dictate what anyone can learn. All I can do is to offer some reasons for granting him recognition, which is a precondition of any bargaining relationship. First of all, anyone who puts before us the threats posed by regimes of fear, however she gets there, matters today. Second, even if we cannot put our attempts at diagnosis in Neumann's conventional terms of imputing "meaning" to "history," we can recognize the metaphorical significance of this old figure, as emblem of the task of constructing rich models of social complexity and social change. Neumann's sober ironies assure us that he is not offering us some holistic schematic.

What I fear in Flyvbjerg's argument (rather than in his examples) is the misleading impression that there is a social-science method to make politics unnecessary in principle, except insofar as in practice those Cicero called "the wicked" in the *Cataline Orations* must somehow be induced to "depart." That is what is entailed by the deproblematization of Weber's methodological theses in the twentieth-century state of the relevant questions. I have tried to follow Neumann's reproblematization of Weber where explorations in ethical possibilities (as embodied in the concept of "political freedom") and "sociological" investigations of power relations are brought together in a strategic political interpretation that presupposes that it will always have to battle against coherent—indeed, "rational"—opposition, as well as resilient patterns of resistances of other kinds. The "truth" of Neumann's political theory is a category that is itself, on Neumann's showing, full of uncertainties and unfulfilled promises. Weber speaks of "courage" at the end of "Politics as a Vocation" but identifies it with a self-abnegation of human desire. Neumann's vision is no less tragic, but he insists on a more intellectual and democratic conception of responsibility. Neumann's last public lecture, on the connection between science and political freedom, given at the Free University a few months before his death, having asserted that "only the political act itself, our activity can bring and secure freedom," closed with the following adaptation of Weber's concept of political responsibility:

One may consider Max Weber's conception of the objectivity of the social sciences as mistaken—as I do—but this principle which he enunciated in "Science as a Profession" I consider to be the only possible one in practice: that all political questions ought to be discussed openly and without rancor, that no scholar and teacher has the obligation of accepting a political system, but that each of them has the obligation, knowing his own prejudices, of discussing openly and rationally every political action and conception. These seem to me to be the connections between intellectual and political freedom. Although it is only one element of the political freedom of man, free scientific inquiry in a free society is indispensable for the self-determination of man (Neumann 1957, 215).

### NOTES

1. The correspondence leading up to the conference is to be found at the Rockefeller Foundation Archives 1952, RG3/910/8/74; the *Proceedings* are in two bound volumes. The Neumann proposal is also at the Rockefeller Foundation Archives 1952, FLN to JHW, RG1.1/200/320/3805 (November 25, 1952), with a copy in the Columbiana Archives at Columbia University: Neumann, Franz L. (Political Science) 1952–1955.

2. Rockefeller Foundation Archives 1952. RG3/910/9/81-2 (November 1–2, 1952): 54–55.

3. Rockefeller Foundation Archives 1952. Neumann to Willits, November 12, 1952, and November 24, 1952, RG3/910/8/75.

# 14

# Finding New Mainstreams

## Perestroika, Phronesis, and Political Science in the United States

## Timothy W. Luke

The entanglements of control and freedom in complicated technological, social, and economic systems cannot be separated from governance, whether it is the exercise of coercive state sovereignty or the implementation of corporate productivity goals. These linkages are extremely complex. So complex, in fact, that almost all researchers in contemporary political science turn away from them. Yet, in doing so, they ignore many social theories about these practices that would enhance the discipline's critical vision and operational utility.

Examining such questions of control and freedom requires unique approaches to critique, and one of the most insightful ones is Foucault's vision of a "critical ontology" of ourselves, which is "the critique of what we are" as well as "the historical analysis of the limits imposed on us and an experiment with the possibility of going beyond them" (1984b, 50). Because Foucault approaches modernity as an "attitude" or an "ethos," he sees the material conditions of control and freedom as being entwined within the means of "relating to contemporary reality; a voluntary choice made by certain people; in the end, a way of thinking and feeling; a way, too, of acting and behaving that at one and the same time marks a relation of belonging and presents itself as a task" (1984a, 39). To make political science matter, one must follow Foucault's mode of critique to explore how modernity intertwines its complex possibilities and prohibitions with the ethos of control and freedom found in the systems of systems that mediate governmentality.

*Making Social Science Matter,* by Bent Flyvbjerg, provides an important intervention in the development of American political science during the twenty-first century, even though its mode of address often drags too much disciplinary detritus from the nineteenth or twentieth centuries into the present. At times, echoes of *Methodenstreiten* over materialism versus idealism, positivism versus historicism, behavioralism versus traditionalism or modernism versus postmodernism clatter around this analysis. Like the rehash of thousands of doctoral prelim questions or hundreds of introductory scope and methods courses, Flyvbjerg's methodological disquisition retraces these struggles in the past before facing today's bigger issues: how and why social science must matter; where, when, and to whom it should matter; and, for whom it will matter? Answers to these queries all too often are lost in the dust with others, but Flyvbjerg does struggle to respond to them. When he asks, "who gains, who loses, by which mechanisms of power" (2001, 162), Flyvbjerg begins cutting into the heart of big questions about power and its operations. And, here is where "making political science matter" becomes most important.

"Making social science matter," as Flyvbjerg emphasizes, is important, but all must recognize how fully "what matters" to social scientists usually has been already made "scientized" and "socialized" before anyone unleashes social science in search of significance. Without the biopolitical scaffolding of matter processed by science, a society rooted in materialist technics, and the expectation of science needing to matter to society, such questions are essentially academic. *In concreto,* however, why and how social science matters, as well as to whom, where, and when, is quite a significant issue, as Flyvbjerg (2001, 166–68) notes. Mattering materially only to small cliques of professional experts intent upon careerist advancement in the academy or to larger public bodies of clients, citizens, or consumers hoping to remake society around scientific practices are two horses of very different colors. Unfortunately, the first engagement of social science has tended to dominate, if not displace entirely, the second for more than a generation (Oren 2003; Luke 1999b, 345–63). And, a new mainstream political science that mobilizes phronesis as its basis for "making social science matter" might do well to find a new third way of even more critical engagement.

Aristotle's politics were an engagement with *phronesis* over *episteme* or *techné,* which Flyvbjerg (2001, 55–60) urges us to remember and embrace. Yet, one must realize how fully *techné* is concretized along with *episteme* in the everyday materiality of built environments, abstract systems, and reified practices where politics happen. When he asks, "who gains, who loses, by which mechanisms of power" (Flyvbjerg 2001, 162), many answers are out there in those actually existing systems of governmentality that are, in too many ways, ignored, neglected, and overlooked by mainstream political science analysis in the United States.

## Governmentality and Freedom

To organize a new social regimen rooted in *techné*, however, reliable practices for simulating the project of "freedom" are needed (Foucault 1980a). The larger tasks of developing a suite of structures and systems to cultivate power over life arguably preserves and enriches human life, although the role of phronesis here is far from clear. Indeed, such "freedom"—to follow Foucault—articulates "a whole series of different tactics that combined in varying proportions the objective of disciplining the body and that of regulating populations" (Foucault 1980a, 146).

Making a transition from human beings suffering an age-old subjection by "Nature" to their liberation in "Society" via the myths of individual and social contract amid the machines of capitalism re-imagines freedom itself to suit collaborative material articulations of disciplined power and knowledge. Centering discourse and practice upon freedom also frames the economy, state, and technology of "Society" within a new historical a priori, or "a series of complex operations that introduce the possibility of a constant order into the totality of representations. It constitutes a whole domain of empiricity as at the same time *describable* and *orderable*" (Foucault 1994, 158). Traditionally, mainstream American political science contributes much to this labor through both popular civic and elite professional education (Flyvbjerg 2001, 9–37). As Foucault suggests, the "framework of thought" behind freedom is another facet of the historical a priori that "delimits in the totality of experience a field of knowledge, defines the mode of being of the objects that appear in that field, provides man's everyday perception with theoretical powers, and defines the conditions in which he can sustain a discourse about things recognized to be true" (Foucault 1994, 158).

A persistent, but also contested, faith in modern modes of enlightenment unfolds as "patient labor giving form to our impatience for liberty" (Foucault 1984b, 50). Reexamining liberal democratic capitalism's means of governmentality returns one, at the same time, to the "archaeological and genealogical study of practices envisaged simultaneously as a techno-logical type of rationality and as strategic games of liberties" (Foucault 1984b, 40) as they play out in the systems of systems that create the allegedly right disposition between people and things. All of these systems of systems have been created through markets in a manner that consti-tutes, in part, many limits imposed upon us and enables, in part, some experiments with new possibilities for us to go, if only in part, beyond them. The logistics of globalism clearly constitute a technological type of rationality, but they also underpin the strategic games implied by the indi-vidual's freedom to act, freedom from action, and freedom through activ-ity as modernity's attitudes (Oren 2003; Adas 1989).

One can assert that the modern regime of bio-power formation, as Foucault first described it, has not been especially attentive to the signifi-cance of liberty in the equations of biopolitics (Foucault 1980a, 138–42). The controlled tactics of inserting human bodies into the machineries of industrial and agricultural production emerged as part and parcel of the process of strategically adjusting the growth in human population num-bers to the development of industrial capitalism. These adjustments are, in part, made through *episteme, techné,* and *phronesis.* Under the bio-power regime, power/knowledge systems have brought life under the ambit of continuous surveillance and explicit calculations (Foucault 1988), but these manifold calculations are never exclusively rooted in an exacting sys-tem of social scientific knowledge (Flyvbjerg 2001, 9–24). Many discourses of state power conjure up a new type of productive agency, resting upon freedom to define how a "transformation of human life" (Foucault 1980a, 145) should unfold along with ongoing industrial revolutions, but they are simultaneously epistemic, technical, and phronetic.

Political inquiry will continue to fail until it acknowledges how fully intertwined unfreedom and freedom have become in the everyday matters of material life that mainstream political science all too often bypasses in its analyses (see Hawkesworth 1988). Freedom, and unfreedom also, forms in, with, through structures and systems of governmentality "in which are articulated the effects of a certain type of power and the reference of a cer-tain type of knowledge, the machinery by which the power relations give rise to a possible corpus of knowledge, and knowledge extends and rein-forces the effects of this power" (Foucault 1980b, 29).

Franklin Delano Roosevelt, for example, set forth the Four Freedoms in his State of the Union Address of January 6, 1941, in which he envi-sioned a new global order that rested upon "four essential human freedoms" that must be extended to all "everywhere in the world" (Rosenman 1938–50, IX, 672). These Four Freedoms are freedom of speech, freedom of worship, freedom from want, and freedom from fear. Seeing the United States as the world's main proponent of the Four Freedoms, FDR pushed America toward the project that JFK advocated a generation later, namely standing ready to "pay any price, bear any burden, meet any hardship, support any friend or oppose any foe to assure the survival and success of liberty." For Roosevelt, the Four Freedoms were a universal set of liberties that represented "the rights of men of every creed and every race, wherever they live," and which marked "the crucial difference between ourselves [the United States] and the enemies [fascism, totalitarianism, national socialism] we face today" (Rosenman 1938–50, X, 287–88).

On the American home front during World War II, for example, the painter Norman Rockwell depicted these goals in the tropes of 1940s Americana: an average Joe holding forth at what appears to be a town meeting; persons of many creeds and races gathered in prayer (with a caption of "each according to the dictates of his own conscience"); a typical Thanksgiving turkey dinner feast; and, two children being tucked into bed by their parents at night (the father grasps a newspaper with headlines about London being bombed). Circulating first in the *Saturday Evening Post,* these images became iconic referents for freedom during the rest of World War II, as well as during the cold war. Today, the administration of President George W. Bush is implicitly using these same constructs of freedom to anchor "the war on terror" by trying to tie the current wars in the Middle East into the tropes of the World War II era, as the president asserted at the World War II Memorial dedication ceremonies in Washington, D.C., and in his commencement speech at the U.S. Air Force Academy, in Maryland, in June 2004.

Foucault, then, is correct about the modern state. It is not "an entity which was developed above individuals, ignoring what they are, or dismissing their daily existence," because its freedoms evolve "as a very sophisticated structure, in which individuals can be integrated, under one condition: that this individuality would be shaped in a new form, and submitted to a set of very specific patterns" (Foucault 1982, 214–15). As Rockwell's paintings and the reception accorded FDR's speech by the public show, freedom is a force field. Its many variations pull new twists into the "very specific patterns" by which governmentality constitutes "a modern matrix of individualization" (Foucault 1982, 215).

At the same time, these governmental practices also indicate how the ethical/moral/political bases of freedom are being, in part, "subpoliticized." By pushing the goals of freedom down into the diverse everyday lifeworlds in which people mostly live their cultural, economic, and political existence as consumers, everyday human politics have become embedded in technified infrastructures. After all, Rockwell's paintings came out in the *Saturday Evening Post* and then went on a nationwide tour whose primary display venues were big downtown department stores. A very narrow politics of expertise now is implied by these venues as "buying" and "selling" folds over too many decisions over how to frame "freedom" and "unfreedom." Those struggles over freedom can, in turn, be derailed by arcane epistemic quibbles over operational scientific assumptions in technical disputes about methodologies of analysis used to manage both individual people and the larger populace, as well as bigger questions of phronesis tied to cultivating the human resources needed by capitalist markets.

### Rethinking the Subpolitical and "Freedom"

To make political science matter, it must ask "where are we going?" (Flyvbjerg 2001, 612). Where we are going is tied to subpolitical expertise, or a tacit consent to trust scientific experts and business owners to do what allegedly is best for the common good in accord with prevailing scientific and business practices. Liberal democratic assumptions about science and capital privilege those with the technology (or the "know-how") valued and/or who have capital (or the "own-how") valued in the economy and society (see Yanow 1996). Yet, these same assumptions ignore how fully those economic and social relations are organized to guarantee that most members in society cannot acquire know-how or accumulate own-how (Tabb 2001; Luke 1989). In fact, the existing regime of power/knowledge in the liberal democratic society of the United States actively works to ensure that most of its individual members do not know-how or own-how it operates, because a subpolitical impulse has largely displaced the political as the driving force in most economies and societies (Baudrillard 1981).

Unlike the larger public goals that allegedly anchor what is usually identified as "the polis," much smaller corporate and professional agendas for private profit and power sustain the broader, deeper, and denser networks at the core of the economy and society, which Beck sees as a realm of "the subpolitical." The financial, professional, and technical networks

behind this subpolis freeze possibilities for collective action and imagination somewhere between a traditional vision of politics and nonpolitics
(Luke 1999a). As Beck asserts, big technological systems, like cybernetic
networks, telecommunications grids, and computer applications, are
becoming the material basis for

> a third entity, acquiring the precarious hybrid status of a *sub-politics*, in
> which the scope of social changes precipitated varies inversely with their
> legitimation. . . . The direction of development and results of technological
> transformation become fit for discourse and subject to legitimation. Thus
> business and techno-scientific action acquire a *new political and moral
> dimension* that had previously seemed alien to technoeconomic activity . . .
> now the potential for structuring society migrates from the political system
> into the sub-political system of scientific, technological, and economic
> modernization. *The political becomes non-political and the non-political
> political.* . . . A revolution under the cloak of normality occurs, which
> escapes from possibilities of intervention, but must all the same be justified
> and enforced against a public becoming critical. . . . The political institu-
> tions become the administrators of a development they neither have
> planned for nor are able to structure, but must nevertheless somehow jus-
> tify. . . . Lacking a place to appear, the decisions that change society become
> tongue-tied and anonymous. . . . What we *do not see and do not want* is
> changing the world more and more obviously and threateningly. (Beck
> 1992, 186–87)

Here, dispersed and discrete decisions made by technicians and tradesmen
are what structure moralities in the economy and society around these
"sub-political systems of scientific, technological, and economic modernization" (Beck 1992, 186), and they are now changing the world without
much, if any, direct state regulation, political planning, or civic legitima-
tion.

From these structural contradictions, the promise of freedom forms as
spaces without boundaries, a place of complete immediacy without shel-
tering barriers, and decentered zones for commercial performance. With
scientific experts carefully engaged in 24/7 surveillance over each segment
of every economy and environment, Flyvbjerg highlights how fully our
civic order has been respatialized in very different manner, such that space
is "an existential and cultural dominant, a thematized or foregrounded
feature or structural principle standing in striking contrast to its relatively

subordinate and secondary . . . role in earlier modes of production" (Jameson 1992, 365).

Decisions taken by experts on one level at a certain scale and tempo in national space, then, rebound on another level for many individuals who live and work in other scales and tempos in highly technified spaces as the structured fields for their everyday practices. Because the subpolitical domain runs beneath, beside, or behind more public national and local structures with their more opaque administrative processes and technified structures, a great deal of public life essentially is subpolitical—both by design and by default. The prerogatives of professional expertise and individual property in liberal democratic societies basically are unquestioned. In turn, the constraints created by the subpolitical are imposed. Liberal codes of property and professional credos of technocracy become shields held up against too many popular efforts to ask the "who" and "whom" question of infrastructures, systems, and technologies in national politics. At the same time, the subpolitics of transnational systems are where the real decisions about "who" and "whom" are made and then made to hold fast (Luke 1999a).

Precise knowledge about subpoliticized space and its hold over inhabitants in this context now guides "the insertion of bodies into global machineries of production and the adjustment of mass populations to economic processes" (Foucault 1980a, 141). Not everyone needs to be inserted or adjusted in same ways to make these mechanisms succeed. Instead, new inequalities and unfreedoms come from ensembles of economic exchange shifting their value-added products to a few privileged locales, leaving their value-detracting by-products in many other places that now divide the world's populations and space in new degraded ways that are taken to be the sine qua non of being "free to choose." In this manner, the practices of governmentality serve as "methods of power capable of optimizing forces, aptitudes, and life in general without at the same time making them more difficult to govern" (Foucault 1980a, 141). Social science can matter in the methods of optimizing such forces, but it all too often does not matter enough in confronting, criticizing or correcting how such governance serves the higher goals of *phronesis.*

Even though all people remains caught as bodies within some face-to-face political system, their civic abilities to exercise effectively any public practices of rule-making, rule-applying, and rule adjudication are highly confined to the political sphere. Indeed, these conditions of "freedom" typically do not map over to the more materially significant subpolitical

260 TIMOTHY W. LUKE

sphere. As the Clinton and Bush years in the United States suggest, democracy can become the engine of collective inaction or, worse, endless spectacles of quasis-theatrical scandal or struggle. The most decisive decisions are being remade globally and locally, as Beck maintains, *"under the cloak of normality"* (1992, 186) in the less transparent realms framed by technics and economics. Therefore, "in contemporary discussions," as Beck suggests, "the alternative society is no longer expected to come from parliamentary debates on new laws, but rather from the application of microelectronics, genetic technology, and information media" (1992, 223).

The superceding of Nature by technologies creates the spatiality of a processed world in which those who own and control the material and mental means of enforcing order concretize new inequalities on an global scale in many landscapes, places, and spaces—urban, rural, suburban, and exurban—which can be neither metropolitan nor peripheral. Without saying so, Flyvbjerg essentially has discovered and disputed the divisions in Beck's subpolitical domain. Indeed, where we are going often derives now from the technology-based and property-driven constraints placed upon people and things caught up within routine technified governmentality. Who gains and who loses are outcomes confused by objects and subjects in big techno-scientific systems. Here one finds the reified regimes in which social science matters, but in which it also must matter—which are global and local, industrial and agricultural, commercial and nonprofit, urban and rural, built and unbuilt (Beck 1997; French 2000; Luke 1989).

Knit together out of technology and property, what should be phronesis conforms now to politicized technocultural practices. And, desirable or not, this praxis constitutes too many of our forms, ways, or standards of living. One example is "the grid"—that system of systems that generate, distribute, and use electricity. Other examples are the food chains, water works, road systems, freight carriers, housing complexes, mass media, and health services that profoundly influence the spaces and sites of urban-industrial life as matter as well as materialized social science. Where we are going, following Flyvbjerg, became a path paved with such artifacts as they came together during the Gilded Age. It congealed—via *episteme, techné, and phronesis*—both to structure agency and to activate structures in those countries that could develop and deploy such systems of systems—water, sewer, gas, electricity, telegraph, telephone, road, and rail—to organize the conduct of both their subjects' and their objects' conduct (Adas

1989). As these modernizing processes unfold, praxes of "the polis" are entwined with clusters of quasified operations embedded in "the subpolis," hybridizations of machinic systems, human populations, and territorial spaces. Indeed, the unfolding of world capitalist markets is part and parcel of a "subpolitical" order that anchors, in part, "freedom to," "freedom from," and "freedom through."

The attainment of popular sovereignty during and after the Enlightenment clearly constituted a major milestone for what is regarded as "liberty" in the North Atlantic Basin, but it also demanded certain correlative forms of subjection, certain types of domination to operate well (Luke 1999a). An empowerment of people through technified media of control, information, and order in the nineteenth and twentieth centuries made society and science central to modes of freedom set forth by the Enlightenment (Foucault 1991). Strangely enough, this transformation was not juridico-political as much as it was techno-economic. Therefore, few, if any, studies by political scientists have investigated all its ramifications. While popular sovereignty plainly marked a transfer of authority to the people, getting "power to the people" through technified means now constitutes the essence of "modernity." Yet, this kind of liberating empowerment rarely is thought about systematically in today's political science.

Of course, societies exist with popular political sovereignty and no subpolitical freedoms, and other societies attain subpolitical freedoms without enjoying popular political sovereignty. In seeking to make it matter, most conventional social science focuses with classical realist categories upon men and women in their quest for power in each national polis by exercising the will to dominate every other polis. A much more realistic reading of these times, however, should look at the subpolis of international, national, regional, and local systems in which "all that is solid melts into air, all that is holy is profaned, and man is at last compelled to face with sober senses, his real conditions of life, and his relations with his kind" (Marx and Engels 1978, 476). There one finds quite different struggles among men and women within the subpolis over how to make possible technified freedoms and then why they should accept reliance upon these mostly nonhuman props in life as normal relations with both their own human kind and other machinic systems. Living well inside the accidental normality of today's advanced built environments is made possible, or impossible, by the power and knowledge embedded in material regimens that run the water, gas, sewer, road, telephone, radio, television, and electricity systems interwoven into subpoliticized spatiality. Here one can, and should, make political science matter, because these systems are, in part, social science materialized.

Yet, on these issues, American political science is, at best, like the search engine Google. This web application does a decent job surveying and searching the 12 billion plus pages on the World Wide Web, but there is a "dark Internet" of up to 500 billion other pages that it misses. Hundreds of intranets cannot be accessed, billions of links are lost, broken, or misspecified, millions of pages are never found or soon decay into "cob web pages," and Google misses much of this material. Political science, in turn, all too often "Googles" only the questions it believes its theories can ask or answer. So when one wishes to know who gains and who loses by which mechanisms of power, political science does not scan "dark power," whose subpolitical regimes of command, coercion, or communication control as much as, or more than, those "light power" mechanisms lit up by conventional methods of disciplinary analysis.

## Technics, Economics, Values Beneath Politics

Creating technified civic spaces could be seen as the unfolding of reason in history, but then, as Lyotard argues, such appeals to rational development do not convince most people these days. Few now believe that progress in knowledge as *techné* will bring "a society emancipated from poverty, despotism, and ignorance. But all of us can see that the development continues to take place without leading to the realization of any of these dreams of emancipation" (Lyotard 1984, 39). Rather, poverty, despotism, and ignorance have become naturalized as background conditions for too many in the world, while a privileged few organize technology and property in the world to realize hyperdeveloped outcomes that openly undercut most of modernity's myths (Tabb 2001). With this eclipse of politics in the system of systems, Lyotard asserts, science and technology are falling under the sway of "another language game, in which the goal is no longer truth, but performativity—that is, the best possible input/output equation" (1984, 46) in synchronizing the productivity of society and space as subpolitics.

Technologies do not simply fall from the sky (Adas 1989; Foucault 1997; Nye 1990). They must instead be fabricated and then mobilized by their owners and/or managers for some profitable business and personal use by enrolling producers, consumers, and advocates in endless new social movements to build global, national, and local systems that promote their utility, tout their necessity, and herald their inevitability as "freedoms to" (Greenfeld 2001). Life in societies organized around sustaining systems of such systems, embedded within a pursuit of performance within commodity markets, is now essentially ignored by mainstream political science. Yet, everyday life requires a broad range of new cultural compliances from everyone's acceding to, or resisting, the governmentality created by the subpolis's many different language games, various skill sets, and several new systemic technocultures (Agger 1989). As a result, the public agenda, when it is understood as politics, rarely moves forward unless it too is shaped to serve the subpolitical interests of what allegedly is "the public." Thus, the system of systems first serves a much smaller subset of highly salient interests espoused by the owners of big companies and/or expert managers of powerful technologies (Virilio 1997).

Corporations operate, because of embedded systems of systems behind global markets, as complex machines (Luke 1996; Greenfeld 2001; Goldstone 2001). Furthermore, producers and consumers in almost all the world's markets must, for the most part, express their goals, find their resources, and generate their life outcomes out of the machine-like operations of these major corporations. The seat of empowerment, understood as the generation of development, modernization, or even civilization, now flows through the accidental normality that rests upon such technified structures. Inasmuch as any modern culture represents corporate acts and company artifacts shaped by particular enterprises in specific settings, the good life promised by the polis is made and remade from ideas and material things mobilized to advance profit-seeking corporate strategies (Luke 1989). Today, for example, many "living on the grid" might see "empowerment" first as getting electricity rather than as attaining popular sovereignty. Before the "powering up" of society, most forms of development and modernization are too hard for many to envision. By the twentieth century, then, it was no accident that attaining "freedom" was believed to require such "power." Clearly, Lenin regarded attaining socialism for the Soviet Union as being equal to "electrification plus Soviet rule," and General Electric in the United States has seen its corporate mission as "bringing good things to life" through electricity.

Empowerment by electrification, motorization, or mechanization, for example, shows how market-based technologies of production and the self co-generate new linkages between objective systemic productivity and subjective idiosyncratic consumption for producers and consumers beneath phronesis in the technified regimens of globalization (Baudrillard 1996). "Plugging in" becomes tacit consent to governmentality's technical dictates as technics conduct one's conduct through multiple technified grids of command, control, and communication as "freedom through" the system. The end users of corporate commodities are redesignated through their purchase of commodities to play the role of capital asset, causing "the ultimate realization of the private individual as a productive force. The system of needs must wring liberty and pleasure from him as so many functional elements of the reproduction of the system of production and the relations of power that sanction it" (Baudrillard 1981, 85). In other words, corporate plans for social transformation achieve life, liberty, and property through the buying decisions of individuals, rather than the other way around. For transnational businesses, the liberation of personal "wants" or individual "needs," as they are allegedly felt by everyone anywhere, is fixed, in turn, by making more and more commodities hitherto inaccessible in many markets available to all who desire them.

Liberating these needs, however, matches capital and its experts with new mobilizations of fresh commodities (Virilio 1997). Subjectivity is redefined through subpolitics as a material need for coexisting with artifacts and systems as commodified goods, and modern subjects are those who can be defined by their material demand for such goods and services freely designed to supply and thereby satisfy them freely (Baudrillard 1996). Disciplinary objectivities, in turn, shape disciplined subjectivity through quasipolitan order. As Baudrillard observes,

> The *consumption* of individuals mediates the *productivity* of corporate capital; it becomes a productive force required by the functioning of the system itself, by its process of reproduction and survival. In other words, there are these kinds of needs because the system of corporate production needs them. And the needs invested by the individual consumer today are just as essential to the order of production as the capital invested by the capitalist entrepreneur and the labor power invested in the wage laborer. It is *all* capital. (1981, 82)

Ideologies of competitive corporate growth realized through the exploitation of labor are inscribed in each commodity, even though these authoritative objects are delivered to compliant consumers as true tokens of the new "freedoms to" find their collective liberation via "the market." Until such circuits are traced through matter by social science, social science will not matter.

When consumers admit that "they're living it," or that products gives them "that feeling," or that buying "the right stuff" truly "gets them connected," it is clear that individual subjects have become repositioned by their possessions in, by, and for "the grid." General Electric historically has prided itself in "bringing good things to life," but today it now asks, "What can GE do for you?" Appliances, applicants, and applications then become "what you can do for GE" as the nexus of electrification serves as a subpolitical bridge for how those good things are brought into life as GE "does" you. Here, Foucault would note, "individuals are vehicles of power, not its points of articulation" (1980b, 98). To make social sciences matter, phronesis must get more deeply into the modernized subjectivities formed, in part, at the cash and commodity nexus with the objects produced, in part, by technified systems of systems (Luke 2005).

Commodities like those fabricated in, by, and for residents of the subpolis beneath nation-states rise and fall in the markets but operate as "a polymorphous disciplinary mechanism" (Foucault 1980b, 106) for corporate and, indirectly, state power. Individually and collectively, the machinic assemblies that carefully produce these artifacts have cultivated over the past century "their own discourse," and "they engender . . . apparatuses of knowledge (*savoir*) and a multiplicity of new domains of understanding" (Foucault 1980b, 106). For the systems of systems, commodities are simultaneously carriers of discourse, circuits of normalization, and conduits of discipline that markets and companies use to possess their individual proprietors with the properties of their systems as reified as artifacts of personal property. This is the "freedom to" choose, and it is—to answer Flyvbjerg—a direction "where are we going" (2001, 162).

## Conclusion

At this juncture, issues of governmentality and their links to negative and positive freedom gain significance because the capillaries of control where social science can matter are so pervasive. That is, questions of freedom in globalizing system of systems always, "lie *across* the distinction between theory and practice, *across* the borders of specialties and disciplines, *across* the specialized competencies and institutional responsibilities, *across* the distinction between value and fact (and thus between ethics and science), and *across* the realms of politics, the public sphere, science and the economy, which are seemingly divided by institutions" (Beck 1992, 70). While their mechanisms are complex, the workings of governmentality unfold at these intersections between the technics of domination and an epistemics for cultivating the self.

Phronesis should examine the conjunction of life, labor, and language in discourses of governmentality, and its workings must lay bare the analytic of power/knowledge "which shows how man, in his being, can be concerned with the things he knows, and know the things that, in positivity, determine his mode of being" (Foucault 1994, 314), articulated through highly focalized professional-technical constructions of permissible "freedoms." The "freedom" given by the economy and society, if we follow Foucault's lines of reasoning, must not be understood either as the naturally given sphere of natural impulses that human powers try to keep under rein or as a mysterious domain of obscure artificial events that human moral knowledge cannot adequately explain. Instead, freedom emerges as a historical artifact that is culturally constructed and ethically elaborated by governmentalizing interventions both to attain technical control and to fulfill scientific explanation. Out of this dense network of interventions into the working of society, a full spectrum of political challenges—ranging from the simulation of space, the intensification of resources, and the incitement of discoveries to the formation of special knowledges, the strengthening of controls, and the provocation of resistances—all are linked to one another as "the empiricities" at stake in moral and political discourses about both negative and positive freedom (Foucault 1994, 362–63).

Truths about freedom are never timeless objective verities, but they mostly conform today to the operational concords of various professional-technical practices produced by the state, society, and science. Such centers of discipline are where "truth," or "a system of ordered procedures for the production, regulation, distribution, circulation, and operation of statements" (Foucault 1980b, 133), arises from knowledge formations, like disciplinary debates over governance, production, or morality, to help steer power formations, like the decision-making bureaucracies of liberal democratic states and capitalist companies. As Foucault asserts, "there are manifold relations of power which permeate, characterize, and constitute the social body, and these relations of power cannot themselves be established, consolidated nor implemented without the production, accumulation, circulation, and functioning of a discourse. There can be no possible exercise of power without a certain economy of discourses of truth which operates through and on the basis of this association" (Foucault 1980b, 95). Social science often is embedded in matter's reified *techné*, but it does not matter enough as phronesis.

The practices of technology and science now implicitly indicate how thoroughly most governmental policies are deeply embedded within "a *sociotechnical* order." As Law suggests, networks of humans and machines, animals and plants, economies and ecologies, which now constitute our environment, are a mixed media of power and knowledge: "what appears to be social is partly technical. What we usually call technical is partly social. In practice nothing is purely technical. Neither is anything purely social" (1991,10). Reimagining the larger social environment as subpoliticized governmentality at work, at the same time, admits that the professional-technical agents of both government and business are, in many ways, trained to operate as "heterogeneous engineers." That is, they must work "not only on inanimate physical materials, but on and through people, texts, devices, city councils, architectures, economics, and all the rest" such that if thir designs are to work as a system, then they must always travel effectively "between these different domains, weaving an emergent web which constituted and reconstituted bits and pieces that it brought together" (Law 1991, 9).

These background conditions of "dark power" in the subpolitical are what conventional political science ignores by fixating on the "light power" of the state, parties, or civil society, even though it is this "dark power" that enables the continuation of "modern politics" in systems of commercialization and technification that infiltrate everyday life (Martin and Schumann, 1997). Flyvbjerg asks, "is it desirable?" (2001, 162). The odd cult of technified practicality in most realms of government action strangely forecloses far too many truly political deliberations and prevents many more genuinely ethical discussions about the desirability of such "freedom" in the register of phronesis. Therefore, this question cannot be easily answered. Flyvbjerg also wonders, "what should be done?" (2001, 162). Plainly, it must do much more than what mainstream political science now does: arguing over minor concerns in various culture wars and quibbling about methodologies for professionally correct research designs. Instead it should begin grappling with the bigger questions of ethics and politics, as well as the regimen of subpolitical governmentality that hides too much of them both. Fortunately, Flyvbjerg (2001, 141–65) endeavors to begin this new mainstream work for political science, and he also invites others to examine specific applications for particular spatial settings in contemporary urban environments; see, for example, Nye (1996), Scott (1998), Luke (1999a), Falk (1999), and Greenfeld (2001). Phronesis today cannot ignore *techné*. Yet, a technified world also must not surrender to a social science seeking legitimacy only as *episteme*, which will not make social science matter. Only when political science returns to phronesis, can one say that the real mainstreams of ethical, political, and social science will be ready to be found.

# References

Abbott, Andrew. 1988. "Transcending General Linear Reality." *Sociological Theory* 6 (Fall): 169–86.

Adams-Miller, Michelle. 2002. *Owning Up: Poverty, Assets, and the American Dream.* Washington, DC: Brookings Institution.

Adas, Michael. 1989. *Machines as the Measure of Men: Science, Technology, and Ideologies of Western Dominance.* Ithaca: Cornell University Press.

Agger, Ben. 1989. *Fast Capitalism.* Urbana: University of Illinois Press.

Alford, John R., and John R. Hibbing. 2004. "The Origin of Politics: An Evolutionary Theory of Political Behavior." *Perspectives on Politics* 2 (December): 707–23.

Alford, John R., Carolyn L. Funk, and John R. Hibbing. 2005. "The Origin of Politics: An Evolutionary Theory of Political Behavior." *American Political Science Review* 99 (May): 153–67.

Alvarez, Sonia. 1990. *Engendering Democracy in Brazil.* Princeton: Princeton University Press.

Anderson, Lisa. 2000. "Response to Ken Wissoker's Negotiating a Passage between Disciplinary Borders: A Symposium." *Items and Issues: Social Science Research Council* 1 (3–4): 8.

Apel, Karl-Otto. 1984. *Understanding and Explanation: A Transcendental Pragmatic Perspective.* Cambridge, MA: MIT Press.

APSA Task Force on Graduate Education. 2004. "Report to the Council." American Political Science Association: 1–15. Available at http://www.apsanet.org/imgtest/graduateeducation.pdf

Arendt, Hannah. 1958. *The Human Condition.* Chicago: University of Chicago Press.

Aristotle. 1976. *The Nicomachean Ethics.* Translated by J. A. K. Thomson, revised with notes and appendices by Hugh Tredennick, introduction and bibliography by Jonathan Barnes. Harmondsworth, UK: Penguin.

Atkinson, Paul, Amanda Coffey, and Sara Delamont. 2003. *Key Themes in Qualitative Research: Continuities and Change.* Walnut Creek, CA: Alta Mira. Press

Axelrod, Robert, and William D. Hamilton. 1981. "The Evolution of Cooperation." *Science,* New Series 211 (4489) (March 27): 1390–96.

Bachrach, Peter, and Morton S. Baratz. 1962. "Decisions and Nondecisions: An Analytical Framework." *American Political Science Review* 57: 641–51.

Balfour, Lawrie. 2004. "Representative Women: Slavery, Citizenship, and Feminist Theory in Du Bois's 'Damnation of Women.'" *Hypatia* 20 (3): 127–48.

Bargh, John A. 1997. "The Automaticity of Everyday Life." In Robert Wyer, Jr., ed., *The Automaticity of Everyday Life: Advances in Social Cognition,* vol. 10. Mahwah, NJ: Erlbaum: 1–62.

Bartky, Sandra Lee. 1990. *Femininity and Domination: Studies in the Phenomenology of Oppression.* New York: Routledge.

Bartlett, Steven J., ed. 1992. *Reflexivity: A Source-Book in Self Reference.* Amsterdam: Elsevier.

Basu, Amrita. 1995. *The Challenge of Local Feminisms: Women's Movements in Global Perpective.* Boulder, CO: Westview Press.

Bates, Robert. 1998. "The International Coffee Organization: An International Institution." In Robert Bates, Avner Greif, Margaret Levi, Jean-Laurent Rosenthal, and Barry R. Weingast, eds., *Analytic Narratives.* Princeton: Princeton University Press: 194–228.

Bates, Robert H., Avner Greif, Margaret Levi, Jean-Laurent Rosenthal, and Barry R. Weingast. 1998. "Introduction." In Robert Bates, Avner Greif, Margaret Levi, Jean-Laurent Rosenthal, and Barry R. Weingast, eds., *Analytic Narratives.* Princeton: Princeton University Press: 3–22.

Baudrillard, Jean. 1981. *For a Critique of the Political Economy of the Sign.* St. Louis, MO: Telos Press.

Baudrillard, Jean. 1996. *The System of Objects.* London: Verso.

Beck, Nathaniel, Jonathan N. Katz, and Richard Tucker. 1998. "Taking Time Seriously: Time-Series-Cross-Section Analysis with a Binary Dependent Variable." *American Journal of Political Science* 42 (4): 1260–88.

Beck, Ulrich. 1992. *The Risk Society.* London: Sage.

Beck, Ulrich. 1997. *The Reinvention of Politics.* Oxford, UK: Polity Press.

Becker, Howard S. 1998. *Tricks of the Trade: How to Think about Your Research While You're Doing It.* Chicago: University of Chicago Press.

Beiner, Ronald. 1983. *Political Judgment.* Chicago: University of Chicago Press.

Beiner, Ronald. 1997. "Do We Need a Philosophical Ethics? Theory, Prudence and the Primacy of Ethos." In *Philosophy in a Time of Lost Spirit: Essays on Contemporary Theory.* Toronto: University of Toronto Press.

Bellah, Robert, Richard Masden, William M. Sullivan, Ann Swidler, and Stephen M. Tipton. 1996. *Habits of the Heart Individualism and Commitment in American Life.* Berkeley: University of California Press.

Benhabib, Seyla. 1992. "Autonomy, Modernity and Community: Communitarianism and Critical Theory in Dialogue." In *Situating the Self.* New York: Routledge: 66–86.

Benhabib, Seyla, and Fred Dallmayr. 1990. *The Communicative Ethics Controversy.* Cambridge, MA: MIT Press.

Berger, Peter, and Thomas Luckman. 1967. *The Social Construction of Reality: A Treatise in the Sociology of Knowledge.* Garden City: Anchor Books.

Berlin, Isaiah. 1996. "On Political Judgment." *The New York Review of Books* 43 (15): 26–30.

Bernstein, Richard. 1985. *Beyond Objectivism and Relativism: Science, Hermeneutics, and Praxis.* Philadelphia: University of Pennsylvania Press.

Bernstein, Richard. 1989. "Interpretation and Solidarity," interview by Dunja Melcic, *Praxis International* 9 (3): 201–19.

Bernstein, Richard J. 1978. *The Restructuring of Social and Political Theory.* Philadelphia: University of Pennsylvania Press.

Bevir, Mark. 2003. "Comments during discussion at the roundtable 'Constructivist and Interpretive Methods.'" Annual Meeting of the American Political Science Association, Philadelphia, August 29.

Bhaskar, Roy. 1975. *A Realist Theory of Science.* London: Verso.

Bhaskar, Roy. 1998. *The Possibility of Naturalism,* 3rd ed. London: Routledge.

Bohman, James. 1993. *New Philosophy of Social Science: Problems of Indeterminacy.* Cambridge, MA: MIT Press.

Boneparth, Ellen, and Emily Stoper, eds. 1988. *Women Power and Policy: Towards the Year 2000.* New York: Pergamon.

Boswell, Thomas. 2004. "In October, Predictions Fall Like Leaves." *The Washington Post,* 5 October, 1.

Boyd, Robert, and Peter J. Richerson. 1985. *Culture and the Evolutionary Process.* Chicago: University of Chicago Press.

Brady, Henry E., and David Collier. 2004. *Rethinking Social Inquiry: Diverse Tools, Shared Standards.* Latham, MD: Rowman and Littlefield.

Brown, Harold. 1977. *Perception, Theory and Commitment: The New Philosophy of Science.* Chicago: Precedent.

Brown, Richard Harvey. 1998. "Modern Science and Its Critics: Toward a Post-Positivist Legitimization of Science." *New Literary History* 29 (3): 521–50.

Brown, Wendy. 1995. *States of Injury: Power and Freedom in Late Modernity.* Princeton: Princeton University Press.

Burckhardt, Sigurd. 1969. *Shakespearean Meanings.* Princeton: Princeton University Press.

Burns, Robert P. 1991. *A Theory of the Trial.* Princeton: Princeton University Press.

Burrell, Gibson. 1997. *Pandemonium: Towards a Retro-Organization Theory.* London: Sage.

Bush, George W., *Radio Address by the President to the Nation,* Saturday, June 9, 2001, available at http://www.whitehouse.gov/news/releases/2001/06/20010608-7.html

Camerer, Colin F., and Eric J. Johnson. 1991. "The Process-Performance Paradox in Expert Judgment: How Can the Experts Know So Much and Predict So Badly?" In K. Anders Erisson and Jacqui Smith, eds., *Toward a General Theory of Expertise*. Cambridge: Cambridge University Press: 195–217.

Campbell, Donald T. 1975. "Degrees of Freedom in the Case Study." *Comparative Political Studies* 8:1, 179.

Carter, Keith, and Sara Delamont, eds. 1996. *Qualitative Research: The Emotional Dimension*. Aldershot, UK: Avebury Press.

Case number 064. In *Documents from 17th and 18th Century Spain*. 064 of 617. Rare Book Division, Princeton University Library.

Chan, Andrew. 2001. *Critically Constituting Organization*. Amsterdam: John Benjamins.

Chappell, Louise. 2002. *Gendering Government*. Vancouver: University of British Columbia Press.

Cheibub, José Antonio, Adam Przeworski, and Sebastian Saiegh. 2004. "Government Coalitions and Legislative Success under Presidentialism and Parliamentarism." *British Journal of Political Science* 34: 565–87.

Churchland, Paul M., and Clifford A. Hooker, eds. 1985. *Images of Science*. Chicago: University of Chicago Press.

Claparede, Edmund. 1951. "Recognition and 'Me-ness.'" In David Rapaport, ed., *Organization and Pathology of Thought, Selected Sources*. New York: Columbia University Press: 58–75.

Claxton, Guy. 1997. *Hare Brain Tortoise Mind: Why Intelligence Increases When You Think Less*. Hopewell, NJ: Ecco Press.

Claxton, Guy. 1998. "Investigating Human Intuition: Knowing Without Knowing Why." *The Psychologist* 11 (5): 217–20.

Clegg, Stewart R. 1975. *Power, Rule and Domination*. London: Routledge and Kegan Paul.

Clegg, Stewart R. 1989. *Frameworks of Power*. London: Sage.

Clegg, Stewart R. 2002. "'Lives in the Balance': A Comment on Professor Hining's and Greenwood's 'Disconnects and Consequences in Organization Theory.'" *Administrative Science Quarterly* 47 (3): 428–41.

Clegg, Stewart R., and Cynthia Hardy. 1996. "Representations." In Stewart R. Clegg, Cynthia. Hardy, and Walter R. Nord, eds., *Handbook of Organization Studies*. London: Sage: 676–707.

Columbiana Archives at Columbia University: Neumann, Franz L. (Political Science) 1952–1955.

Columbiana Collection, Columbia University. Minutes of Political Science Faculty, April 15, 1955.

Connolly, William. 1992. *Identity/Difference: Democratic Negotiations of Political Paradox*. Ithaca: Cornell University Press.

Cornell, Drucilla. 1998. *At the Heart of Freedom.* Princeton: Princeton University Press.

Cruikshank, Barbara. 1999. *The Will to Empower: Democratic Citizens and Other Subjects.* Ithaca: Cornell University Press.

Cunningham, Frank. 1973. *Objectivity in Social Science.* Toronto: University of Toronto Press.

Dahl, Robert. 1957. "The Concept of Power." *Behavioral Science* 2: 201–15.

Darier, Éric, ed. 1998. *Discourses of the Environment.* Oxford, UK: Blackwell.

Dawes, Robyn M., David Faust, and Paul E. Meehl. 1989. "Clinical Versus Actuarial Judgment." *Science,* New Series, 243 (4899) (March 31): 1668–74.

Dean, Mitchell. 1991. *The Constitution of Poverty: Toward a Genealogy of Liberal Governance.* London: Routledge.

Dean, Mitchell. 1999. *Governmentality: Power and Rule in Modern Society.* Thousand Oaks, CA: Sage.

Dean, Mitchell, and Barry Hindess, eds. 1998. *Governing Australia: Studies in Contemporary Rationalities of Government.* Cambridge, UK: Cambridge University Press.

Denton, Nancy A. 2001. "Housing as a Means of Asset Accumulation: A Good Strategy for the Poor?" In Thomas M. Shapiro and Edward N. Wolff, eds., *Assets for the Poor: The Benefits of Spreading Asset Ownership.* New York: Russell Sage Foundation: 232–66.

Devereux, Daniel T. 1986. "Particular and Universal in Aristotle's Conception of Practical Knowledge." *Review of Metaphysics* 39 (March): 483–504.

Dewey, John. 1929. *Character and Events.* New York: Holt.

Diamond, Jared. 1998. *Guns, Germs and Steel: A Short History of Everybody for the Last 13,000 Years.* New York: Vintage.

Diesing, Paul. 1991. *How Does Social Science Work? Reflections on Practice.* Pittsburgh: University of Pittsburgh Press.

Dietz, Mary G. 2002. *Turning Operations: Feminism, Arendt, and Politics.* New York: Routledge.

DiStefano, Christine. 1991. *Configurations of Masculinity.* Ithaca: Cornell University Press.

Donzelot, Jacques. 1979. *The Policing of Families.* New York: Pantheon.

Dreyfus, Hubert L. 1982. "Why Studies of Human Capacities Modeled on Ideal Natural Science Can Never Achieve Their Goal." Revised edition of a paper presented at The Boston Colloquium for the Philosophy of Science. October.

Dreyfus, Hubert. 1991. "Defending the Difference: The Geistes/Naturwissenschaften Distinction Revisited." In *Akademie der Wissenschaften zu Berlin, Einheit der Wissenschaften, Internationale Kolloquium der Akademie der Wissenschaften zu Berlin, Bonn, 25–27 June 1990.* Berlin: Walter de Gruyter: 463–85.

Dreyfus, Hubert, and Stuart Dreyfus. 1990. "What Is Morality: A Phenomenological Account of the Development of Expertise." In David Rasmussen, ed., *Universalism vs. Communitarianism.* Cambridge, MA: MIT Press: 237–64.

Dreyfus, Hubert, and Stuart Dreyfus. 1991. "Sustaining Non-rationalized Practices: Body-Mind, Power, and Situational Ethics." Interview by Bent Flyvbjerg. *Praxis International* 11 (1): 93–113.

Dreyfus, Hubert, Stuart Dreyfus, and Tom Athanasiou. 1988. *Mind over Machine: The Power of Human Intuition and Expertise in the Era of the Computer.* New York: Macmillan.

Dryzek, John S. 1986. "The Progress of Political Science." *Journal of Politics* 48 (2): 301–20.

Dryzek, John S. 1990. *Discursive Democracy: Politics, Policy and Political Science.* Cambridge, UK: Cambridge University Press.

Dryzek, John, James Farr, and Stephen T. Leonard, eds. 1995. *Political Science and History: Research and Political Traditions.* Cambridge, UK: Cambridge University Press.

Duerst-Lahti, Georgia, and Rita Mae Kelly. 1995. *Gender Power, Leadership and Governance.* Ann Arbor: University of Michigan Press.

Easton, David. [1953] 1971. *The Political System: An Inquiry into the State of Political Science,* 2nd ed. New York: Knopf.

Eckstein, Harry. 1975. "Case Study and Theory in Political Science." In Fred Greenstein and Nelson Polsby, eds., *Handbook of Political Science,* vol. 7. Reading, MA: Addison-Wesley: 79–138.

Ellis, Henry, and R. Hunt. 1993. *Fundamentals of Cognitive Psychology,* 5th ed. Madison: Brown and Benchmark.

Elster, Jon. 1998. "A Plea for Mechanisms." In Peter Hedstrøm and Richard Swedberg, eds., *Social Mechanisms: An Analytical Approach to Social Theory.* Cambridge, UK: Cambridge University Press: 45–73.

Elster, Jon. 1999. *Alchemies of the Mind: Rationality and the Emotions.* Cambridge, UK: Cambridge University Press.

Emirbayer, Mustafa. 1997. "Manifesto for a Relational Sociology." *American Journal of Sociology* 103 (2): 281–317.

Enloe, Cynthia. 1990. *Bananas, Beaches and Bases: Making Feminist Sense of International Politics.* Berkeley: University of California Press.

Enloe, Cynthia. 1993. *The Morning After: Sexual Politics at the End of the Cold War.* Berkeley: University of California Press.

Enloe, Cynthia. 2000. *Maneuvers: The International Politics of Militarizing Women's Lives.* Berkeley: University of California Press.

Epstein, Seymour, Rosemary Pacini, Veronika Denes-Raj, and Harriet Heier. 1996. "Individual Differences in Intuitive-Experiential and Analytical-Rational Thinking Styles." *Journal of Personality and Social Psychology* 71: 390–405.

Ericsson, K. Anders, and Jacqui Smith. 1991. "Prospects and Limits in the Empirical Study of Expertise: An introduction." In K. Anders Ericsson and Jacqui Smith, eds., *Toward a General Theory of Expertise: Prospects and Limits*. Cambridge, UK: Cambridge University Press: 1–38.

Ewald, François. 1986. *L'Etat Providence*. Paris: B. Grasset.

Ewald, François. 1996. *Histoire de l'Etat Providence: Les Origines de la solidarité*. Paris: Grasset.

Falk, Richard. 1999. *Predatory Globalization: A Critique*. Cambridge, UK: Polity Press.

Fay, Brian. 1975. *Social Theory and Political Practice*. Boston: Allen and Unwin.

Fearon, James D., and David D. Laitin. 2003. "Ethnicity, Insurgency and Civil War," *American Political Science Review* 97 (1): 75–90.

Fearon, James D., and David D. Laitin. Forthcoming. "Sons of the Soil." Stanford University, available at www.stanford.edu/~dlaitin/

Feldman, Leonard. 2004. *Citizens Without Shelter: Homelessness, Democracy, and Political Exclusion*. Ithaca: Cornell University Press.

Ferrara, Alessandro. 1988. *Reflective Authenticity: Rethinking the Project of Modernity*. New York: Routledge.

Ferrara, Alessandro. 1989. "Critical Theory and Its Discontents: On Wellmer's Critique of Habermas," *Praxis International* 8 (3): 305–20.

Finlay, Linda, and Brendan Gough, eds. 2003. *Reflexivity: A Practical Guide for Researchers in Health and Social Sciences*. Oxford, UK: Blackwell.

Flammang, Janet. 1997. *Women's Political Voice*. Philadelphia: Temple University.

Flyvbjerg, Bent. 1998a. *Rationality and Power: Democracy in Practice*. Chicago: University of Chicago Press.

Flyvbjerg, Bent. 1998b. "Habermas and Foucault: Thinkers for Civil Society?" *British Journal of Sociology* 49 (2): 208–33.

Flyvbjerg, Bent. 2001. *Making Social Science Matter: Why Social Inquiry Fails and How It Can Succeed Again*. Cambridge, UK: Cambridge University Press.

Flyvbjerg, Bent. 2004a. "A Perestroikan Straw Man Answers Back: David Laitin and Phronetic Political Science." *Politics and Society* 32 (3): 389–416.

Flyvbjerg, Bent. 2004b. "Five Misunderstandings About Case Study Research." In Clive Seale, Giampietro Gobo, Jaber F. Gubrium, and David Silverman, eds., *Qualitative Research Practice*. London: Sage: 420–34.

Flyvbjerg, Bent, Nils Bruzelius, and Werner Rothengatter. 2003. *Megaprojects and Risk: An Anatomy of Ambition*. Cambridge, UK: Cambridge University Press.

Flyvbjerg, Bent, Mette K. Skamris Holm, and Søren L. Buhl. 2002. "Underestimating Costs in Public Works Projects: Error or Lie?" *Journal of the American Planning Association* 68 (3): 279–95.

Ford Foundation Archives. 1951. FF Reel 489, Grant 51-41.

Foucault, Michel. 1973. *The Order of Things: An Archaeology of the Human Sciences.* New York: Vintage.

Foucault, Michel. 1977a. *Discipline and Punish.* Harmondsworth, UK: Penguin.

Foucault, Michel. 1977b. *Language, Counter-Memory, Practice: Selected Essays and Interview.* Ithaca: Cornell University Press.

Foucault, Michel. 1980a. *History of Sexuality: Vol. I.* New York: Vintage.

Foucault, Michel. 1980b. *Power/Knowledge: Selected Interviews & Other Writings, 1972–1977.* New York: Pantheon.

Foucault, Michel. 1982. "The Subject and Power." In Hubert Dreyfus and Paul Rabinow, eds., *Michel Foucault: Beyond Structuralism and Hermeneutics.* Brighton, UK: Harvester: 214–32.

Foucault, Michel. 1984a. "Space, Knowledge, and Power." Interview by Paul Rabinow, in Paul Rabinow, ed., *The Foucault Reader.* New York: Pantheon: 239–56.

Foucault, Michel. 1984b. "What Is Enlightenment?" In Paul Rabinow, ed., *The Foucault Reader.* New York: Pantheon: 32–50.

Foucault, Michel. 1988a. *Politics, Philosophy, Culture: Interview and Other Writings 1977–1984.* London: Routledge.

Foucault, Michel. 1988b. *Technologies of the Self.* Amherst: University of Massachusetts Press.

Foucault, Michel. 1991. *The Foucault Effect: Studies in Governmentality,* ed. Graham Burchell, Colin Gordon and Peter Miller. Chicago: University of Chicago Press.

Foucault, Michel. 1994. *The Order of Things: An Archaeology of the Human Sciences.* New York: Vintage.

Foucault, Michel. 1997. *"Society Must Be Defended": Lectures at the Collège de France, 1975–1976.* New York: Picador.

Fraser, Nancy. 1989. "Women, Welfare, and the Politics of Need Interpretation." In *Unruly Practices.* Minneapolis: University of Minnesota Press: 144–60.

Freeman, Jo. 2000. *One Room at a Time.* Lanham, MD: Rowman and Littlefield.

French, Hilary F. 2000. *Vanishing Borders: Protecting the Planet in the Age of Globalization.* New York: Norton.

Gadamer, Hans-Georg. 1974. *Truth and Method.* New York: Seabury Press.

Gadamer, Hans Georg. 1976. *Philosophical Hermeneutics.* Berkeley: University of California Press.

Gadamer, Hans-Georg. 1983. "What Is Practice." In *Reason in the Age of Science.* Translated by Frederick G. Lawrence. Cambridge, MA: MIT Press.

Galison, Peter. 1987. *How Experiments End.* Chicago: University of Chicago Press.

Garfinkel, Harold. 1967. *Studies in Ethnomethodology.* Englewood Cliffs, NJ: Prentice Hall.

Gasking, Douglas A. T., and A. C. Jackson. 1967. "Wittgenstein as a Teacher." In L. Fann, ed., *Ludwig Wittgenstein: The Man and His Philosophy.* Sussex, UK: Harvester: 49–55.

Geddes, Barbara. 1990. "How the Cases You Choose Affect the Answers You Get: Selection Bias in Comparative Politics." *Political Analysis* 2: 131–50.

Geertz, Clifford. 1973. "Thick Description: Toward and Interpretive Theory of Culture." In *The Interpretation of Cultures: Selected Essays*. New York: Basic Books: 3–31.

Geertz, Clifford. 1983. *Local Knowledge*. New York: Basic Books.

Giddens, Anthony. 1986. *The Constitution of Society: Outline of a Theory of Structuration*. Berkeley: University of California Press.

Giddens, Anthony. 1993. *New Rules of Sociological Method: A Positive Critique of Interpretive Methodologies,* 2nd ed. Stanford: Stanford University Press.

Gilens, Martin. 1999. *Why Americans Hate Welfare: Race, Media, and the Politics of Antipoverty Policy.* Chicago: University of Chicago Press.

Gilovich, Thomas, Dale Griffin, and Daniel Kahneman, eds. 2002. *Heuristics and Biases: The Psychology of Intuitive Judgment.* Cambridge, UK: Cambridge University Press.

Glymour, Clark. 1980. *Theory and Evidence.* Princeton: Princeton University Press.

Glynn, Ian. 1999. *An Anatomy of Thought: The Origin and Machinery of the Mind.* Oxford, UK: Oxford University Press.

Goldberg, Elkhonon. 2001. *The Executive Brain: Frontal Lobes and the Civilized Mind.* New York: Oxford University Press.

Goldstone, Patricia. 2001. *Making the World Safe for Tourism.* New Haven: Yale University Press.

Gould, Stephen Jay. 2003. *Triumph and Tragedy in Mudville: A Lifelong Passion for Baseball.* New York: Norton.

Gramsci, Antonio. 1971. *Selections from the Prison Notebooks.* Edited and translated by Quintin Hoare and Geoffrey Nowell Smith. New York: International Publishers.

Green, Donald, and Ian Shapiro. 1994. *Pathologies of Rational Choice Theory: A Critique of Applications.* New Haven: Yale University Press.

Greene, Joshua, and Jonathan Haidt. 2002. "How (and Where) Does Moral Judgment Work?" *Trends in Cognitive Sciences* 6 (12): 517–23.

Greene, Joshua D., R. Brian Sommerville, Leigh E. Nystrom, John M. Darley, and Jonathan D. Cohen. 2001. "An FMRI Investigation of Emotional Engagement in Moral Judgment." *Science* 293 (5537): 2105–8.

Greenfeld, Liah. 2001. *The Spirit of Capitalism: Nationalism and Economic Growth.* Cambridge, MA: Harvard University Press.

Greenwald, Anthony, and Mahzarin Banaji. 1995. "Implicit Social Cognition: Attitudes, Self-Esteem, and Stereotypes." *Psychological Review* 102 (1): 4–27.

Grossberg, Lawrence. 1997. "Cultural Studies: What's in a Name? (One More Time)." In *Bringing It All Back Home: Essays in Cultural Studies.* Durham, NC: Duke University Press.

Gunnell, John G. 1993. "Relativism: The Return of the Repressed." *Political Theory* 21: 563–84.

Gunnell, John G. 1998. *The Orders of Discourse: Philosophy, Social Science and Politics.* Lanham, MD: Rowman and Littlefield.

Habermas, Jürgen. 1971. *Knowledge and Human Interests.* Translated by Jeremy J. Shapiro. Boston: Beacon.

Habermas, Jürgen. 1973. *Theory and Practice.* Boston: Beacon Press.

Habermas, Jürgen. 1981. *Theory of Communicative Action: Volume 1.* Boston: Beacon Press.

Habermas, Jürgen. 1988. *On the Logic of the Social Sciences.* Cambridge, MA: MIT Press.

Habermas, Jürgen. 1990. "Reconstruction and Interpretation in the Social Sciences." In *Moral Consciousness and Communicative Action.* Cambridge, MA: MIT Press: 21–42.

Habermas, Jürgen. 1993. *Between Facts and Norms: Contributions to a Discourse Theory of Law and Democracy.* Cambridge, MA: MIT Press.

Haidt, Jonathan. 2001. "The Emotional Dog and Its Rational Tail: A Social Intuitionist Approach to Moral Judgment." *Psychological Review* 108 (4): 814–34.

Harcourt, Bernard E. 2001. *Illusion of Order: The False Promise of Broken Windows Policing.* Cambridge, MA: Harvard University Press.

Hardin, Russell. 1995. *One for All: The Logic of Group Conflict.* Princeton: Princeton University Press.

Harding, Sandra. 1993. "Rethinking Standpoint Epistemology: What Is 'Strong Objectivity'?" In Linda Alcoff and Elizabeth Potter, eds., *Feminist Epistemologies.* New York: Routledge: 49–82.

Harre, Rom. 1986. *Varieties of Realism.* Oxford, UK: Basil Blackwell.

Hartman, Chester. 1974. *Yerba Buena. Land Grab and Community Resistance in San Francisco.* San Francisco: Glide.

Haskell, Thomas L. 2000. *The Emergence of Professional Social Science: The American Social Science Association and the 19th-Century Crisis of Authority.* Baltimore: Johns Hopkins University Press.

Hawkesworth, Mary. 1988. *Theoretical Issues in Policy Analysis.* Albany: SUNY Press.

Hawkesworth, Mary. 2001. "Democratization: Reflections on Gendered Dislocations in the Public Sphere." In Rita Mae Kelly, Jane Bayes, Mary Hawkesworth, and Brigitte Young, eds., *Gender, Globalization and Democratization.* Lanham, MD: Rowman and Littlefield.

Hawkesworth, Mary. 2003a. "Congressional Enactments of Race-Gender: Toward a Theory of Raced-Gendered Institutions." *American Political Science Review* 97 (4): 529–50.

Hawkesworth, Mary. 2003b. "Political Science in a New Millennium: Issues of Knowledge and Power." In Mary Hawkesworth and Maurice Kogan, eds., *Encyclopedia of Government and Politics*, 2nd ed. London: Routledge.

Hawkesworth, Mary. 2006. "Contending Conceptions of Science and Politics: Methodology and the Constitution of the Political." In Dvora Yanow and Peregrine Schwartz-Shea, eds., *Interpretation and Method: Empirical Research Methods and the Interpretive Turn*. Armonk, NY: M. E. Sharpe.

Heidegger, Martin. 1962. *Being and Time*. New York: Harper and Row.

Heller, Agnes. 1990. *Can Modernity Survive?* Berkeley: University of California Press.

Hillier, Amy, and Dennis Culhane. 2003. *Closing the GAP: Housing (Un)Affordability in Philadelphia*. Philadelphia: Cartographic Modeling Laboratory, University of Pennsylvania.

Hindess, Barry. 1996. *Discourses of Power: From Hobbes to Foucault*. Oxford, UK: Blackwell.

Hobbes, Thomas. 1962. *Leviathan, or the Matter, Forme and Power of a Commonwealth Ecclesiasticall and Civil*, edited by Michael Oakeshott. New York: Collier Books.

Hoffman, James E. 1986. "The Psychology of Perception." In Joseph Ledoux and William Hirst, eds., *Mind and Brain: Dialogues in Cognitive Neuroscience*. Cambridge, UK: Cambridge University Press: 7–32.

Hogarth, Robin. 2001. *Educating Intuition*. Chicago: University of Chicago Press.

Honig, Bonnie. 1994. *Political Theory and the Displacement of Politics*. Ithaca: Cornell University Press.

Horgan, John. 1999. *The Undiscovered Mind*. New York: Free Press.

Horkheimer, Max. 1941. Max Horkheimer Archiv, Archiv IX. January 17, 1941. Protocol.

Ingersoll, Virginia Hall, and Guy B. Adams. 1992. *The Tacit Organization*. Greenwich, CT: JAI Press.

Isaac, Jeffrey. 1987. *Power and Marxist Theory: A Realist View*. New York: Cornell University Press.

Isaac, Jeffrey. 2003. "Conceptions of Power." In Mary Hawkesworth and Maurice Kogan, eds., *Encyclopedia of Government and Politics*, 2nd ed. London: Routledge.

Jackson, Patrick Thaddeus, and Daniel H. Nexon. 2002. "Globalization, the Comparative Method, and Comparing Constructions." In Daniel M. Green, ed., *Constructivism and Comparative Politics*. Armonk, NY: M. E. Sharpe: 88–120.

Jameson, Fredric. 1992. *Postmodernism, or the Cultural Logic of Late Capitalism*. Durham: Duke University Press.

Janis, Irving L. 1989. *Crucial Decisions: Leadership in Policymaking and Crisis Management*. London: Free Press.

Jaquette, Jane, ed. 1989. *The Women's Movement in Latin America: Feminism and the Transition to Democracy*. Boston. Unwin Hyman.

Jaquette, Jane, and Sharon Wolchik. 1998. *Women and Democracy: Latin America and Central and Eastern Europe.* Baltimore: Johns Hopkins University Press.

Jeydel, Alana, and Andrew Taylor. 2003. "Are Women Legislators Less Effective? Evidence from the U.S. House in the 103rd–105th Congress." *Political Research Quarterly* 56 (March): 19–27.

Kabeer, Naila. 2003. *Reversed Realities: Gender Hierarchies in Development Thought.* London: Verso.

Kahn, Roger. 1972. *The Boys of Summer.* New York: Harper and Row.

Kahneman, Daniel, and Amos Tversky. 1979. "Prospect Theory: An Analysis of Decisions Under Risk." *Econometrica* 47: 263–91.

Kahneman, Daniel, and Amos Tversky. 1981. "The Psychology of Preferences." *Scientific American* 346: 160–72.

Kahneman, Daniel, Paul Slovic, and Amos Tversky, eds. 1982. *Judgment Under Uncertainty: Heuristics and Biases.* Cambridge, UK: Cambridge University Press.

Kathlene, Lyn. 1989. "Uncovering the Political Impacts of Gender: An Exploratory Study." *Western Political Quarterly* 42 (November): 397–421.

Kathlene, Lyn. 1994. "Power and Influence in State Legislative Policymaking: The Interaction of Gender and Position in Committee Hearing Debates." *American Political Science Review* 88 (September): 560–76.

Katznelson, Ira. 2001. *Desolation and Enlightenment: Political Knowledge After Total War, Totalitarianism, and the Holocaust.* New York: Columbia University Press.

Kelly, Rita, Jane Bayes, Mary Hawkesworth, and Brigitte Young, eds. 2001. *Gender, Globalization and Democratization.* Boulder, CO: Rowman and Littlefield.

Kenney, Sally. 1996. "New Research on Gendered Political Institutions." *Political Research Quarterly* 49 (June): 445–66.

Kettler, David. 1957. "Dilemma of Radicalism." *Dissent* (Autumn): 386–92.

Kettler, David. 1974. "The Vocation of Radical Intellectuals." In Ira Katznelson, ed., *The Politics and Society Reader.* New York: David McKay.

Kettler, David. 2001. *Domestic Regimes, Rule of Law, and Democratic Social Change.* Berlin: Galda and Walsh.

King, Gary, Robert O. Keohane, and Sidney Verba. 1994. *Designing Social Inquiry: Scientific Inference in Qualitative Research.* Princeton: Princeton University Press.

Kleinmuntz, Benjamin, David Faust, Paul Meehl, and Robyn Dawes. 1990. "Comment." *Science,* New Series, 247 (4939): 146–47.

Kleinmuntz, Benjamin, David Faust, Paul Meehl, and Robyn M. Douglas. 1990. "Clinical and Actuarial Judgment." *Science,* New Series, 247 (4939): 146–47.

Knorr-Cetina, K. 1981. *The Manufacture of Knowledge: An Essay on the Constructivist and Contextual Nature of Science.* Oxford, UK: Pergamon. Press.

Koh, Kyunghee, and David E. Meyer. 1991. "Function Learning: Induction of Continuous Stimulus-Response Relations." *Journal of Experimental Psychology: Learning, Memory, and Cognition* 17: 811–36.

Kreps, David, and Robert Wilson. 1982. "Reputation and Imperfect Information." *Journal of Economic Theory* 27: 253–79.

Kuhn, Thomas S. 1970. *The Structure of Scientific Revolutions,* 2nd ed., enlarged. Chicago: University of Chicago Press.

La Rochefoucauld. 1959. *Maxims.* Translated by Leonard Tanock. London: Penguin Books: #67.

Laitin, David D. 1995. "Disciplining Political Science." *American Political Science Review* 89 (2): 454–56.

Laitin, David D. 1997. "Language Conflict and Violence." *Archives Européennes de Sociologie* 41 (1): 97–137.

Laitin, David D. 2002. "Comparative Politics: The State of the Subdiscipline." In Ira Katznelson and Helen Milner, eds., *Political Science: The State of the Discipline.* New York: Norton, 2002: 630–59.

Laitin, David. 2003. "The Perestroikan Challenge to Social Science." *Politics and Society* 31 (1) (March): 163–84.

Lakatos, Imre. 1970. "Falsification and the Methodology of Scientific Research Programmes." In Imre Lakatos and Richard Musgrave, eds., *Criticism and the Growth of Knowledge.* Cambridge, UK: Cambridge University Press: 91–196.

Lapid, Yosef. 2003. "Through Dialogue to Engaged Pluralism: The Unfinished Business of the Third Debate." *International Studies Review* 5 (1): 128–31.

Lasswell, Harold. 1950. *Politics: Who Gets What, When, How.* New York: P. Smith.

Lasswell, Harold. 1971. *A Preview of Policy Science.* New York: Elsevier.

Latour, Bruno. 1987. *Science in Action.* Cambridge, MA: Harvard University Press.

Latour, Bruno, and Steve Woolgar. 1979. *Laboratory Life: The Social Construction of Scientific Facts.* Beverly Hills, CA: Sage; 2nd ed., Princeton: Princeton University Press, 1986.

Laudan, Larry. 1990. *Science and Relativism.* Chicago: University of Chicago Press.

Laumann, Edward O., John H. Gagnon, Robert T. Michael, and Stuart Michaels. 1994. *The Social Organization of Sexuality.* Chicago: University of Chicago Press.

Law, John, ed. 1991. *A Sociology of Monsters: Essays on Power, Technology, and Domination.* London: Routledge.

Lemert, Charles. 2001. *Social Things.* Lanham MD: Rowman and Littlefield.

Lewicki, Pavel, Maria Czyzewska, and Hunter Hoffman. 1987. "Unconscious Acquisition of Complex Procedural Knowledge." *Journal of Experimental Psychology: Learning, Memory, and Cognition* 13: 523–30.

Lewicki, Pavel, Thomas Hill, and Maria Czyzewska. 1992. "Nonconscious Acquisition of Information." *American Psychologist* 47: 796–801.

Lewis, Michael. 2003. *Moneyball: The Art of Winning an Unfair Game.* New York: Norton.

Lieberman, Matthew D. 2000. "Intuition: A Social Cognitive Neuroscience Approach." *Psychological Bulletin* 126 (1): 109–37.

Lindenfeld, David L. 1997. *The Practical Imagination: The German Sciences of State in the Nineteenth Century.* Chicago: University of Chicago Press.

Longino, Helen. 1990. *Science as Social Knowledge.* Princeton: Princeton University Press.

Lord, Carnes, and David K. O'Connor, eds. 1991. *Essays on the Foundations of Aristotelian Political Science.* Berkeley: University of California Press.

Luke, Timothy W. 1989. *Screens of Power: Ideology, Domination, and Resistance in Informational Society.* Urbana: University of Illinois Press.

Luke, Timothy W. 1996. "Identity, Meaning and Globalization: Space-Time Compression and the Political Economy of Everyday Life." In Scott Lash, Paul Heelas, and Paul Morris, eds., *Detraditionalization: Critical Reflections on Authority and Identity.* Oxford, UK: Blackwell: 109–33.

Luke, Timothy W. 1999a. *Capitalism, Democracy, and Ecology: Departing from Marx.* Urbana: University of Illinois Press.

Luke, Timothy W. 1999b. "The Discipline as Disciplinary Normalization: Networks of Research." *New Political Science* 21 (3): 345–63.

Luke, Timothy W. 2005. "Caught Between Confused Critics and Careerist Co-Conspirators: *Perestroika* in American Political Science." In Kristen Renwick Monroe, ed. *Perestroika! The Raucous Rebellion in Political Science,* ed. Kristen Renwick Monroe. New Haven: Yale University Press: 468–88.

Lukes, Steven. 1974. *Power: A Radical View.* London: Blackwell.

Lynch, Michael. 1985. *Art and Artifact in Laboratory Science.* London: Routledge and Kegan Paul.

Lyotard, Jean-Francois. 1984. *The Postmodern Condition: A Report on Knowledge.* Minneapolis: University of Minnesota Press.

Macintyre, Alasdair. 1984. *After Virtue: A Study in Moral Theory,* 2nd ed. South Bend: Notre Dame University Press.

Marcus, George E., W. Russell Neuman, and Michael MacKuen. 2000. *Affective Intelligence and Political Judgment.* Chicago: University of Chicago Press.

Markovits, Andrei S., and Steven L. Hellerman. 2001. *Offside: Soccer and American Exceptionalism.* Princeton: Princeton University Press.

Marshall, Catherine, and Gretchen B. Rossman. 1999. "Defending the Value and Logic of Qualitative Research." In *Designing Qualitative Research,* 3rd ed. Thousand Oaks, CA: Sage: 191–203.

Martin, Hans-Peter, and Harald Schumann. 1997. *The Global Trap: Globalization and the Assault on Democracy and Prosperity.* London: Zed Press.

Marton, Ference, Peter Fensham, and Seth Chaiklin. 1994. "A Nobel's Eye View of Scientific Intuition." *International Journal of Science Education* 16 (4): 457–73.

Marx, Karl. 1964. *The Economic and Philosophical Manuscripts of 1844.* Translated by Martin Milligan and edited by Dirk G. Straits. New York: International Publishers.

Marx, Karl. 1976. *Capital.* Harmondsworth, UK: Penguin.

Marx, Karl, and Friedrich Engels. 1978. "The Communist Manifesto." In Robert C. Tucker, ed., *The Marx-Engels Reader.* New York: Norton: 335–53.

Masters, Richard S. W. 1992. "Knowledge, Knerves and Know-how: The Role of Explicit vs. Implicit Knowledge in the Breakdown of a Complex Skill Under Pressure." *British Journal of Psychology* 83: 343–58.

Maynard-Moody, Steven, and Michael Musheno. 2006. "Stories for Research." In Dvora Yanow and Peregrine Schwartz-Shea, eds., *Interpretation and Method: Empirical Research Methods and the Interpretive Turn.* Armonk, NY: M. E. Sharpe.

Mazur, Amy. 2002. *Theorizing Feminist Policy.* Oxford, UK: Oxford University Press.

McAdam, Doug, Sidney Tarrow, and Charles Tilly. 2001. *Dynamics of Contention.* Cambridge, UK: Cambridge University Press.

McClintock, Anne. 1995. *Imperial Leather.* New York: Routledge.

McDonagh, Eileen. 2002. "Political Citizenship and Democratization: The Gender Paradox." *American Political Science Review* 96 (3): 535–52.

McKelvey, Bill. 2002 "From Fields to Science." In Robert Westwood and Stewart Clegg, eds., *Debating Organizations: Point/Counterpoint: Central Debates in Organization Theory.* London: Blackwell.

McMackin, John, and Paul Slovic. 2000. "When Does Explicit Justification Impair Decision-Making?" *Journal of Applied Cognitive Psychology* 14 (6): 527–41.

Mearsheimer, John J. 2001. "Methodological Parochialism vs. Methodological Pluralism." Paper presented at Panel 7-1, "Perestroika: Undisciplined, Unpunished." APSA Meetings, San Francisco, CA., August 31.

Miller, Richard. 1987. *Fact and Method: Confirmation and Reality in the Natural and the Social Sciences.* Princeton: Princeton University Press.

Mills, C. Wright. 1959. *The Sociological Imagination.* Oxford, UK: Oxford University Press.

Minson, Jeffrey. 1993. *Questions of Conduct: Sexual Harassment, Citizenship and Government.* London: Macmillan.

Mitchell, Timothy. 2002. *Rule of Experts: Egypt, Techno-politics, Modernity.* Berkeley: University of California Press.

Monroe, Kristen Renwick, ed. 2005. *Perestroika! The Raucous Revolution in Political Science.* New Haven: Yale University Press.

Moon, J. Donald. 1975. "The Logic of Political Inquiry: A Synthesis of Opposed Perspectives." In F. I. Greenstein and N. W. Polsby, eds., *Handbook of Political Science: Political Science, Scope and Theory.* Reading, MA: Addison-Wesley: 131–228.

Mouffe, Chantal. 1993. *The Return of the Political.* London: Verso.

Murray, Thomas. 1983. "Partial Knowledge." In Daniel Callahan and Bruce Jennings, eds., *Ethics, The Social Sciences and Policy Analysis.* New York: Plenum.

Myers, David G. 2002. *Intuition: Its Powers and Perils.* New Haven: Yale University Press.

Nehamas, Alexander. 1985. *Nietzsche: Life as Literature.* Cambridge, MA: Harvard University Press.

Neumann, Franz L. 1944. *Behemoth: The Structure and Practice of National Socialism 1933–1944,* 2nd ed. New York: Oxford University Press.

Neumann, Franz L. 1957. *The Democratic and the Authoritarian State.* Glencoe, IL: Free Press.

Neumann, Franz L. 1986. *The Rule of Law: Political Theory and the Legal System of Modern Society.* Dover, NH: Berg.

Neumann, Iver. 1999. *Uses of the Other.* Minneapolis: University of Minnesota Press.

Newton-Smith, W. H. 1981. *The Rationality of Science.* London: Routledge.

Nietzsche, Friedrich. 1920–29. *Gesammelte Werke,* vol. 16. Munich: Musarion.

Nietzsche, Friedrich. 1968a. *Twilight of the Idols: or How to Philosophize with a Hammer.* Translated by R. J. Hollingdale. New York: Penguin.

Nietzsche, Friedrich. 1968b. *The Will to Power.* Translated by Walter Kaufmann and R. J. Hollingdale. New York: Vintage.

Nietzsche, Friedrich. 1969. *On the Genealogy of Morals.* New York: Vintage.

Nietzsche, Friedrich. 1974. *The Gay Science.* Translated by Walter Kaufmann. New York: Vintage.

Nisbet, Richard E., and Thomas D. Wilson. 1977. "Telling More Than We Can Know: Verbal Reports on Mental Processes." *Psychological Review* 84 (3): 231–59.

Norretranders, Tor. 1998. *The User Illusion.* Translated by Jonathan Sydenham. New York: Viking.

Norton, Anne. 2004. *95 Theses on Politics, Culture, and Method.* New Haven: Yale University Press.

Nussbaum, Martha C. 1990. "The Discernment of Perception: An Aristotelian Conception of Private and Public Rationality." In *Love's Knowledge: Essays on Philosophy and Literature.* Oxford, UK: Oxford University Press: 54–105.

Nye, David E. 1990. *Electrifying America: Social Meanings of a New Technology.* Cambridge, MA: MIT Press.

Nye, David E. 1996. *The Technological Sublime.* Cambridge, MA: MIT Press.

Oakeshott, Michael. 2001. *The Voice of Liberal Learning: Michael Oakeshott on Education.* Indianapolis: Liberty Fund.

Oren, Ido. 2003. *Our Enemies & US: America's Rivalries and the Making of Political Science.* Ithaca: Cornell University Press.

Parsons, Talcott. 1954. "The Present Position and Prospects of Systematic Theory in Sociology." In *Essays in Sociological Theory.* New York: Free Press: 212–37.

Pateman, Carole. 1988. *The Sexual Contract.* Cambridge, UK: Polity Press.

Pearl, Judea. 2000. *Causality.* Cambridge, UK: Cambridge University Press.

Peirce, Charles Sanders. 1940. *The Philosophy of Peirce,* edited by Justus Buchler. New York: Harcourt, Brace.

Pennington, Bill. 2003. "Rich Get Richer and Poor Are Undecided." *New York Times,* 5 August, D1.

Peterson, Spike. 1992. *Gendered States: Feminist (Re)Visions of International Relations Theory.* Boulder, CO: Lynne Rienner.

Peterson, Spike, and Anne Sisson Runyan. 1999. *Global Gender Issues,* 2nd ed. Boulder, CO: Westview Press.

Pickering, Andrew. 1992. *Science as Practice and Culture.* Chicago: University of Chicago Press.

Piven, Frances Fox, and Richard A. Cloward. 1971. *Regulating the Poor: The Functions of Public Welfare.* New York: Vintage Books.

Piven, Frances Fox, and Richard A. Cloward. 1977. *Poor People's Movements: Why They Succeed, How They Fail.* New York: Vintage Books.

Piven, Frances Fox, and Richard A. Cloward. 2000. *Why Americans Still Don't Vote: And Why Politicians Want It That Way.* Boston: Beacon Press.

Pizarro, David, and Paul Bloom. 2001. "The Intelligence of the Moral Intuitions: A Reply to Haidt." *Psychological Review* 110 (1): 193–96.

Polanyi, Michael. 1966. *The Tacit Dimension.* New York: Doubleday.

Polanyi, Michael. 1969. *Knowing and Being,* edited by Majorie Greene. Chicago: University of Chicago Press.

Polanyi, Michael, and Harry Prosch. 1975. *Meaning.* Chicago: University of Chicago Press.

Political Science Faculty. Columbiana Collection. 1955. Minutes of the Political Science Faculty. April 15. Columbia University.

Post-autistic Economics Network. 2004. Available at http://www.paecon.net/

Procacci, Giovanna. 1993. *Gouverner la misère: La question sociale en France (1789–1848).* Paris: Éditions du Seuil.

Przeworski, Adam, Michael E. Alvarez, José Antonio Cheibub, and Fernando Limongi. 2000. *Democracy and Development: Political Institutions and Well-Being in the World 1950–1990.* Cambridge, UK: Cambridge University Press.

Putnam, Hilary. 1981. *Reason, Truth, and History.* Cambridge, UK: Cambridge University Press.

Putnam, Hilary. 1983. *Realism and Reason.* Cambridge, UK: Cambridge University Press.

Putnam, Hilary. 1988. *Representation and Reality.* Cambridge, MA: MIT Press.

Putnam, Hilary. 1990. *Realism with a Human Face.* Cambridge, MA: Harvard University Press.

Putnam, Robert D. 2001. *Bowling Alone: The Collapse and Revival of American Community.* New York: Simon and Schuster.

Putnam, Robert D., and Lewis Feldstein. 2003. *Better Together: Restoring the American Community.* New York: Simon and Schuster.

Putnam, Robert D., with Robert Leonardi and Raffaella Y. Nanetti. 1993. *Making Democracy Work: Civic Traditions in Modern Italy.* Princeton: Princeton University Press.

Rabinow, Paul, and William M. Sullivan, eds. 1979. *Interpretive Social Science: A Reader.* Berkeley: University of California Press.

Ramachandran, V. S., and Sandra Blakeslee. 1998. *Phantoms in the Brain.* New York: Morrow.

Reber, Arthur. 1967. "Implicit Learning of Artificial Grammars." *Journal of Verbal Learning and Verbal Behavior* 6: 317–27.

Reber, Arthur. 1993. *Implicit Learning and Tacit Knowledge: An Essay on the Cognitive Unconscious.* New York: Oxford University Press.

Reid, Carolina Katz. 2004. *Achieving the American Dream? A Longitudinal Analysis of the Homeownership Experiences of Low-Income Households.* Seattle: Center for Studies in Demography and Ecology, University of Washington, Working Paper 04-04, April.

Retsinas, Nicolas P., and Eric S. Belsky, eds. 2002. *Low-Income Homeownership: Examining the Unexamined Goal.* Washington, DC: Brookings Institution.

Ridley, Matt, 1994. *The Red Queen: Sex and the Evolution of Human Nature.* New York: Macmillan.

Rockefeller Foundation Archives. 1951–1952.

Rohe, William M., Shannon Van Zandt, and George McCarthy. 2002. "Homeownership and Access to Opportunity." *Housing Studies* 17 (1): 51–61.

Rorty, Richard. 1991. *Objectivity, Relativism, and Truth.* Cambridge, UK: Cambridge University Press.

Rorty, Richard. 1997. "Thomas Kuhn, Rocks, and the Laws of Physics." *Common Knowledge* 6: 6–16.

Rose, Nikolas. 1985. *The Psychological Complex: Psychology, Politics and Society in England, 1869–1939.* London: Routledge and Kegan Paul.

Rose, Nikolas. 1996. *Inventing Our Selves: Psychology, Power and Personhood.* Cambridge, UK: Cambridge University Press.

Rosenman, Samuel I., ed. 1938–1950. *The Public Papers and Addresses of Franklin Delano Roosevelt,* vol. IX: G72.

Rosenman, Samuel I., ed. 1938–1950. *The Public Papers and Addresses of Franklin Delano Roosevelt,* vol. X: 287–88.

Rosenthal, Cindy Simon. 2000. "Gender Styles in State Legislative Committees: Raising Their Voice and Resolving Conflict." *Women and Politics* 21 (2): 21–45.

Rosenthal, Cindy Simon. 2002. *Women Transforming Congress.* Norman: University of Oklahoma Press.

Ross, Dorothy. 1992. *The Origins of American Social Science.* Cambridge, UK: Cambridge University Press.

Ruderman, Richard S. 1997. "Aristotle and the Recovery of Political Judgment." *American Political Science Review* 91 (2): 409–20.

Rule, James B. 1997. *Theory and Progress in Social Science.* Cambridge, UK: Cambridge University Press.

Rule, Wilma, and Joseph Zimmerman. 1994. *Electoral Systems in Comparative Perspective: Their Impact on Women and Minorities.* Westport, CT: Greenwood Press.

Rumelhart, David E., James L. McClelland, and the PDP Research Group. 1986. *Parallel Distrubuted Processing: Explorations in the Microstructure of Cognition,* vol. 1. Cambridge, MA: MIT Press.

Schlesinger, James R. 1968. "Uses and Abuses of Analysis." *Survival* 10 (October): 334–42.

Schmitt, Carl. 1996. *The Concept of the Political.* Translated by George Schwab. Chicago: University of Chicago Press.

Schmidt, Mary R. 1993. "Grout: Alternative Kinds of Knowledge and Why They Are Ignored." *Public Administration Review* 53 (6): 525–30.

Schon, Donald. 1983. *The Reflective Practitioner.* New York: Basic Books.

Schooler, Jonathan, and Tonya Engstler-Schooler. 1990. "Verbal Overshadowing of Visual Memories: Some Things Are Better Left Unsaid." *Cognitive Psychology* 22: 36–71.

Schram, Sanford F. 2002. *Praxis for the Poor: Piven and Cloward and the Future of Social Science in Social Welfare.* New York: New York University Press.

Schram, Sanford F. 2003. "Return to Politics: Perestroika, Phronesis, and Post-paradigmatic Political Science." *Political Theory* 31 (6) (December): 835–51.

Schram, Sanford F. 2004. "Beyond Paradigm: Resisting the Assimilation of Phronetic Social Science." *Politics & Society* 32 (3) (September): 417–33.

Schram, Sanford F. 2006. *Welfare Discipline: Discourse, Governance, and Globalization.* Philadelphia: Temple University Press.

Schutz, Alfred. 1962. "Common-Sense and Scientific Interpretation of Human Action." In Maurice Natanson, ed., *The Problem of Social Reality: Collected Papers,* vol. 1. The Hague: Nijhoff: 3–47.

Schwandt, Thomas A. 2001. *Dictionary of Qualitative Inquiry,* 2nd ed. Thousand Oaks, CA: Sage.

Schwartz-Shea, Peregrine. 1983. "Normative Rhetoric and the Definition of Cooperation." Ph.D. diss., University of Oregon.

Schwartz-Shea, Peregrine. 2003. "Is This the Curriculum We Want? Doctoral Requirements and Offerings in Methods and Methodology." *PS: Political Science and Politics* 36 (3): 379–86.

Schwartz-Shea, Peregrine. 2005. "The Graduate Student Experience: 'Hegemony' or Balance in Methodology Training?" In Kristen R. Monroe, ed., *Perestroika! The Raucous Revolution in Political Science.* New Haven: Yale University Press: 374–402.

Schwartz-Shea, Peregrine, and Dvora Yanow. 2002. "'Reading' 'Methods' 'Texts':
   How Research Method Texts Construct Political Science." *Political Research
   Quarterly* 55 (2): 457–86.
Scott, James C. 1990. *The Moral Economy of the Peasant: Rebellion and Subsistence
   in Southeast Asia.* New Haven: Yale University Press.
Scott, James C. 1998. *Seeing Like a State: How Certain Schemes to Improve the
   Human Condition Have Failed.* New Haven: Yale University Press.
Scott, Joan W., and Debra Keates, eds. 2001. *Schools of Thought: Twenty-five Years
   of Interpretive Social Science.* Princeton: Princeton University Press.
Seidel, Michael. 1988. *Streak: Joe DiMaggio and the Summer of '41.* New York: Pen-
   guin.
Selten, Reinhard. 1978. "The Chain-Store Paradox." *Theory and Decision* 9:
   127–59.
Selten, Reinhard, and Peter Hammerstein. 1994. "Game Theory and Evolutionary
   Biology." In Robert J. Aumann and Sergiu Hart, eds.. *Handbook of Game The-
   ory* vol. 2. Amsterdam: Elsevier: 929–93.
Sennett, Richard. 1995. "'Sex, Lies and Social Science': An Exchange." *New York
   Review of Books,* April 20, 28.
Sent, Esther-Mirjam. 2002. "Review of *Making Social Science Matter: Why Social
   Inquiry Fails and How It Can Succeed Again* by Bent Flyvbjerg." *Southern Eco-
   nomic Journal* 68 (3): 732–34.
Shapiro, Ian. 2002. "Problems, Methods, and Theories in the Study of Politics, or:
   What's Wrong with Political Science and What to Do About It." *Political The-
   ory* 30 (4): 596–619.
Shapiro, Ian. 2005. *The Flight from Reality in the Human Sciences.* Princeton:
   Princeton University Press.
Shapiro, Ian, Rogers M. Smith, and Tarek E. Massoud, eds. 2004. *Problems and
   Methods in the Study of Politics.* New York: Cambridge University Press.
Shdaimah, Corey, Roland Stahl, and Sanford Schram. 2004. *Low-Income Home
   Repair Policies in Philadelphia: Addressing Severe Home Repair Problems.* Pre-
   liminary report prepared for the Women's Community Revitalization, funded
   by the William Penn Foundation.
Shlay, Ann. 2004. *"Low-Income Homeownership: American Dream or Delusion."*
   Paper presented at the 2004 Annual Meetings of the Urban Affairs Association,
   Washington, DC. April 1.
Shlay, Anne B., and Gordon Whitman. 2004. *Research for Democracy: Linking
   Community Organizing and Research to Leverage Blight Policy.* Available at
   http://commorg.utoledo.edu/papers.htm.
Shotter, John. 1993. *Cultural Politics of Everyday Life.* Toronto: University of
   Toronto Press.
Simonton, Dean Keith. 1999. *Origins of Genius: Darwinian Perspectives on Creativ-
   ity.* New York: Oxford University Press.

Smith, Rogers M. 2002. "Should We Make Political Science More of a Science or More about Politics?" *PS: Political Science and Politics* 35 (2) (June): 199–201.

Smooth, Wendy. 2001. "African American Women State Legislators: The Impact of Gender and Race on Legislative Influence." Ph.D. diss., University of Maryland.

Sollner, Alfons. 2004. "Hannah Arendt's *The Origins of Totalitarianism* in Its Original Context." *European Journal of Political Theory* 3 (2) (April): 219–38.

Sollner, Alfons. 2005. "'Political Culturism': Adorno's 'Entry-Point' in the Cultural Concert of German Post-War History." In David Kettler and Gerhard Lauer, eds., *Exile, Science, and Bildung: The Contested Legacies of German Émigré Intellectuals.* London: Macmillan.

Somech, Anit. 1999. "Tacit Knowledge in Academia: Its Effects on Student Learning and Achievement." *Journal of Psychology* 133 (6): 605–16.

Soss, Joe. 2006. "Talking Our Way to Meaningful Explanations: A Practice-Centered View of Interviewing for Interpretive Research." In Dvora Yanow and Peregrine Schwartz-Shea, eds., *Interpretation and Method: Empirical Research Methods and the Interpretive Turn.* Armonk, NY: M. E. Sharpe.

Stablein, Ralph. 1996. "Data in Organization Studies." In Stewart R. Clegg, Cynthia Hardy, and Walter R. Nord, eds., *Handbook of Organization Studies.* London: Sage: 509–25.

Stadler, Michael, and Peter Frensch, eds. 1998. *Handbook of Implicit Learning.* Thousand Oaks: Sage.

Stanley, Liz, and Susan Wise. 1983. *Breaking Out: Feminist Consciousness and Feminist Research.* London: Routledge and Kegan Paul.

Steans, Jill. 1998. *Gender and International Relations: An Introduction.* New Brunswick, NJ: Rutgers University Press.

Stevens, Jacqueline. 2002. "Symbolic Matter: DNA and Other Linguistic Stuff." *Social Text* 20 (Spring): 105–36.

Stewart, Sharla A. 2003. "Revolution from Within." *University of Chicago Magazine* 95, no. 5, available at http://magazine.uchicago.edu/0306/features/index.shtml

Stockman, Norman. 1983. *Anti-Positivist Theories of Science: Critical Rationalism, Critical Theory and Scientific Realism.* Dordrecht: D. Reidel.

Stone, Randall. 2002. *Lending Credibility.* Princeton: Princeton University Press.

Tabb, William. 2001. *The Amoral Elephant: Globalization and the Struggle for Social Justice in the Twenty-First Century.* New York: Monthly Review Press.

Tajfel, Henri, and John C. Turner. 1979. "An Integrative Theory of Intergroup Conflict." In W. G. Austin and S. Wrochel, eds., *The Social Psychology of Intergroup Relations.* Monterey, CA: Brooks/Cole: 33–47.

Tambiah, Stanley. 1986. *Sri Lanka: Ethnic Fratricide and the Dismantling of Democracy.* Chicago: University of Chicago Press.

Tambiah, Stanley. 1992. *Buddhism Betrayed?* Chicago: University of Chicago Press.

Tambiah, Stanley. 1996. *Leveling Crowds.* Berkeley: University of California Press.

Tambiah, Stanley. 1997. "Continuity, Integration and Expanding Horizons" (interview with Mariza Peirano). *Série Antropologia,* no. 230, Departamento de Antropologia, Universidade de Brasília: 8–10

Tamerius, Karin. 1995. "Sex, Gender, and Leadership in the Representation of Women." In Georgia Duerst-Lahti and Rita Mae Kelly, eds., *Gender Power, Leadership and Governance.* Ann Arbor: University of Michigan Press: 93–114.

Tarrow, Sidney. 2004. "Bridging the Quantitative-Qualitative Divide." In Henry E. Brady and David Collier, eds., *Rethinking Social Inquiry: Diverse Tools, Shared Standards.* Latham, MD: Rowman and Littlefield.

Taylor, C. C. W. 1995. "Politics." In Jonathan Barnes, ed., *The Cambridge Companion to Aristotle.* Cambridge, UK: Cambridge University Press: 233–58.

Taylor, Charles. 1977. "Interpretation and the Sciences of Man." In Fred R. Dallmayr and Thomas McCarthy, eds., *Understanding and Social Inquiry.* Notre Dame: Notre Dane University Press: 101–31.

Taylor, Charles. 1989. *Sources of the Self: The Making of the Modern Identity.* Cambridge, MA: Harvard University Press.

Tello, María del Pilar. 1983. *O Revolución? Hablan los Militares del 68* [Coup or Revolution? The Military Officers of '68 Speak]. 2 vols. Lima: Ediciones SAGSA.

ten Bos, Rene. 2000. *Fashion and Utopia in Management Thinking.* Amsterdam: John Benjamins.

Thomas, Sue. 1994. *How Women Legislate.* New York: Oxford University Press.

Tickner, J. Ann. 1991. "Hans Morgenthau's Principles of Political Realism: A Feminist Reformulation." In Rebecca Grant and Kathleen Newland, eds., *Gender and International Relations.* Bloomington: Indiana University Press.

Tickner, J. Ann. 1992. *Gender in International Relations.* New York: Columbia University Press.

Tickner, J. Ann. 2001. *Gendering World Politics: Issues and Approaches in the Post–Cold War Era.* New York: Columbia University Press.

Tilly, Charles. 1995. "To Explain Political Processes." *American Journal of Sociology* 100 (6): 1594–1610.

Tilly, Charles. 1998. *Durable Inequality.* Berkeley: University of California Press.

Tilly, Charles. 2002. *Stories, Identities, and Political Change.* Lanham, MD: Rowman and Littlefield.

Topper, Keith. 2005. *Disorder of Political Inquiry.* Cambridge, MA: Harvard University Press.

Toth, Jeffrey P. 2000. "Nonconscious Forms of Human Memory." In Endel Tulving and Fergus Craik, ed., *The Oxford Handbook of Memory.* Oxford, UK: Oxford University Press: 245–61.

Toulmin, Stephen. 2001. *Return to Reason.* Cambridge, MA: Harvard University Press.

Tversky, Amos, and Daniel Kahneman. 1981. "The Framing of Decisions and the Rationality of Choice." *Science* 211: 453–58.

Underwood, Geoffrey, ed. 1996. *Implicit Cognition.* Oxford, UK: Oxford University Press.

University Seminars. 1946–47. *The State.* Minutes of the Columbia University Seminar: 401–2.

Üsdiken Behlul, and Yorgo Pasadeos. 1995. "Organizational Analysis in North America and Europe: A Comparison of Co-citation Networks." *Organization Studies* 16 (3): 503–26.

van Fraasen, Bas. 1980. *The Scientific Image.* Oxford: Oxford University Press.

Virilio, Paul. 1997. *Open Sky.* London: Verso.

Vivas, Elisio 1960. "Science and the Studies of Man." In H. Schoek and J. Wiggans, eds., *Scientism and Values.* Princeton: Van Nostrand.

von Dietze, Erich. 2001. *Paradigms Explained: Rethinking Thomas Kuhn's Philosophy of Science.* Westport, CT: Praeger.

Waltz, Kenneth. 1979. *Theory of International Politics.* New York: McGraw-Hill.

Weber, Max. 1917/1919/1994. *Wissenschaft als Beruf: Politik als Beruf.* Edited by W. J. Mommsen and W. Schluchter. Tübingen: J. C. B. Mohr.

Weber, Max. 1918/1946. "Science as a Vocation." Speech given at Munich University in 1918, published in Hans H. Gerth and C. Wright Mills (translated and edited), *Max Weber: Essays in Sociology.* New York: Oxford University Press: 129–56.

Weber, Max. 1949. *The Methodology of the Social Sciences.* Translated and edited by Edward Shils and Henry Finch. New York: Free Press.

Weber, Max. 1978. *Economy and Society.* Berkeley: University of California Press.

Weinberg, Steven. 2001. "What Science Can Explain." *New York Review of Books,* September 20: 97.

Wellmer, Albrecht. 2000. *Endgames: The Irreconcilable Nature of Modernity: Essays and Lectures.* Cambridge, MA: MIT Press.

Wendt, Alexander E. 1999. *Social Theory of International Politics.* Cambridge, UK: Cambridge University Press.

White, Stephen K. 2002. "Review of *Making Social Science Matter: Why Social Inquiry Fails and How It Can Succeed Again.*" *American Political Science Review* 96 (1): 179–80.

Whitehead, Alfred North. 1911. *Introduction to Mathematics.* London: Williams and Norgate.

Whyte, William Foote, and Kathleen King Whyte. 1988. *Making Mondragon: The Growth and Dynamics of the Worker Cooperative Complex.* Ithaca: Cornell University Press.

Wicks, Andrew C., and Edward R. Freeman. 1998. "Organization Studies and the New Pragmatism: Positivism, Anti-positivism, and the Search for Ethics." *Organization Science* 9 (2): 123–40.

Wildavsky, Aaron. 1979. *Speaking Truth to Power: The Art and Craft of Policy Analysis.* Boston: Little Brown.

Williams, Bernard. 1985. *Ethics and the Limits of Philosophy.* Cambridge, MA: Harvard University Press.

Willingham, Daniel B., and Laura Preuss. 1995. "The Death of Implicit Memory." *Psyche* 2 (15), available at http://psyche.cs.monash.edu.au/v2/psyche-2-15-willingham.html

Wilson, Robert. 1982. "Reputation and Imperfect Information." *Journal of Economic Theory* 27: 253–79.

Wilson, Thomas D., and Jonathan W. Schooler. 1991. "Thinking Too Much: Introspection Can Reduce the Quality of Preferences and Decisions." *Journal of Personality and Social Psychology* 60 (2): 181–92.

Wilson, Timothy. 2002. *Strangers to Ourselves: Discovering the Adaptive Unconscious.* Cambridge, MA: Belknap Press.

Winch, Peter. 1958. *The Idea of a Social Science and Its Relation to Philosophy.* London: Routledge and Kegan Paul.

Wittgenstein, Ludwig. 1922 *Tractatus Logico-Philosophicus.* London: Routledge and Kegan Paul.

Wittgenstein, Ludwig. 1999. *Philosophical Investigations,* 3rd ed. Englewood Cliffs: Prentice Hall.

Wolfe, Alan. 1970. "The Professional Mystique." In Marvin Surkin and Alan Wolfe, eds., *An End to Political Science: The Caucus Papers.* New York: Basic Books: 288–309.

Wolfe, Alan. 2005. "Reality in Political Science." *Chronicle of Higher Education/The Chronicle Review* 52 (11) (November 4): 819.

Wolin, Sheldon. 1969. "Political Theory as a Vocation." *American Political Science Review* 63: 1062–82.

Woolhouse, Leanne S., and Rowan Bayne. 2000. "Personality and the Use of Intuition: Individual Differences in Strategy and Performance on an Implicit Learning Task." *European Journal of Personality* 14 (2): 157–69.

Yanow, Dvora. 1996. *How Does a Policy Mean? Interpreting Policy and Organizational Acts.* Washington, DC: Georgetown University Press.

Yanow, Dvora. 1997. "Passionate Humility in Interpretive Policy and Administrative Analysis." *Administrative Theory and Praxis* 19: 171–77.

Yanow, Dvora. 2000. *Conducting Interpretive Policy Analysis.* Newbury Park, CA: Sage.

Yanow, Dvora. 2003. *Constructing "Race" and "Ethnicity" in America: Category-Making in Public Policy and Administration.* Armonk, NY: M. E. Sharpe.

Yanow, Dvora. 2004. "Translating Local Knowledge at Organizational Peripheries." *British Journal of Management* 15 (Special Issue) (March): S15–S25.

Young, Iris. 1994. "Gender as Seriality: Thinking About Women as a Social Collective," *Signs* 19 (3): 713–38.

Zimmerman, Manfred. 1989. "The Nervous System in the Context of Information Theory." In R. F. Schmidt and G. Thews, eds., *Human Physiology,* 2nd ed. Berlin: Springer-Verlag: 166–73.

# About the Contributors

BRIAN CATERINO is an interdisciplinary social theorist who currently works in public television. He has taught at the University of Rochester and in the New School DIAL program. His most recent publications include "Marketing Critical Theory," *New Political Science* 25 (3) (September 2003): 435–49, and "Interpretation and Institution," in Kristen Renwick Monroe, ed., *Perestroika! The Raucous Revolution in Political Science* (Yale University Press, 2005). He currently studies the role of status and reputation in academic publishing.

STEWART CLEGG is Professor at the University of Technology, Sydney. He has published more than one hundred refereed publications, most in top-tier international journals He has published nearly forty books, his most recent being *Power and Organization,* co-authored with David Courpasson and Nelson Phillips (Sage, 2006).

BENT FLYVBJERG is Professor of Planning at Aalborg University, Denmark, where he teaches urban policy and planning. He was twice a Visiting Fulbright Scholar to the United States, where he did research at the University of California at Los Angeles and Berkeley and at Harvard University. He is the author of numerous publications in seventeen languages. His books in English include *Megaprojects and Risk: An Anatomy of Ambition* (Cambridge University Press, 2003), *Making Social Science Matter* (Cambridge University Press, 2001), and *Rationality and Power: Democracy in Practice* (University of Chicago Press, 1998). He is currently doing research on the role of lying in policy and planning.

MARY HAWKESWORTH is Professor of Women's and Gender Studies at Rutgers University. Her teaching and research interests include feminist theory, women and politics, contemporary political philosophy, philosophy of science, and social policy. Her most recent books are *Globalization and Feminist Activism* (Rowman and Littlefield, 2006) and *Feminist Inquiry: From Political Conviction to Methodological Innovation* (Rutgers University Press, 2006).

PATRICK THADDEUS JACKSON is Assistant Professor in the School of International Service at American University. He is the author of "Defending the West: Occidentalism and the Formation of NATO," *Journal of Political Philosophy* 11 (3) (September 2003): 223–52; and "Hegel's House, or, 'People are States Too,'" *Review of International Studies* 30 (2004): 281–87. His book *Civilizing the Enemy: German Reconstruction and the Invention of the West* is forthcoming from the University of Michigan Press.

GREGORY J. KASZA has appointments in Political Science and East Asian Languages and Cultures at Indiana University. He is the author of *The State and the Mass Media in Japan, 1918–1945* (University of California Press, 1988); *The Conscription Society: Administered Mass Organizations* (Yale University Press, 1995) and *One World of Welfare: Japan in Comparative Perspective* (Cornell University Press, forthcoming, 2006).

DAVID KETTLER is Research Professor at Bard College, New York, and Professor Emeritus in Political Studies and Cultural Studies at Trent University (Ontario) He was Chair of the Caucus for a New Political Science, 1969–1971. Recent book publications include *Karl Mannheim and the Crisis of Liberalism* (with Volker Meja) (Transaction, 1995); *Domestic Regimes, the Rule of Law, and Democratic Social Change* (Galda and Wilch, 2001); *Adam Ferguson: Social and Political Thought* (Transaction, 2004); and *Karl Mannheim's Sociology as Political Education* (with Colin Loader) (Transaction, 2002); as well as four edited volumes arising out the "Contested Legacies" project: *Contested Legacies: The German-Speaking Intellectual and Cultural Emigration to the United States and United Kingdom, 1933–45* (Galda and Wilch, 2002); *Political Theory and the Hitler Regime* (special issue of the *European Journal of Political Theory*) (with Tom Wheatland); *Exile, Science, and Bildung: The Contested Legacies of German Intellectual Émigrés* (with Gerhard Lauer)(Palgrave-Macmillan, 2005); and *Limits of Exile* (with Zvi Ben-Dor) (special issue of the *Journal of the Interdisciplinary Crossroads*, 2006).

DAVID D. LAITIN is the Watkins Professor of Political Science at Stanford University. He received his B.A. from Swarthmore College and his Ph.D. from the University of California, Berkeley. He has conducted field research on issues of language, religion, and nationalism in Somalia, Yorubaland (Nigeria), Catalonia (Spain), and Estonia. His books include *Politics, Language and Thought: The Somali Experience* (1977); *Hegemony and Culture: Politics and Religious Change Among the Yoruba* (1986); *Somalia: Nation in Search of a State* (1987, with Said Samatar); *Language Repertoires and State Construction in Africa* (1992); and *Identity in Formation: The Russian-speaking Populations in the Near Abroad* (1998). He has also published, in collaboration with James Fearon, "Ethnicity, Insurgency and Civil War," *American Political Science Review* 97 (1) (February 2003): 75–90.

TIMOTHY W. LUKE is University Distinguished Professor of Political Science at Virginia Polytechnic Institute and State University in Blacksburg, Virginia. He also is the Program Chair for Government and International Affairs in the School of Public and International Affairs and a member of the faculty in the Department of Science and Technology in Society. His latest books are *Capitalism, Democracy, and Ecology: Departing from Marx* (University of Illinois Press, 1999); *The Politics of Cyberspace,* ed. with Chris Toulouse (Routledge, 1998); *Ecocritique: Contesting the Politics of Nature, Economy, and Culture* (University of Minnesota Press, 1997); and, most recent, *Museum Politics: Power Plays at the Exhibition* (University of Minnesota Press, 2002).

THEODORE SCHATZKI is Professor and Chair of Philosophy at the University of Kentucky. He is the author of *Social Practices* (1996), The *Site of the Social* (2002), and *Heidegger: Theorist of Space* (forthcoming, Steiner Verlag).

SANFORD F. SCHRAM teaches social theory and policy in the Graduate School of Social Work and Social Research at Bryn Mawr College. He is the author of several books and numerous scholarly articles, including *Words of Welfare: The Poverty of Social Science and the Social Science of Poverty* (University of Minnesota Press, 1995), which won the Michael Harrington Award from the American Political Science Association, and *Welfare Discipline: Discourse, Governance, and Globalization* (Temple University Press, 2006).

PEREGRINE SCHWARTZ-SHEA is Associate Professor of Political Science at the University of Utah. She has published on methodological issues central to Perestroika in *Political Research Quarterly* and *PS: Political Science and Politics*. She is co-editor, with Dvora Yanow, of *Interpretation and Method: Empirical Research Methods and the Interpretive Turn* (M. E. Sharpe, 2006).

COREY S. SHDAIMAH is Assistant Professor in the School of Social Work, University of Maryland at Baltimore. She is the author of "'Progressive' Lawyering: Dilemmas of Power and Hierarchy,'" in Austin Sarat and Stuart Scheingold, eds., *The Worlds Cause Lawyers Make* (Stanford University Press, 2005).

ROLAND W. STAHL is a doctoral candidate at the Graduate School of Social Work and Social Research at Bryn Mawr College. He currently is completing his doctoral thesis on sanctions and client outcomes in welfare-to-work programs.

LESLIE PAUL THIELE is Professor of Political Science at the University of Florida. His publications include *Environmentalism for a New Millennium* (Oxford University Press, 1999) and *Thinking Politics* (2nd ed., Congressional Quarterly Press, 2003). His most recent work is *The Heart of Judgment: Practical Wisdom, Neuroscience, and Narrative* (Cambridge University Press, 2006).

# Index

Aalborg, 28, 29, 34, 41, 57
Academic journals, 230
Advocates vs. researchers, 105
Agency, 173
Agger, Ben, 132
Algorithm, 37
Alternative methodologies, 66
American political science, 253
American Political Science Association, 231, 241
American Political Science Review, 35, 231, 232
Analytical reason, 202
Andocentric, 162
Anti-democratic, 237
APSA task force on Graduate education, 210, 211
Arendt, Hannah, 135, 235; *Origins of Total-itarianism,* 235
Aristotelian, 68, 72, 126, 153, 171, 226
Aristotle, 8, 9, 10, 27, 33, 52, 73, 74, 125, 144, 159, 243, 244, 249
Art, 69
Authoritarian rule, 156

Background conditions of social science, 121
Background practices, 65
Background skills, 63

Baseball, 86, 89, 92, 93
Bates, Robert, 48
Baudrillard, Jean, 263, 264
Beck, Martin, 259, 260
Behavioralism, 3, 4, 167
Beiner, Ronald, 135
Bellah, Robert, 28, 131; *Habits of the Heart,* 131
Bernstein, Richard, 7, 74, 75
Bias, 157
Bioethics, 20
Bio-power, 255
Bodin, Jean, 249
Bordieu, Pierre, 4, 8, 27, 28, 34, 41, 124, 139
Brady, Henry, 6
Bureaucracy, 239
Bush, George W., President, 107

Capitalism, liberal democratic, 254
Cartographic metaphor, 181
Case study research, 7, 26, 56
Caucus for a New Political Science, 6
Causal: explanation, 3; mechanisms, 8, 51, 52, 91; hypotheses, 19; inferences, 41; phenomena, 176. *See also* Causality
Causality, 5
Chamber of Industry and Commerce, 48, 59, 143, 147, 148